The Hulton Getty Picture Collection

The American Millennium

1,000 Remarkable Years
of Incident and Achievement

The Hulton Getty Picture Collection

The American Millennium

1,000 Remarkable Years of Incident and Achievement

Nick Yapp

KÖNEMANN

Frontispiece: Walking on the nose of a president. A maintenance worker dangles from ropes in front of one of the four faces of Mount Rushmore, Abraham Lincoln, high above the South Dakota landscape.

First published in 2000 by Könemann Verlagsgesellschaft mbH,
Bonner Strasse 126, D-50968 Köln

This book was produced by The Hulton Getty Picture Collection,
Unique House, 21–31 Woodfield Road, London W9 2BA

Design: Mick Hodson and Alan Price
Project manager and editor: Richard Collins
Picture editor: Sophie Spencer-Wood
Proof reader and indexer: Liz Ihre
Editorial assistance: Tom Worsley, Gill Hodson
Scanning: Antonia Hille, Dave Roling, Mark Thompson

Publishing director: Peter Feierabend

Typesetting by Mick Hodson Associates
Colour separation by Omniascanners srl
Printed and bound by Star Standard Industries Ltd
Printed in Singapore
ISBN 3-8290-6010-6
10 9 8 7 6 5 4 3 2 1

Based on an original idea and concept by Ludwig Könemann

CONTENTS

General Introduction

No other country has so mastered the art of self-promotion. The United States invented modern advertising, PR, packaging, 'spin' and mass-marketing – an entire way of life that is gift-wrapped. Politics, art, sex, leisure and even science are all part of the entertainment conglomerate that is 'United States Inc.'

American heroes (and anti-heroes) are all larger than life – Daniel Boone, Davy Crockett, Elvis Presley, Henry Ford, Marilyn Monroe, Al Capone, Teddy Roosevelt, JFK, Casey Jones, Bonnie and Clyde, George Armstrong Custer, Calamity Jane and thousands more. That is how they are presented; that is how the public wants them; that is how some of them were. In reality, some may have been modest people, but American history has often sought to avoid reality.

The vast continent is criss-crossed with paths of glory. A thousand years ago Native Americans followed trails that wandered across the Plains, dragging their dwellings after them. Five hundred years later, Spanish and French and British explorers hacked their trails through forests the size of the countries they had left behind them, staggered over deserts, pioneered faltering routes over mountains in search of El Dorado. Wherever they went, they found instead every other conceivable richness, but this did not stop them. They moved on further, until they reached another ocean and the limits of what had seemed an infinite land. Four hundred years after them, millions of refugees arrived, fleeing from persecution, poverty and pogroms in Europe. They boarded the crowded trains that chugged out of New York and went where there were jobs, or where they had been told to go. And in more modern times come the hosts of Mexicans, South Americans and people of the Pacific Rim, creeping across the border, avoiding the security cameras and the guards. Some fly into this brave new world, scenting, beyond the perimeter fences of airports from Newark to Los Angeles, the same riches that lured their predecessors.

The end product of this ceaseless influx of new Americans is a country abounding in talent and self-confidence. No other civilisation has produced such breadth of culture, so many brilliant ideas, and such a heart-stopping mixture of courage and foolishness in its dreams. Never before has the world witnessed such glory. No warriors of the past have been so all-conquering.

There are drawbacks. The responsibility of being the strongest power in the world has unnerved the US. The Vietnam débâcle scarred the American soul. But Americans bounce back with a resilience that is breathtaking. It is as though the last one thousand years have been but the prologue to what is still The Greatest Show on Earth.

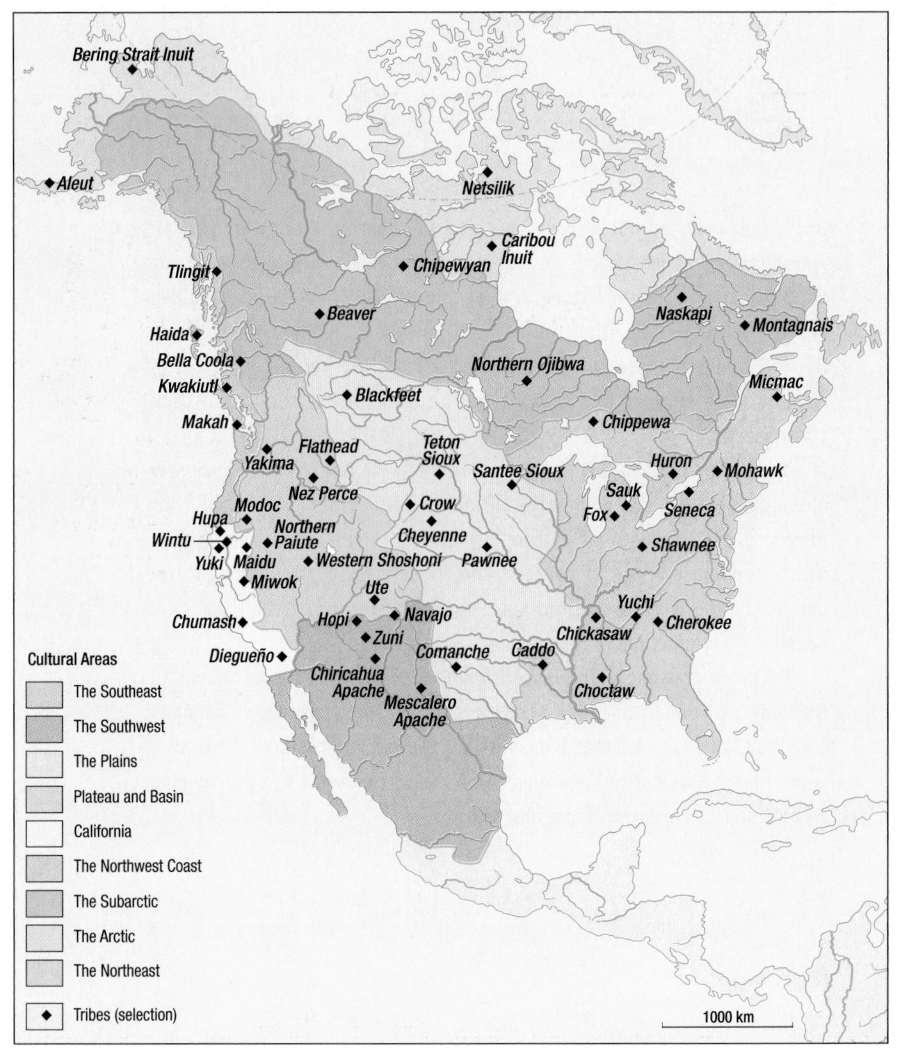

Map 1 Nine Cultural Areas of Native American Tribes (including some notable tribes)

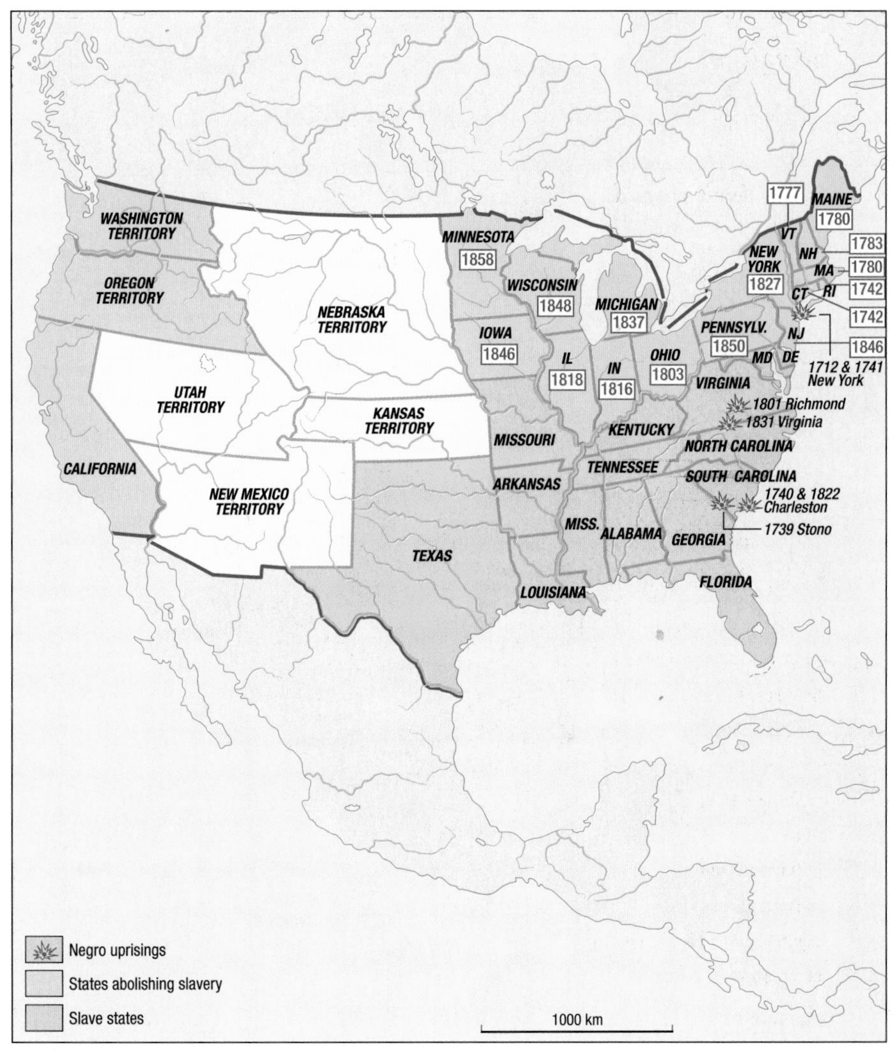

Map 2 The Abolition of Slavery

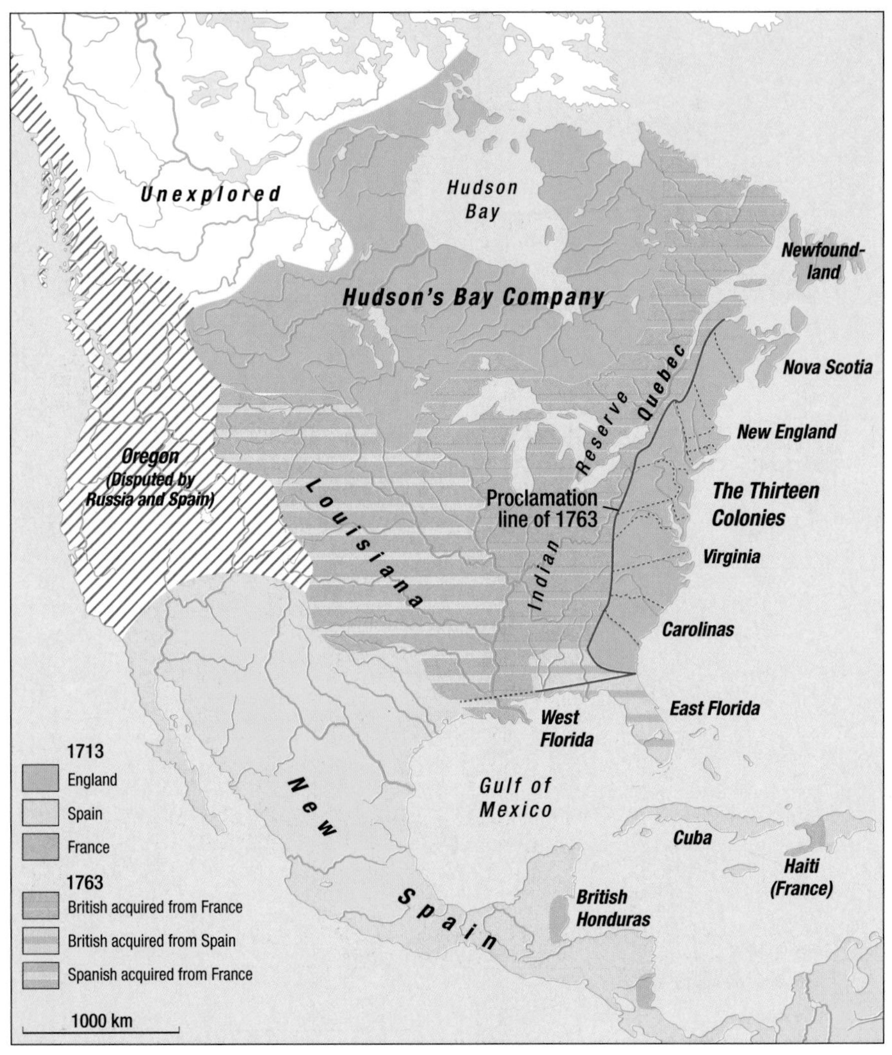

Map 3 The Struggle for Empire, 1713–1763

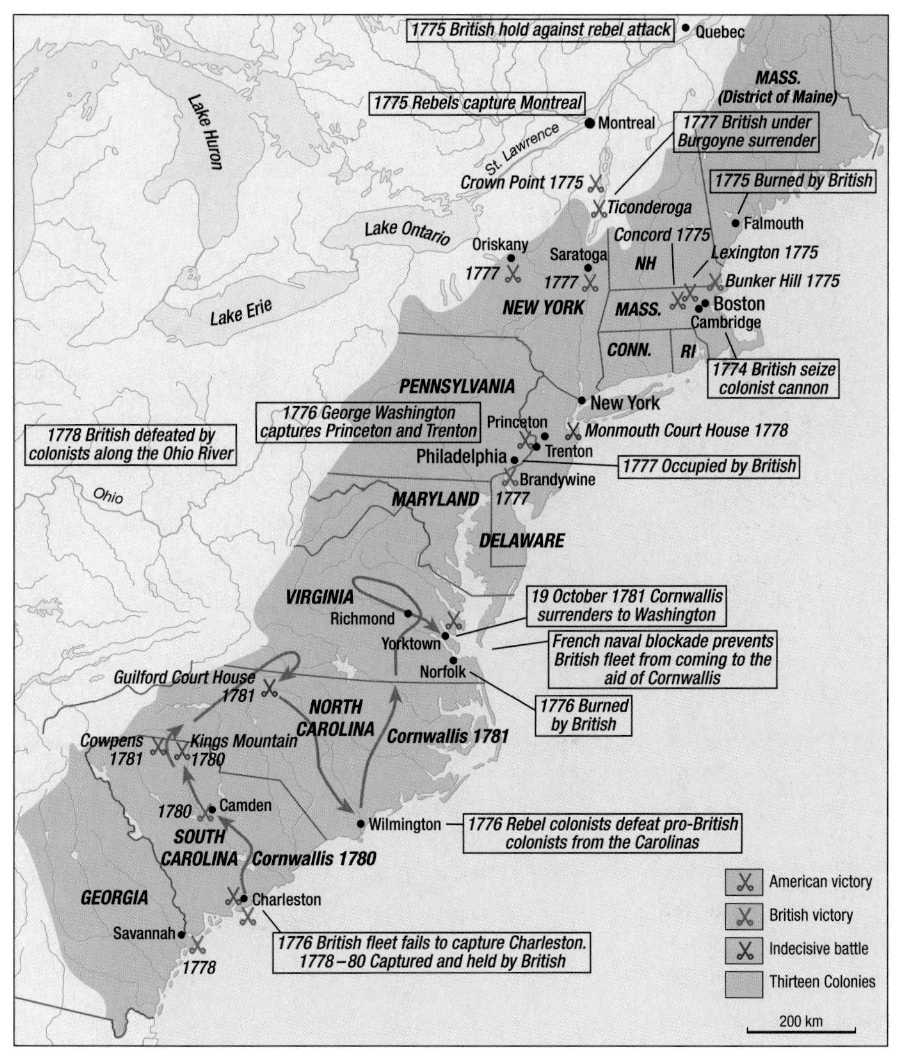

Map 4 New England and the War of Independence

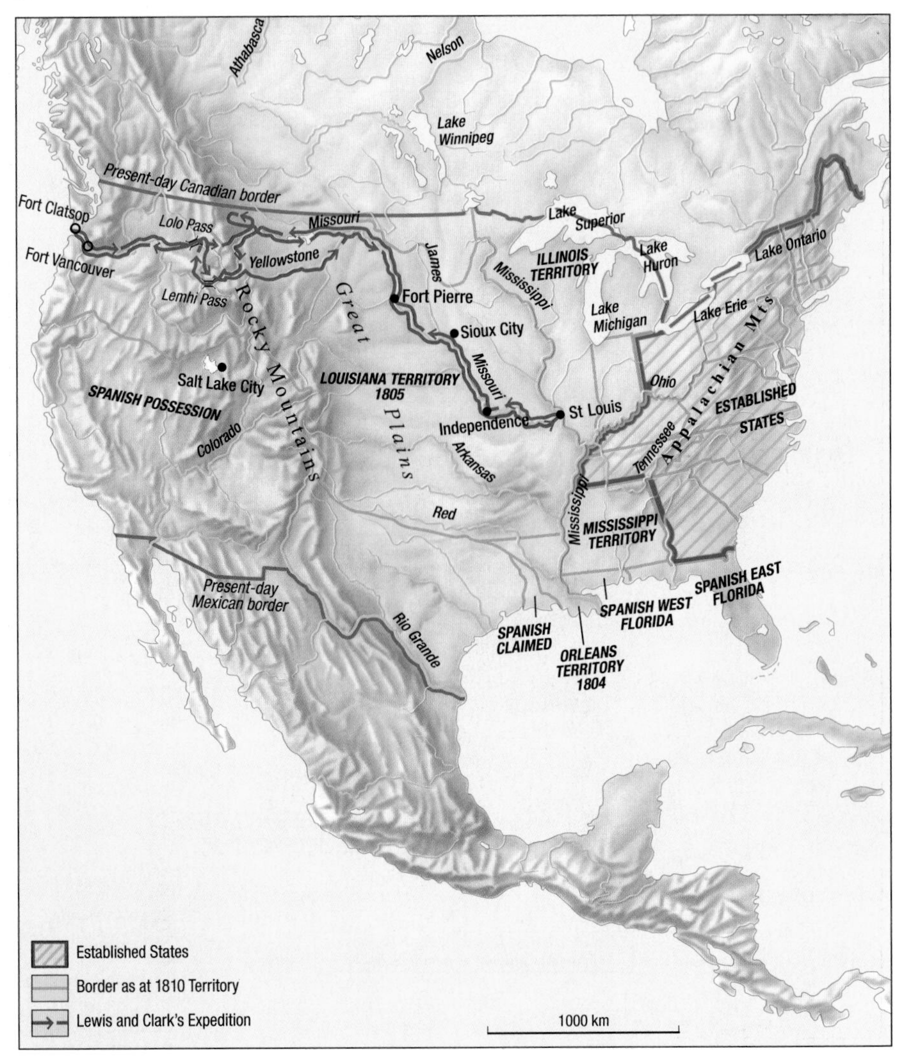

Map 5 Lewis and Clark's Expedition, 1804–1806

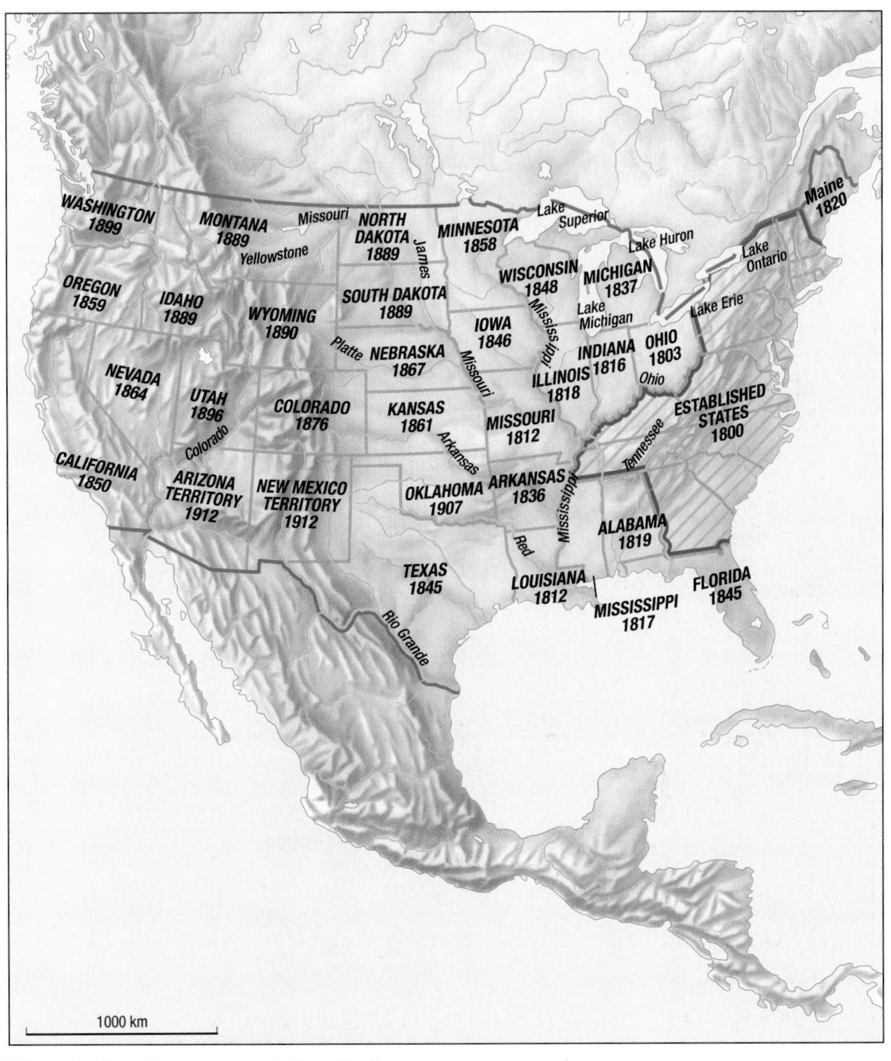

Map 6 The States and the Union

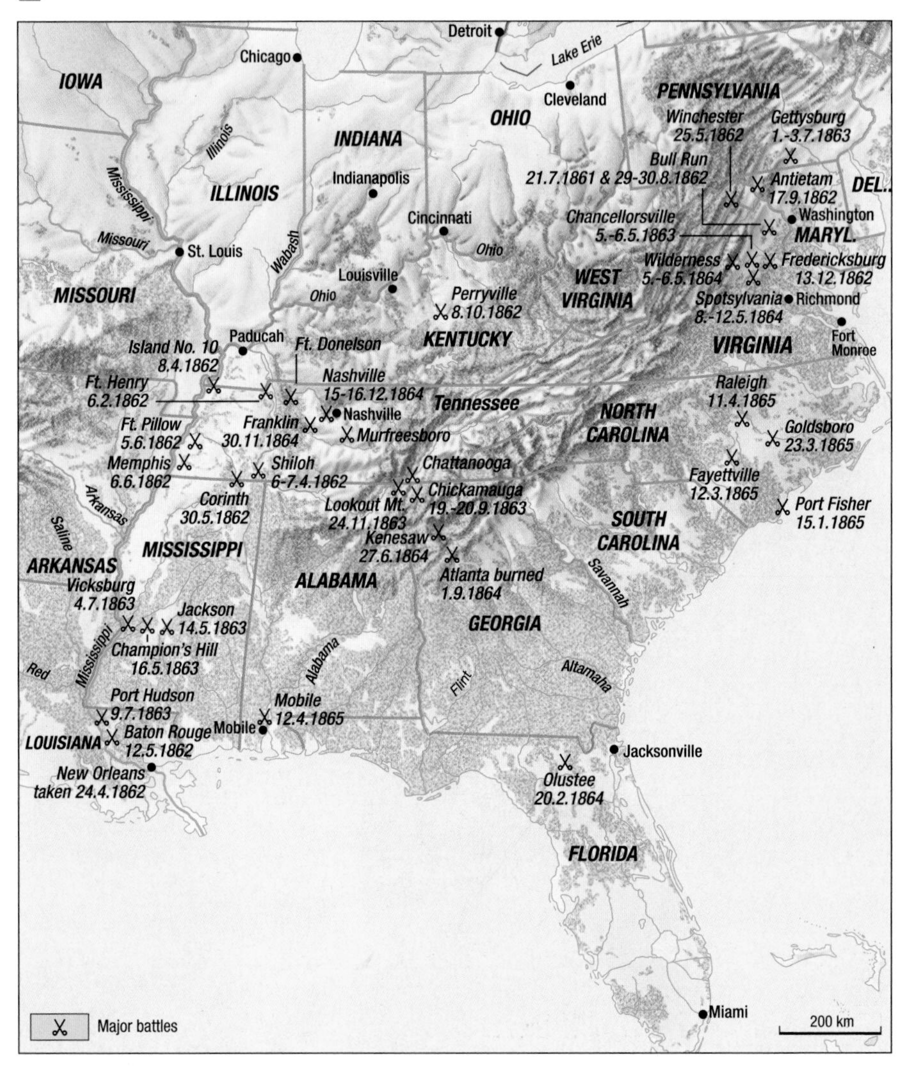

Map 7 The Civil War, 1860-1870

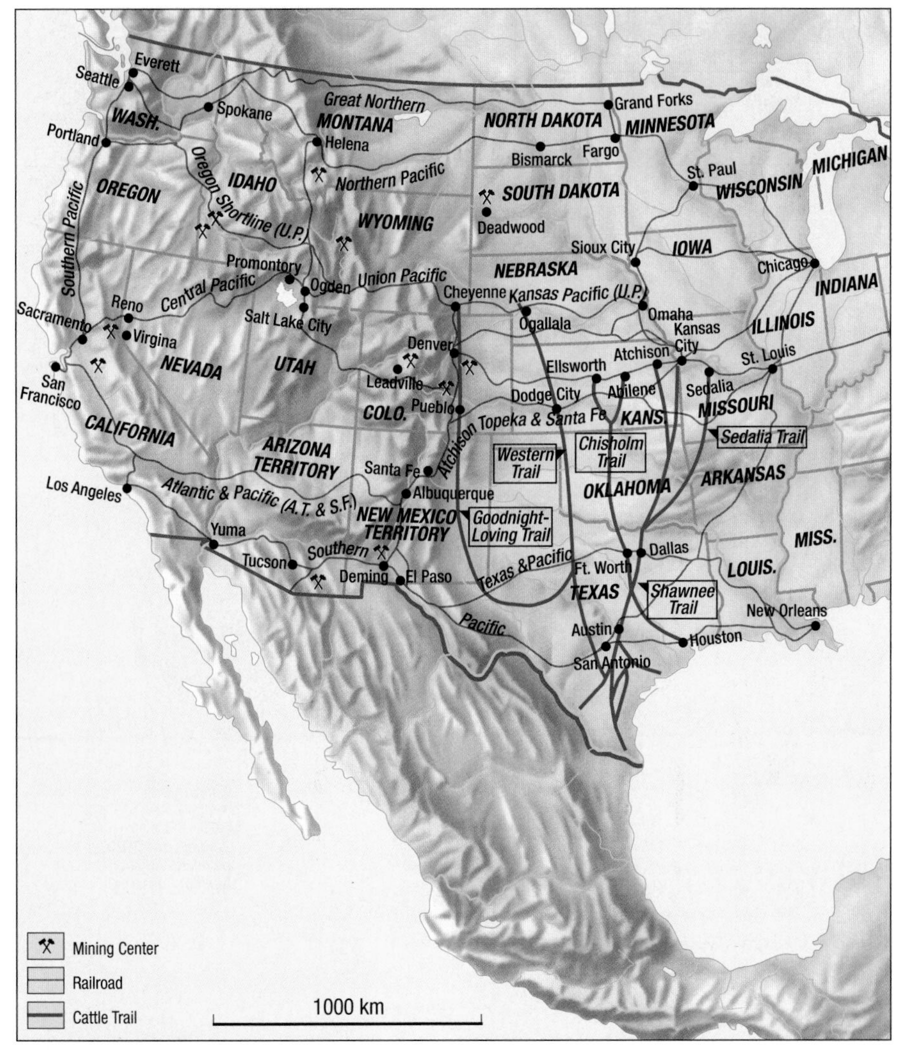

Map 8 Go West, Young Man, 1870–1900

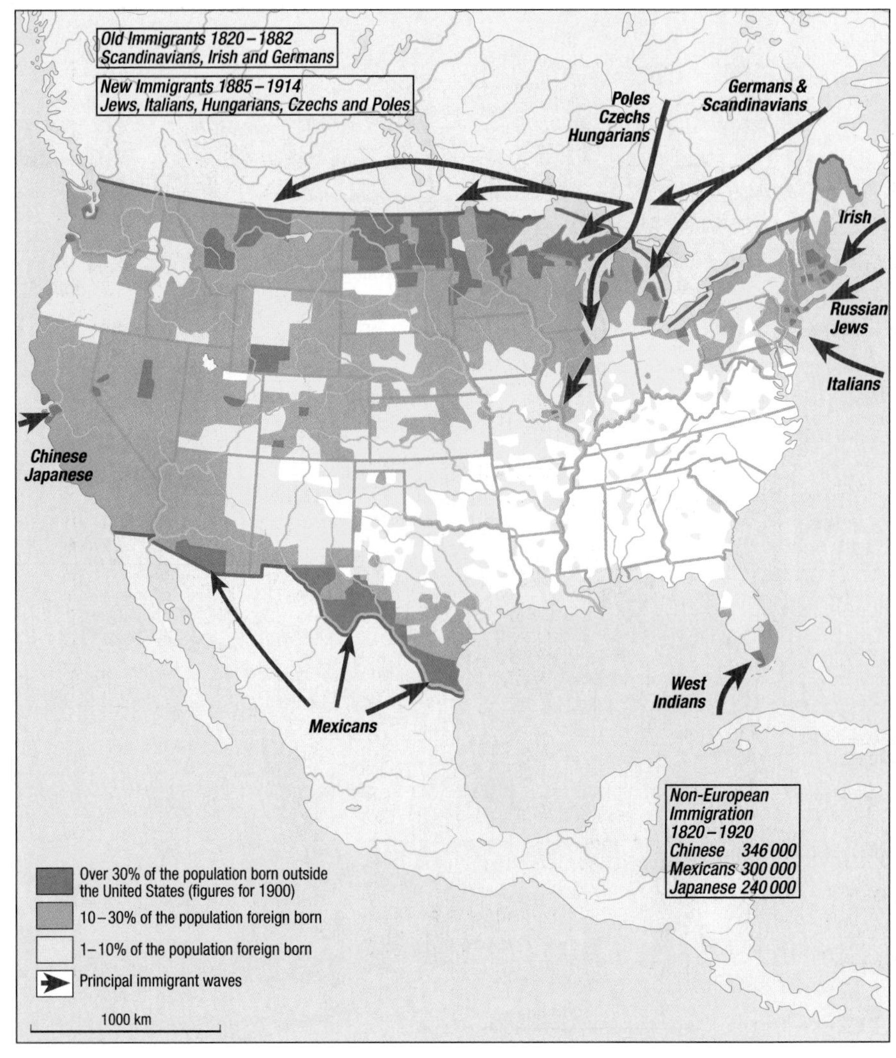

Map 9 The New Americans

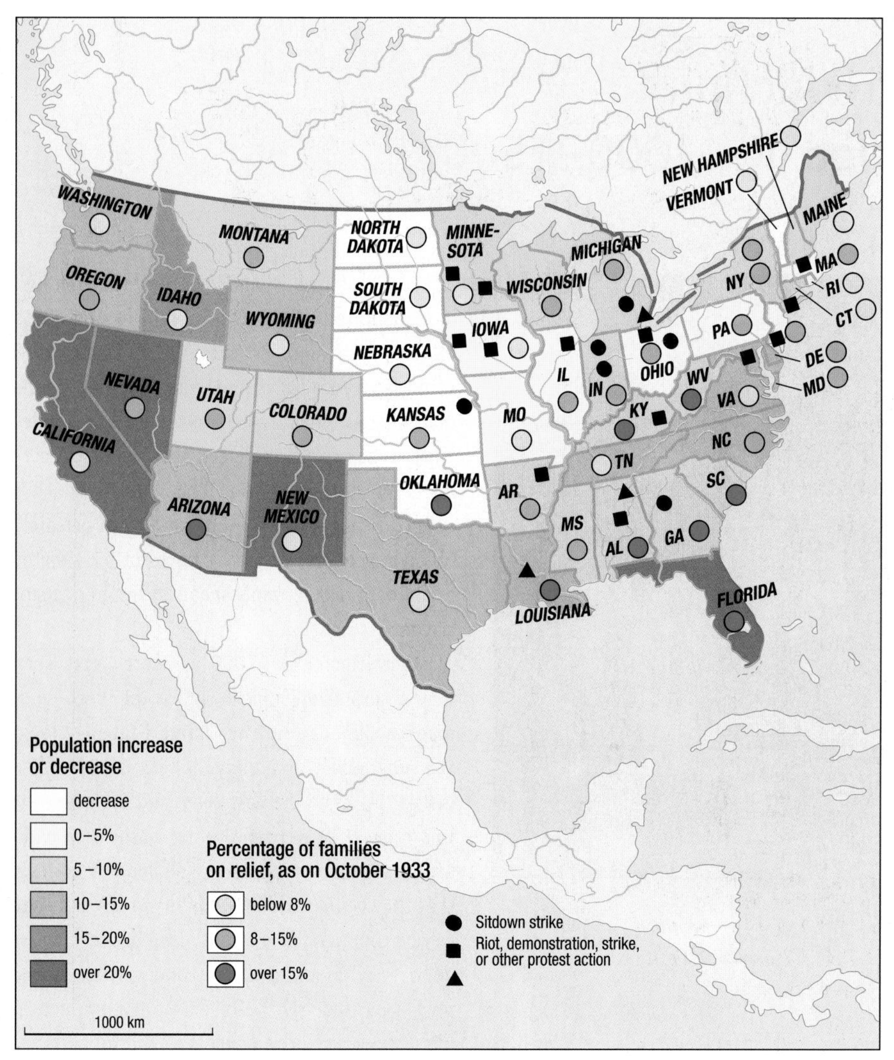

Map 10 The Great Depression, 1929-1939

Introduction to Period 1 – 1000–1500

No one knows when North America was first inhabited. Estimates vary from 10,000 to 70,000 years ago. Whenever they came, they came from Asia, at a time when the two continents were joined by a land bridge 1,000 miles wide. It is possible, therefore, that the first Americans did not cross from Siberia to Alaska, but much further south. They were almost certainly following sources of food – flocks of birds, herds of animals, and certainly shoals of fish in rivers or streams.

Over the next 10,000 or more years they moved surprisingly quickly across the vastness of modern Canada and the United States – down the west coast and then fanning out over the central plains to the east coast and the south. At this time, they were all hunter-gatherers, living off nuts, berries, roots, fruit, fish and any animals that they could trap. They had no horses, but they were accompanied by dogs. They killed smaller animals with darts, arrows and spears. Larger prey – particularly the bison – were trapped in pits they dug or driven over the edges of cliffs.

Their methods of marking time were, of

course, completely different from those of Europe, though the Creeks of the south-eastern United States did divide the year into winter and summer, and into roughly twelve months. The year started with the corn harvest in the month of Much Heat (August), followed by Little Chestnut, Big Chestnut, Frost, Big Winter (December), Little Winter, Wind, Little Spring, Big Spring, Mulberry, Blackberry and Little Heat (July). By AD 1000 (in European terms), almost the entire continent was inhabited, with a diversity of cultures that was at least as broad as that in Europe, though basically divided into three or four distinct ways of life.

In the southern, northern and central plains the Kiowa, Comanche, Cheyenne and Crow lived almost exclusively by hunting. The vast herds of bison supplied them with their dwellings, clothes, food and even heat, for they used dried bison dung as the fuel for their fires. Other tribes – the Sioux, Shawnee and Delaware – lived by a mixture of hunting and farming. Around the coasts were tribes that lived primarily by fishing for salmon and cod, collecting shellfish and, occasionally and bravely, hunting whales. In the south west and in the Mississippi basin were the tribes who lived almost exclusively by farming, though they were not averse to eating some of the small and far from tasty rodents of the scrubland around them.

By 1300 the population had reached roughly 10 million. It probably never exceeded this number, for, though the Native Americans were spared the plagues and fevers that festered in Europe (at least until the arrival of Europeans), a large area of land was needed to support each individual. By 1500, most Native Americans lived by farming. Early farming methods were simple. Tribes in the forests of what are now the northern United States used the slash and burn method of clearing land: in the autumn they cut a circle of bark from a tree. By the following spring the tree was dead. A year or so later they burned the dead trees, thus gradually clearing the land for planting. Their principal crops were beans and potatoes, a diet they supplemented with wild nuts and berries, the occasional (equally wild) bear or deer, and the passenger pigeon. This bird was later hunted to extinction by Europeans, but before then it filled the skies above New England with flocks that numbered hundreds of thousands at a time.

Tribes in the south grew mainly maize (more commonly known in America as corn) and squash, both of which originally came from Mexico. The Natchez people of the Mississippi basin were already cultivating maize sometime after AD 800, and were themselves emigrants from Mexico some 2,000 or more years earlier with the Hohokam, Anasazi and Mogollon. The Anasazi were perhaps the most advanced of these peoples. They settled in the 'Four Corners' area of the United States – where Utah, Colorado, Arizona and New Mexico meet. They were the ancestors of the modern Pueblo tribes, best known for their multi-storey adobe apartment houses, capable of housing many families.

The greatest agency for change throughout all tribes, apart from the prolific spread of maize, was trade. Traders arrived regularly from Mexico, selling decorative and luxury items: copper bells and jewellery, precious stones, ornamental seashells and brightly coloured macaws. In the south west, they journeyed as far north as Colorado and, among the stops on their route were the Anasazi towns at Chaco Canyon, Aztec, Salmon, Canyon de Chelly and Mesa Verde.

But it was maize that revolutionised life for many Native American tribes. By the 11th and 12th centuries, its cultivation had moved up the banks of the Mississippi, into Arkansas and Oklahoma. It was farmed in Tennessee, South Carolina and Florida. It had crossed the Ohio River and flourished as far north as the climate permitted. Even the Huron of southern Ontario became maize farmers.

And there was at least one great city in North America at this time. It was Cahokia, built just a few miles from the modern city of St Louis. Nobody knows quite how big it was, but conservative estimates suggest that more than 20,000 people lived inside the vast wooden palisade that surrounded it – roughly equivalent to the population of London at the time. It was an advanced community in trade, in the amount of food it supplied, in knowledge of astronomy and irrigation, and in the manufacture of everything from cooking utensils to jewellery.

Just as no one is certain when the first Asians moved into North America, so no one knows when Europeans first set foot on the continent. It seems likely that, near the beginning of the 11th century, Norsemen or Swedes or Danes (or perhaps all three) landed on the east coast. Here they found 'self-sown wheat-fields and wild grapes, out of which a very good wine can be made'. The land became known as Vinland, and may have been Nova Scotia, though it is a long time since vineyards have produced great wine that far north.

What is known is that on 12 October 1492, the *Santa Maria* (100 tons in weight and 25 metres long), the *Niña* and the *Pinta* dropped anchor off the island of San Salvador. The commander of the expedition was Christopher Columbus, and he spent the next few weeks exploring Haiti and Cuba. He found spices, cotton, weird birds, and people with 'copper-coloured' skin. What he was looking for was gold, and he was told that there was plenty of it – to the west, inland, to the north, further away. The fate of early North American civilisation was sealed.

1
HUNTERS AND FARMERS 1000–1300

The ancient cliff dwellings at Mesa Verde, Colorado (*right*). The culture of the Anasazi, who fashioned and inhabited these astonishing buildings, came to maturity around the end of the first millennium. For the next two hundred and fifty years they flourished, with similar settlements spread through New Mexico over an area of some 60,000 square miles. Many of them were connected by a series of roads, designed for foot traffic only, but in places some 30 feet wide.

Introduction

The Hopewell people farmed and lived in the valleys of the Illinois and Ohio rivers. They grew maize (corn), squash, beans and tobacco. They wove cloth from the threads of soft bark, and decorated their clothing with freshwater pearls and ornaments made from copper and mica. They traded and travelled – west to the Rocky Mountains, south to the Gulf of Mexico – searching for the much-prized obsidian which could be split to produce a razor-sharp edge for tools and weapons.

The Hopewells also built mounds. These mounds were very like the 'mottes' of 11th and 12th-century European castles – simple, conical-shaped piles of earth. They stood some 30 feet high (10 metres), and were used as burial chambers. As time went by the Hopewells began to construct much larger mounds, in the shapes of birds or animals, which may well have been the base for temples and places of worship.

There were other mound builders in North America. On the site of the old city of Cahokia, in the Mississippi basin, are the remains of nineteen 'platform' mounds, flat-topped and larger than most. The largest of them was Monks Mound. Today, after several hundred years of erosion, Monks Mound is still 90 feet (30 metres) high, covering an area roughly the size of two football pitches. In southern Ohio is the Great Serpent Mound, a quarter of a mile long, in the shape of a snake swallowing an egg.

The mounds mark a significant point in the development of North American culture, for they could not have been made without coordinated labour on a large scale. They give the lie to the idea, first voiced by a French Jesuit missionary as early as 1612, that the North American natives 'roamed through rather than occupied' the landscape – though that idea appealed greatly to those who later herded the survivors into grim reservations and stole the land from them.

How far such civilisations might have developed we shall never know, for sometime around the year 1300 (a time when much of northern Europe suffered a mini ice age) disasters seem to have struck throughout North America. The Anasazi people left Chaco Canyon and their sandstone homes. Whole communities from the Mississippi basin fled south to seek shelter in Cahokia. There was much inter-tribal warfare in the south west and north east. Various reasons have been given for this sudden unrest – drought, floods, the sudden invasion of waves of migrating people from Alaska and Canada.

Whatever the reason, the great age of the mound builders was over.

(*Above*) Death Valley, California. If America was later to be seen by European settlers as 'God's Promised Land', and a new earthly paradise, this was hell. It is the hottest place on earth, with an average daily temperature in summer of almost 50° Celsius. The ground comes near to boiling point. Rocks and sand dunes, pools loaded with chloride and sulphates and harshly sculptured hills form an inhospitable, inhuman environment. Not until 1849, when gold fever was at its height, did the white man brave this awful place, and then simply to pass through it as quickly as possible.

(*Above*) The fiery sandstone towers of Monument Valley, on the borders of Arizona and Utah. The red-rock buttes and jagged pinnacles have become known to the rest of the world in dozens of Western films, from John Ford's *Stagecoach* onwards. Nowadays, most of the valley is on the Navajo Reservation, but when the Navajo first came here sometime after 1300, they were a free, wandering people, one of seven Apachean tribes.

(*Above*) The Grand Canyon of the Colorado River, Arizona, more than a mile deep and between four and eighteen miles across. At the bottom are the oldest exposed rocks in the world. And the Canyon is slowly getting deeper and deeper. In the last millennium the river has sunk by just over an inch (1.3 centimetres), though the erosion of the sandstone and limestone is largely the work of wind, not water. There is evidence of human presence here as early as 2000 BC, and the Anasazi certainly passed through.

(*Above*) The Great Serpent Mound in Adams County, Ohio. The figure is nearly a quarter of a mile (350 metres) long, and represents a serpent swallowing an egg. Some 1500 years or more since it was made, nobody understands its symbolic significance. The original inhabitants of Ohio were the Iroquoians, a wandering tribe who passed through this area as they moved east across America, looking for 'a land that pleased them'.

Some of the finest surviving examples of early North American native art are the petroglyphs (rock carvings) that exist in the caves of Utah and Arizona. Long before the arrival of Columbus, unknown artists carved these stylised and abstract shapes. (*Above*) Carvings of a horned animal on a cave wall in Monument Valley, Arizona. (*Opposite, above*) A variety of forms, many animal but some undoubtedly human, also from Monument Valley. (*Opposite, below*) Human and abstract forms from the caves of Canyon de Chelly, Arizona. All photographs are by Ernst Haas.

(*Left*) The remains of an Anasazi pueblo in Canyon de Chelly, Arizona. Settlements such as these may have housed up to two hundred people. They were often built on the north side of valleys, opening towards the south for passive solar heat. They were built by hand, with few tools and no machinery, and the materials were hauled to the site by hand, for there were no draught animals in Canyon de Chelly or any other Anasazi developments.

(*Above*) The remains of another Anasazi pueblo in Mesa Verde, Colorado, photographed in 1890. The largest of these villages, and there were well over one hundred and twenty of them, was Pueblo Bonito, which had more than eight hundred rooms, layered on four floors, constructed in terraces. It remained the largest residential building in North America until the New York apartment blocks of the 19th century. As well as their considerable construction skills, the Anasazi were able farmers. They used a variety of water-control devices – contour terraces, check dams, ditches for irrigation and reservoirs.

At the height of its development, the Anasazi civilisation produced richly decorated pottery bowls and vases. (*Left, above and below*) Two views of a vase from Chevlon, Arizona – 8 inches in diameter. (*Opposite left, above and below*) Food bowls from Four-Mile Ruin, Arizona – the top bowl is 9.5 inches across, the bottom bowl 10.5 inches. (*Opposite right, top to bottom*) Four more food bowls from Four-Mile Ruin.

2
BEFORE THE STORM
1300–1500

(*Below*) A pictograph of aspects of Native American life, probably dating from around the year 1400. The pictograph is clear evidence that the people who drew it were hunters as it shows the weapons they used and their prey. It also shows that they used fire, and that they travelled in large canoes, judging from the number of paddles represented. It is impossible to tell whether the canoe was made of birch-bark stretched over a wooden frame, or whether it was of the dug-out variety, hewn from a single piece of timber. In either case, few canoes held more than a dozen people.

Introduction

War was not the prime concern of the North Americans. Even the hunters saw trading as essential to their way of life. Small bands would meet in summer at pre-arranged times and places to hold the equivalent of European medieval fairs – exchanging presents, merry-making, holding wedding ceremonies and meeting together. At the Dalles on the Columbia River, sixty miles east of present-day Portland, Oregon, there was a permanent market. The staple diet of the people who lived here was salmon from the river itself, and this was traded for shellfish, whalebone, obsidian, tools, feathers, skins, baskets and plants. When the Athapascans (later presented by Hollywood as the villainous Apaches) surged south from the north west, sometime around the year 1400, they were tamed by the peaceful Pueblos, who taught them horticulture, weaving and shepherding.

Most of the time, peace prevailed in North America. There were occasionally skirmishes between warriors from different tribes, but, in general, good relations existed between the farming and hunting communities. In the north east, where tribes lived in closer proximity to one another than in most other parts of the continent, the farming Hurons and the hunting Algonquins established good relations. They traded with one another, exchanging maize, nets and tobacco for furs, dried fish and meat. In exceptionally cold winters one tribe would shelter another. The Plains Indians often intered among the Pueblos of the south west.

The people were slow to anger. Unlike the Aztecs of Mexico, who punished their children by scratching their bodies (and even their tongues) with sharp thorns, North American parents treated their children with tenderness. The children were allowed great freedom to play, and were spoken to gently, even when they had misbehaved. If soft words had no effect, parents showed their displeasure by pouring a bowl of cold water over the offender.

Late in the 14th century, however, some tribes began to band together in leagues or federations to increase their fighting strength. Over the next one hundred and fifty years, the number and frequency of wars increased. An atmosphere of hostility was created, especially in the north east, setting up a situation ripe for the 'divide and conquer' attitude of many later European expeditions.

Ways of life that had existed for thousands of years were about to be destroyed. For the moment, the European presence was felt only in Mexico and the Caribbean. The first five hundred Amerindian slaves were shipped back to Seville in Spain in 1494. Smallpox reached the mainland from Cuba in 1520. A year later, Poncé de Leon landed in Florida.

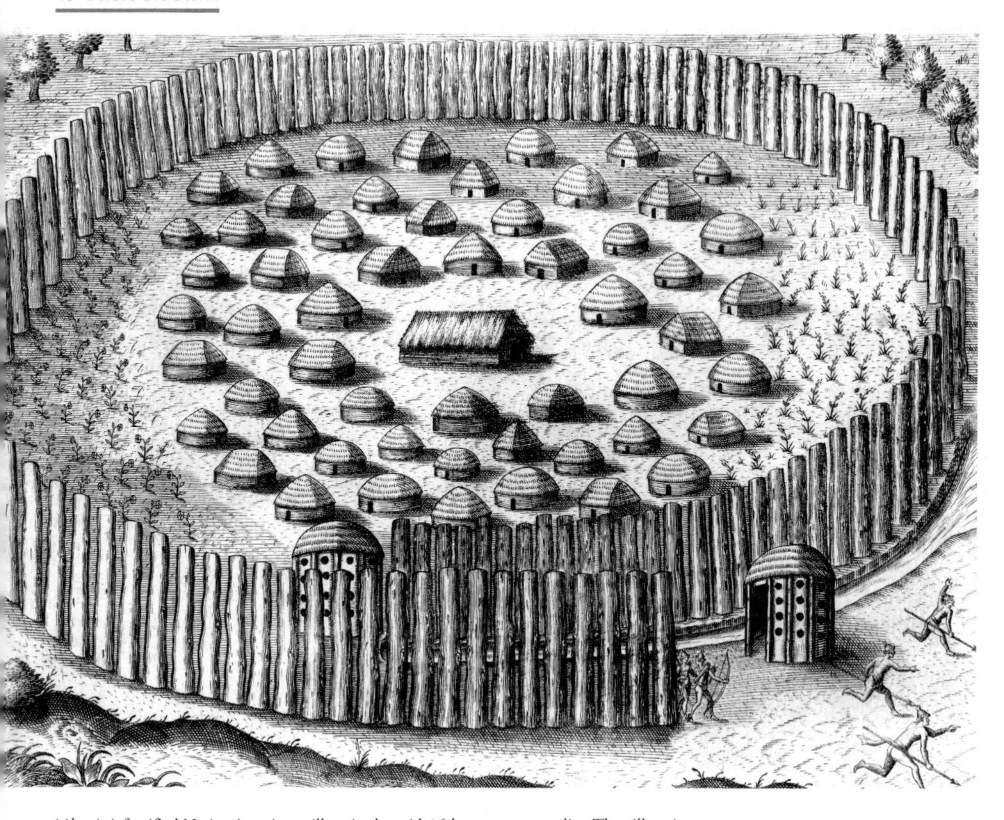

(*Above*) A fortified Native American village in the mid-16th century, or earlier. The village is protected by a palisade of thick palings. On either side of the entrance there is a guardhouse, and a stream has been diverted, probably to provide a water supply rather than to act as a moat. The largest hut, in the centre, is the chief's house. Such villages were most common in the north east of America, where there were plentiful supplies of wood. The nomadic tribes of the Great Plains built lodges of buffalo hides (teepees), but some – notably the Pawnee of the central Plains – often built their homes of earth.

(*Above*) Warriors declare war on an enemy by fastening locks of hair to the notches of arrows and planting them along the side of a path – from an illustration by Nicholas de Challeaux. Warfare was not common among the tribes of North America. Occasionally disputes would arise about rights over hunting ground. In times of famine and hardship there was always the risk of a raid by warriors desperate for food. As a general rule, colonists from Europe were received hospitably, unless relations had already been soured by raiding parties of white slavers.

For many tribes, hunting was a way of life. There were plenty of Native Americans who lived entirely by hunting, migrating with the seasons in search of food – anything from the mighty bison to the humble rabbit. Although skilled with the spear, the preferred weapon for hunting animals was the bow. The Native American bow was shorter than the European longbow, but had considerable penetrative power. (*Above*) Native Americans hunt deer by a stream. The hunters have disguised themselves with the skins of previous catches, enabling them to approach to within easy bow shot of their quarry.

(*Above*) Curing meat for the coming winter. The hunters have brought home a mixed bag. Arranged on the wood grill are fish, reptiles, a snake, and what may be a young deer. Meat cured in this fashion would be tough to eat, and would have lost much of its flavour, but in winter, when times were hard and there was little game to be had, it might just be enough to support life.

(*Above*) Nicholas de Challeaux's illustration of a group of Native Americans preparing for a feast in the mid-16th century or earlier. In the background, women are sorting through beans and pulses, and on the left a man is grinding herbs. To the right of the picture, a man carries a pitcher of water. In the centre, one man fans the wood fire while another pours beans into the large earthenware cauldron resting on the burning wood.

(*Above*) Jacques le Moyne's illustration of a group of Native Americans bringing surplus supplies of fruit and vegetables to a large storehouse. These public granaries were built beside water, in the hope that this would keep the supplies cool and fresh. Abundant harvests were few and far between. Many North American civilisations lived on the brink of famine most of the time, and it was common for entire settlements to be abandoned when drought struck.

(*Above*) A group of Native American youths take time out from hunting and working. Some are fishing on the lake in the background. Others are competing in running races. On the left young warriors sharpen their skills in archery. In the centre and foreground, five young men are playing what may well be the forerunner of basketball. The aim is to throw a stone to hit the square target on the top of the tall pole.

(*Above*) Men and women perform a Native American ritual dance. Dance played an important part in the culture of many tribes. There were dances to bring rain, to bring the sun, to appease the gods, to protect the tribe, to ensure the strength and fertility of the tribe. The figureheads at the top of the poles may well be those of past members of the tribe, who had brought glory, peace or prosperity to the community.

(*Left*) Christopher Columbus, the Italian explorer widely regarded as the discoverer of America. Columbus was forty-one when he set out in the *Santa Maria* to find a new route to the Indies for the King and Queen of Spain. His courage, and his stubborn insistence that he knew what he was doing, enabled him to convince his doubting crew that there was no need to turn back, even after weeks at sea.

(*Above*) A highly imaginative picture of Columbus reassuring his suffering (and complaining) crew, at the very moment when one of the sailors (right, background) sights land. The land was one of the Bahamas. Columbus named the island San Salvador (Blessed Saviour). According to Columbus's reckoning, they had at last reached the Indies, so he called the islanders *indios* (Indians). When he eventually made contact with the inhabitants, he described them as 'very well made, of very handsome bodies and very good'.

(*Left*) An early illustration of the departure of the *Santa Maria* (foreground), the *Pinta* and the *Niña* from Palos, 3 August 1492. In the background, King Ferdinand and Queen Isabella wave a fond farewell to the bold adventurer, and anxiously hope that he can fulfil his promises.

(*Above*) A 15th-century illustration of the arrival of Columbus's expedition in the Bahamas, 12 October 1492. Columbus lived another fourteen years, and never knew that he had failed to reach the Indies but had been one of the first Europeans to set foot on the continent of America. King Ferdinand (seated left) encourages Columbus from the shores of the Old World.

Although Amerigo Vespucci (*left*) was born in the same year as Columbus, and financed the 1492 expedition, it was not until 1499 that he made his first voyage to America. Vespucci's first name was given to the continent by a young German cartographer, Martin Waldseemüller.

News of Columbus's return sparked a sea-borne gold rush across the Atlantic. Within a few years European nations came to blows in their greed to exploit the riches of the New World. Pope Alexander VI, concerned lest Catholic nations should go to war with each other, drew a line across a rudimentary map of the Americas, granting all land east of the line to Portugal, all line west of the line to Spain. (*Above*) By the Treaty of Tordesillas, 1494, Pope Alexander defines the spheres of Spanish and Portuguese influence in the New World.

Though many of them were hunters, the Native Americans had a great respect for wildlife. Each creature was admired for its special qualities – be it strength, courage, speed or patience. The squirrel (*below, left*) was a totem animal of the Sioux. European explorers, too, were impressed by many of the animals they saw. (*Above, left*) A woodcut of a North American bison, from Francisco de Gomara's *La Historia General de las Indians,* 1554.

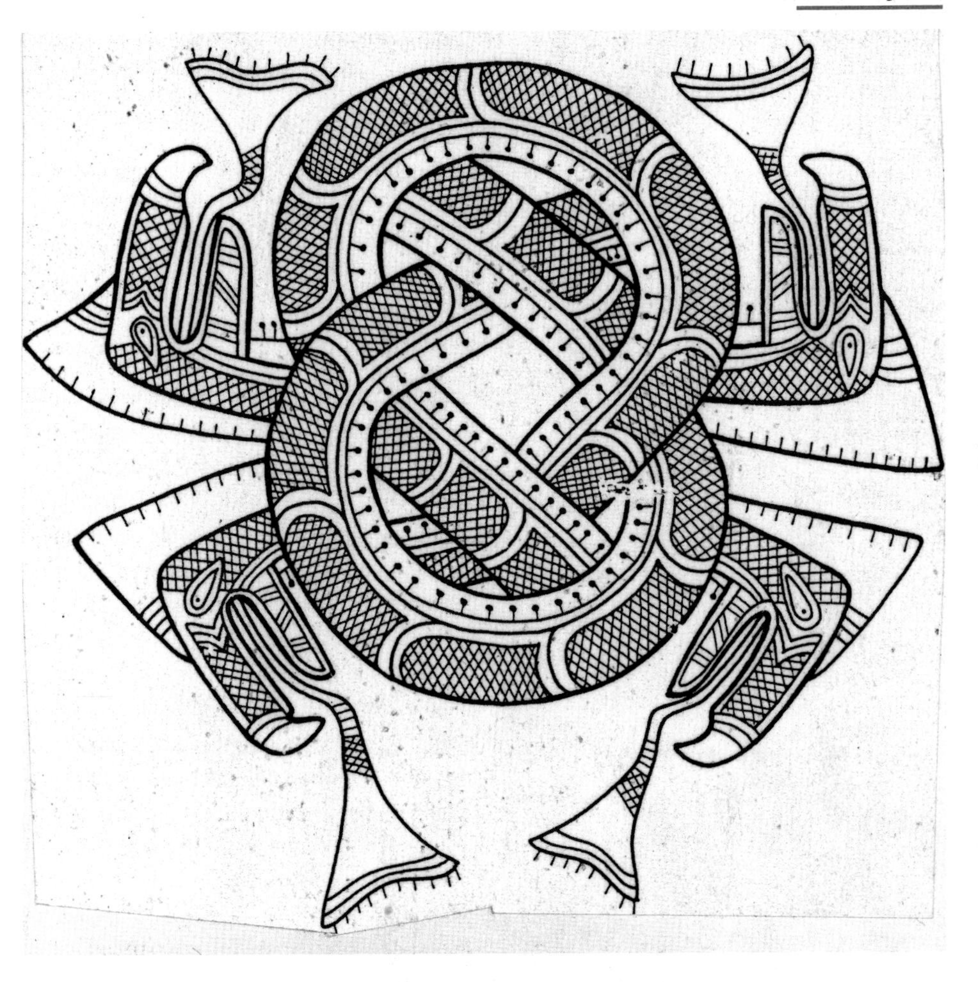

Of all creatures, the snake was perhaps the most feared as well as admired. It was cunning, dangerous, often deadly, and could survive in the most desolate of places – all qualities that a good warrior needed. (*Above*) A snake design etched on a shell by Apalachee Indians of the Missouri basin, c.1500.

Introduction to Period 2 – 1500–1825

When the invasion came, the raiders were a mixed bunch – Spanish missionaries, British pirates, French fishermen, freebooters, farmers, soldiers, convicts, ne'er do wells, traders and some very brave and hardy women. All that they shared was greed. The few jewels and trinkets that Columbus took back to Ferdinand and Isabella only served to whet the appetites of every prince and adventurer in Europe. Rumours of the riches of the Americas echoed through every palace and prison. Spanish rumours spoke of El Dorado (the Land of Gold), or at least of Cibola (the Seven Cities of Gold) where precious jewels dripped from the trees and the very chamber pots were made of gold, and where Judas took his holidays from Hell. French rumours spoke of Saguenay, another land of gold, but far to the north. British rumours spoke more realistically of Spanish gold, carried in slow-moving treasure hulks across the Atlantic Ocean.

From first to last, in the eyes of most Europeans, America has been a land of gold. In the 16th and early 17th centuries, settlers and explorers thought of little else, but gradually British,

French, Dutch and Portuguese alike realised that New France, New Spain, New England (and even New Scotland) had other forms of wealth to offer. It was a land teeming with good things, a vast supermarket stacked with furs, fish, tobacco, timber and opportunity, and with remarkably naïve and gullible staff at the checkouts.

The Dutch bought Manhattan for a pittance in 1624. The British snatched Virginia, sending cargoes of tobacco back to King James, who personally hated the stuff. The French took their time to survey as much of the wilderness as possible. Champlain became the 'founder of Canada'. Cartier explored the St Lawrence. La Salle pushed further west to the Mississippi, sailed down that great river and reached the Gulf of Mexico. But all the while, the French shopped as they went.

The Spanish made the greatest and the longest lasting impression on the continent, though not necessarily the most admirable. They came for plunder, bringing with them the horse, cannon, Catholicism and a language which is now the tongue of the vast majority of all Americans. They left a trail of missions in California and unpleasant memories of their behaviour at the Alamo in the Texan war of independence.

But it was the British who emerged as the final victors in the scramble for North America, though they arrived a little late on the scene. In April 1607 three ships financed by the London Company moored in Chesapeake Bay, and those on board went on to found the first British settlement, at Jamestown in Virginia. Within a short while they had established the first American self-governing body – the House of Burgesses. These officers were elected by every inhabitant; that is, by every male over the age of sixteen regardless of whether or not he owned property. And it was a broader based democratic institution than any in Britain at the time. Virginia became the first state to abolish the British system of primogeniture, whereby the eldest son automatically inherited his father's entire estate. Life in early Virginia offered opportunities such as never existed in Britain. Adam Thoroughgood, who went to Virginia as a servant, rose in fifteen years to be the owner of a plantation of some 5,300 acres (2,000 hectares) of land.

Plantations grew in number and size, stretching right down the coastlines of Virginia and Carolina, exporting not only tobacco, but also rice and indigo. On the eve of the American Revolution, Carolina alone shipped over a million pounds of indigo back to England. From the very beginning, the hard labour on these plantations was done by black slaves, the first sad cargo reaching Virginia from Africa around 1620. Sixty years later, black slaves were arriving at the rate of 60,000 a year.

1620 was a momentous year in the history of the United States. For on 19 September in that year, the *Mayflower* set sail from Plymouth with one hundred and forty-nine people on board, the vast majority of them seeking a new life in a new land. They took with them furniture, animals and chickens, salt beef, vegetables and hogsheads of beer, and they reached Cape Cod on 23 November. Their first winter in America was a disaster, but enough of them survived to proclaim their right to self-government in the Mayflower Compact. It was the beginning of the end of British rule in America.

Ten years later John Winthrop of Groton Manor in Suffolk joined them. He was a Puritan, though his reasons for leaving England were largely financial – he objected to the high taxes he paid and the low rents he received. He was a mixture of entrepreneur and preacher, adopting a high moral tone (he criticised the colony of Virginia for having as its main aim that which was 'carnal, not religious') but acting practically and pragmatically.

In the late 17th and early 18th centuries, British dissidents and non-conformists, men of ambition and men of tolerance, created a string of colonies that ran from Massachusetts to Virginia. By 1733 there were thirteen of them: New Hampshire, Massachusetts, Connecticut, Rhode Island, New Jersey, New York, Pennsylvania, Delaware, Maryland, Virginia, North Carolina, South Carolina and Georgia. Back in London, the Hanoverian kings George II and III and successive governments had little understanding of the creators of these colonies and even less of the strength and nature of their convictions.

This ignorance grew at a time when the

French power in North America was finally broken, by the British capture of Quebec and the terms of the Peace of Paris in 1763. It had cost a considerable amount of money to maintain the armies that had defeated the French, and the British Government wanted its money back. In 1765 Parliament in London passed the Stamp Act, taxing every legal document, newspaper and contract in the American colonies. The Americans howled with disapproval, and the Stamp Act was quickly repealed.

But the British had not learnt their lesson, and a few years later they imposed import duties on paper, glass and tea. The colonists boycotted all three. The duties on paper and glass were removed – that on tea remained. In Boston a minor riot ensued in which five people were killed. The next day broadsheets appeared with graphic descriptions and bloodthirsty pictures of the Boston massacre. On 16 December 1773, patriots swarmed aboard a ship in Boston harbour and threw its cargo of tea overboard. On 19 April 1775 shots were exchanged between British troops and American citizens at Lexington. The Revolution had started.

The end came with the British surrender at Yorktown six and a half years later. Those who had masterminded the Revolution then sat down to draw up the Constitution of the new United States. There were fifty-five of them in all, among them some of the greatest names in American history – Washington, Madison, Hamilton, Franklin, Adams, Mason and Henry. It took them seventeen weeks.

3
COLONIAL BEGINNINGS 1500–1650

Columbus never knew that he had made his landfall on an immense new continent, and many years elapsed before Europeans had any idea of the size of America. Early settlers and traders nibbled round the edges of this great New World. Almost a hundred years after Columbus, maps revealed little more than the coastline. Bays and river mouths were marked, and the sea creatures that inhabited the Atlantic Ocean and the Gulf of Mexico were graphically illustrated. (*Right*) John White's map of the east coast, from Virginia to Washington, 1587. White was one of the first settlers, a companion of Grenville, Raleigh and Drake, and a watercolour artist who recorded life in Virginia.

39
38
37
36
35
34
33
32
31
30
28
27

Introduction

The men who led early European expeditions in America were not young. Columbus was in his mid-forties when he first crossed the Atlantic. Poncé de Leon was over fifty when he landed in Florida and marched inland searching for gold and the fountain of youth. Samuel de Champlain, Cartier and de Soto were all over forty when they set out on their several journeys into the unknown. Henry Hudson was sixty when he embarked on his last and fatal voyage.

The youngest was Francisco Vasquez de Coronado, who was barely thirty when he put on his gilded armour and headed north from Compostela, Mexico, in February 1540. With him were two hundred and fifty horsemen, seventy foot soldiers, one thousand 'Indians', a train of priests, and a motley collection of goats, sheep and cattle. Two and a half years later, the survivors returned to Mexico having marched up the coast of the Gulf of California, through Arizona, New Mexico and Texas, into Kansas and as far north as the Nebraska border, before turning back. They were 'very sad and very weary, completely worn out and shamefaced'.

Most of these treasure hunts ended in disappointment, many of them in death. De Leon never found his fountain of youth. Raleigh never discovered El Dorado. Jacques Cartier never reached the legendary kingdom of Saguenay, said to have mines overflowing with gold and silver, and to be populated by men who flew about like bats despite being weighed down with rubies.

Greater wealth awaited those who established colonies and trading posts. By 1580 fishing in North American waters had become one of Europe's largest industries, with over five hundred vessels a year crossing the Atlantic for cod, salmon and shellfish. The colonists of Virginia made their fortunes from a single crop – tobacco. The Dutch snapped up (and later sold) a bargain when they bought Manhattan from the Native Americans in 1624. Honest men and villains alike filled their pockets and their bank accounts in the early days of Massachusetts, Maryland and the Carolinas.

Few of them had the idea of making their fortunes in New France, New Spain or New England and then returning to the old countries. From the very beginning, the colonists preferred to put down roots, to build new lives, to raise families and to stay. Occasionally fever or 'Indian' attacks wiped out a colony in its early days, but in general there was nothing temporary about the little settlements so lovingly and painstakingly built along the estuaries and bays of both east and west coasts.

And, in the east especially, those who had faced religious persecution in the Old World were determined to take strong hold of the New.

It was not long before Spanish adventurers began the conquest of mainland America. This Aztec figure of Death (*above*) from central America survived, though the Aztec empire was destroyed by the Spanish. In many ways, such destruction was a taste of what was to come. (*Right*) A petroglyph in Canyon de Chelly, Arizona, depicts the Spanish with their horses, lances and dogs.

In 1511 Vasco Núñez de Balboa joined an expedition to Darien on the Isthmus of Panama as a stowaway. Following an insurrection, Balboa took command and became the first European to sight the Pacific Ocean, in 1513 (*opposite, and above, left*). Like Columbus, Giovanni da Verrazano (*above, right*) came from Genoa. Francis I, King of France, commissioned him to discover a northern route to the Indies. Verrazano got no further than the north-east coast, exploring Chesapeake Bay, the Hudson River and Newfoundland.

In May 1539, Fernando de Soto (*above*, on horseback) anchored in Tampa Bay. He had been sent with an expedition of six hundred to find the gold that Charles V of Spain was convinced littered the New World. For three years de Soto and his ever-dwindling force tramped the Mississippi basin without success. In 1542 de Soto died of fever. To conceal his death from the Indians, his men lowered his body at midnight into the dark waters of the river he had discovered. Barely half the expedition survived to return to Mexico.

(*Above*) Francisco Vasquez de Coronado (on horseback) and his men cross the plains of Kansas in their search for Cibola, the 'Seven Cities of Gold', 1541. As a treasure hunt, it was a grim failure. As a feat of endurance it was an heroic odyssey. Coronado and his men fought their way through the American south west. They suffered from haemorrhoids and fistulas. Their bodies were covered in sores. On their backs they carried 30 lbs of armour. And they never found the land where the 'trees dripped with gold'.

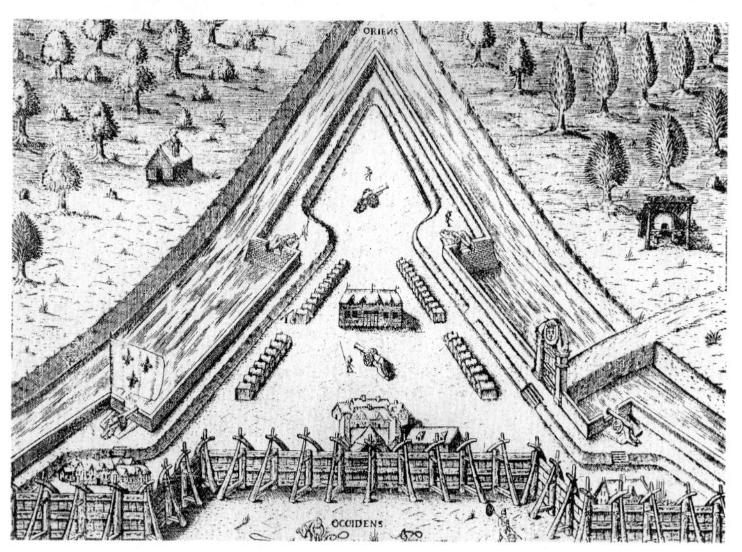

By the mid-16th century, the French had established a string of settlements along the south-east coast of America. Jean Ribaut led a Huguenot expedition that landed in what was to become South Carolina *(above, left)*. (*Below, left*) The French Fort Caroline on the St John's River, Florida. The triangular strong-post contained a granary, a barracks, and the residence of the commander, René Goulaine de Laudonnière.

Not all the new arrivals sought plunder. Many Spanish missions were established, providing shelter for the poor as well as a bridgehead for Christianity. (*Right*) The Spanish fort at St Augustine, Florida. St Augustine is the oldest continuously inhabited city in the United States.

Samuel de Champlain (*left*) was one of the boldest of the French explorers of North America. He made his first voyage to the north-east coast of America in 1603, and, though much of his time was spent mapping the new continent, there was little of the soft touch about Champlain. (*Above*) Champlain and his Montaignais and Huron allies make a surprise attack on an Iroquois camp, 1609. It is said that when Champlain's men fired their muskets at the Iroquois, they kindled a hatred of the French that was to last for more than a hundred years.

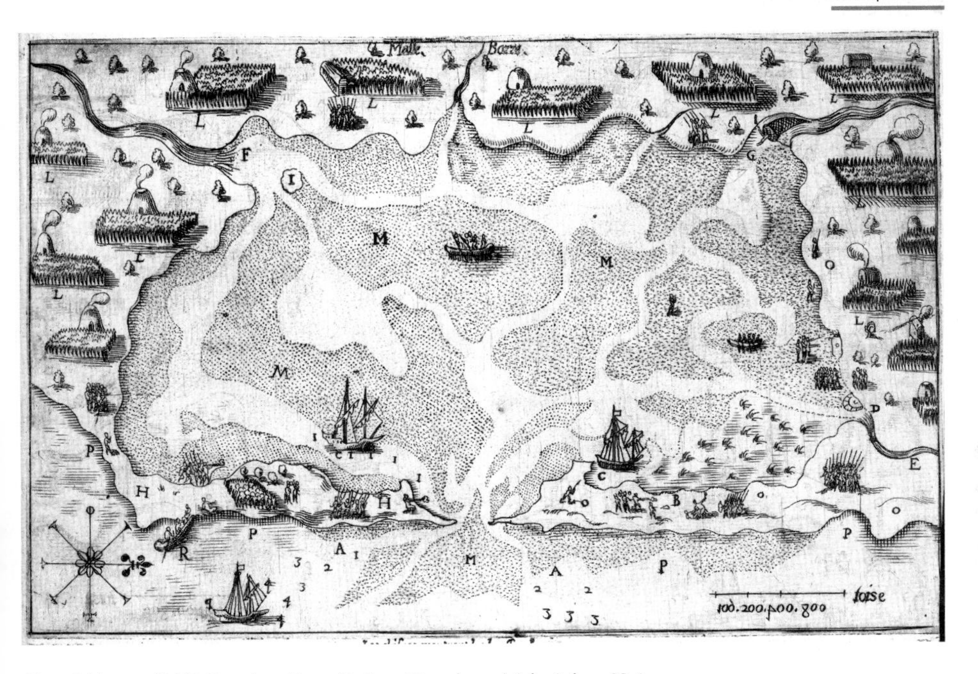

Champlain's map of Malle Barre (now Nauset Harbour, Massachusetts) (*above*) shows Native American encampments and another skirmish between French soldiers and Iroquois warriors. Champlain also founded the French settlement at Quebec. After Quebec was seized by the English in the Anglo-French War, Champlain negotiated its return to French control. Later he became known as 'the founder of Canada'.

The English explorer Henry Hudson (*above*) established better relations with the Iroquois. In 1609 Hudson sailed one hundred and thirty miles from the mouth of the river that was named after him to the site of Albany, New York. Here Hudson, his crew and a party of Mohawks made merry with a bottle of brandy. (*Right*) Hudson and his crew head for the shore.

The Five Nations of the Iroquois controlled much of the land around the St Lawrence River. By the mid-17th century, they had cleared most of their enemies from the east shore of Lake Huron and the north and south shores of Lake Erie (*opposite, below right*), and now sought to expand their territory into New England. (*Left*) An Iroquois warrior.

In earlier times, the Five Nations had been separate, warring factions. This was the work of Atotarho, an Onondaga sorcerer with a twisted body and snakes in his hair (*right*, seated). The other figures in the picture are Hiawatha and Dekanawida, who cured Atotarho's mind and body, and united the Iroquois. (*Below, left*) The totem of the Five Nations.

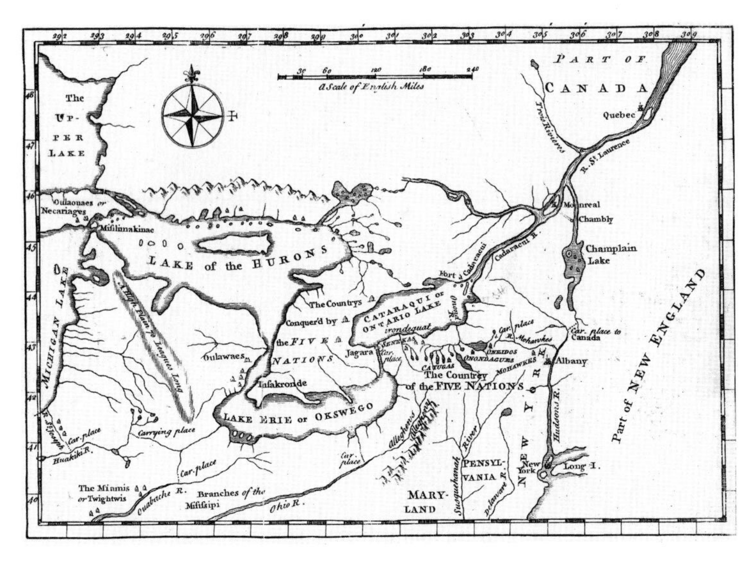

Some of the most beautiful, and probably the most accurate, portraits of Native Americans towards the end of the 16th century are to be found among the watercolours of the English artist John White. (*Left*) Hororoans, wife of Chief Pomece, and her daughter.

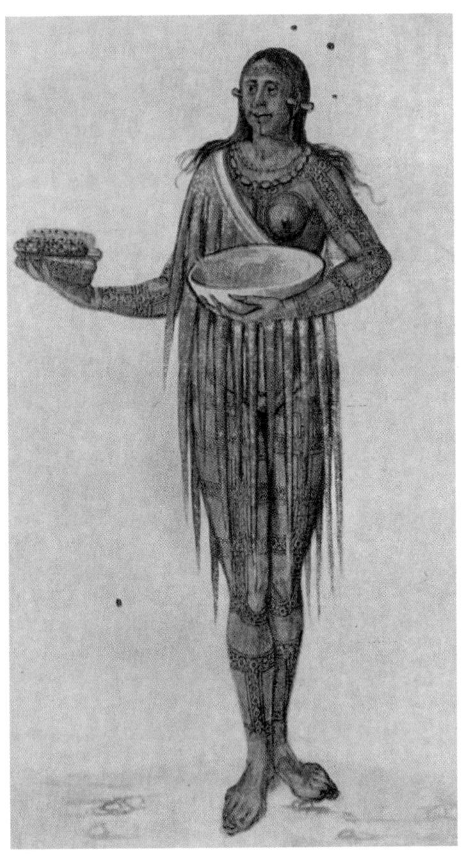

White sketched and painted scenes from Indian and early colonial life, as well as the flora and fauna of Virginia and Florida. In 1587 he was appointed governor of the settlement on Roanoake Island. White then sailed back to England, leaving his daughter and grand-daughter, Virginia Dare, the first English child born in the New World. When he returned in 1590, no trace of the colony could be found. White's paintings of an Indian woman from Florida (*above, left*) and an Indian chief (*above, right*).

The English colony of Jamestown, Virginia, was founded in 1607. After precarious beginnings, the colony prospered through the export of tobacco (*opposite, above and below*). The House of Burgesses in Jamestown was the first elected assembly in North America (*above*). In 1621 the Virginia Company recruited and sent out unmarried female settlers (*left*) to 'improve morale'.

The story of Princess Pocahontas and captain John Smith is one of the most romantic tales to come from early colonial days in North America. Pocahontas (*left*) – whose Indian name was Matoaka – was the daughter of Powhathan, king of the Pamaunkee people, a confederacy of the Tidewater tribes.

John Smith was an English soldier and adventurer whose harsh discipline saved the colony of Jamestown in its early days. According to Smith, Pocahontas saved his life on two occasions, when he had fallen into the hands of the Pamaunkee people. On the first occasion, Smith was on a hunting expedition when he was captured. Just as he was about to be put to death, Pocahontas intervened, begging for his life (*above*). Smith was spared.

Ætatis suæ 21. A°. 1616.

Smith was later captured a second time by the Pamaunkee (*above, top left*), and again Pocahontas pleaded with her father to spare Smith's life (*above, top right*). In 1612, Pocahontas was persuaded to join the Jamestown colony, where she was baptised Rebecca. The following year she married John Rolfe, Governor of Jamestown, and went to live in England (*opposite*). (*Above, bottom left and right*) Further images from the same series of engravings of Native American and colonial life.

It was the very success of the colony that led to one of the greatest tragedies in early colonial history. The colonists sought to cultivate more and more land to increase their tobacco harvest, which was making a great deal of wealth for the Virginia Company. The easiest way to do this was to take over land that the Indians had already cleared. In 1622 the Indians, led by Opechancanough, took up arms to repel the land-grabbing English. The outcome was the Jamestown massacre (*left*), in which some three hundred and fifty colonists were slaughtered, including John Rolfe.

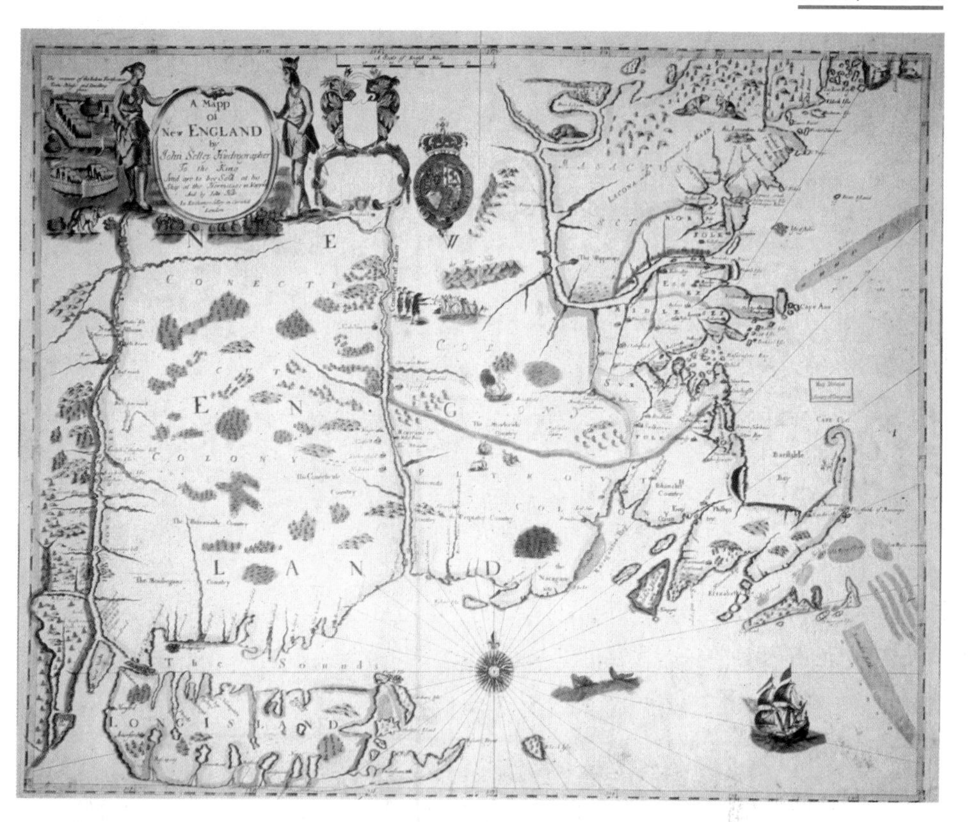

On 16 September 1620, the *Mayflower* set sail from Plymouth harbour in south-west England (*opposite*). On board were one hundred and forty-nine people, as well as goats, chickens, furniture, salted beef, vegetables and hogsheads of beer. One passenger and four of the crew died on the sixty-five-day voyage across the Atlantic. The rest landed safely at Cape Cod, Massachusetts, where, in the words of William Bradford (the ship's chronicler): 'they cried unto the Lord, and he heard their voice and looked upon their adversities'. (*Above*) An early map of New England, showing Cape Cod (far right) and Long Island (bottom left).

(*Opposite, above*) The Pilgrim Fathers pray before leaving Plymouth in September 1620. (*Above, right*) The landing at Plymouth Harbour in America, November 1620. The following winter over half the expedition died. (*Below, right*) William Bradford reads the Mayflower Compact to his fellow passengers on board the *Mayflower*. They agreed that all should be bound into a 'civil body politic', abiding by majority rule. (*Opposite, below*) Miles Standish marches at the head of a party from the Mayflower Colony.

The first task for any arrivals in the New World was to build a stockade (*below*). Once that was done, it was possible to trade with the local native population (*bottom*). For the first colonists at Jamestown life was harsh. They did not find the land of bounty and beauty that they had been promised by the promoters of the expedition – 'Virginia, earth's only paradise...' (*Left*) Coat-of-arms of the Virginia Company. After two years only thirty-eight of the one hundred and forty-nine who had set sail were still alive, and all they had to eat were the animals they trapped or shot in the woods, and the maize they obtained from the natives.

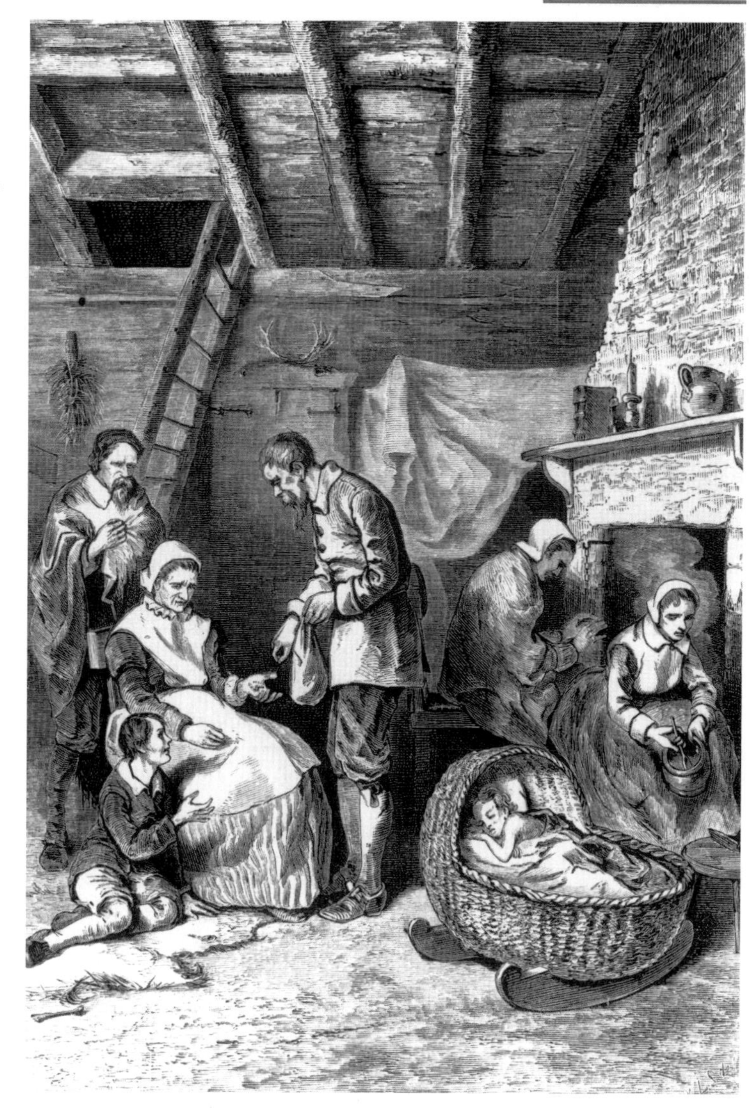

(*Right*) The first winter in 'Earth's only paradise' – a settler doles out part of the meagre supply of maize to his family in Jamestown. They had arrived too late in the year to plant food for an autumn harvest, and were living off what little food they had brought with them.

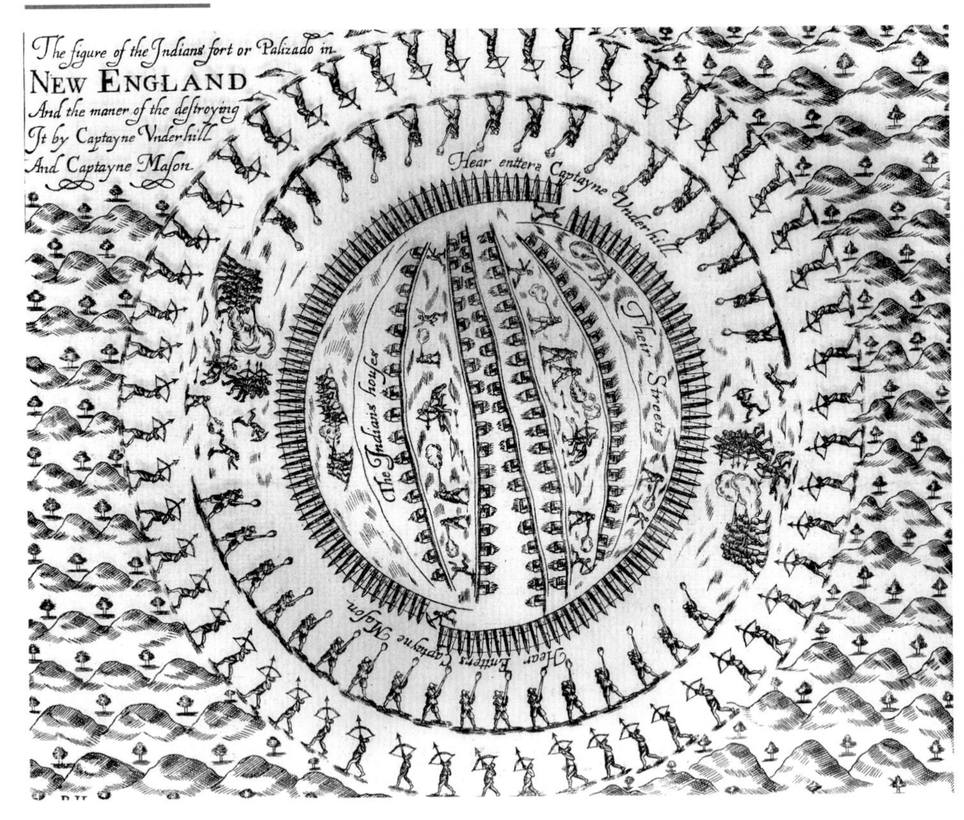

The early colonists were not the only ones to suffer hardship. The diseases they brought with them from Europe devastated the native population. In New England smallpox killed up to 75 per cent of Native Americans within the space of two generations. Those Indians who survived and refused to yield their land were often driven from it by force. In 1636 white settlers in Massachusetts accused a Pequot of murdering a colonist. In revenge, the settlers attacked and burnt a Pequot village (*opposite*), killing men, women and children. Only seven Indians escaped the carnage.

Sassacus, the Pequot chief, organised the survivors among his tribe and counter-attacked the settlers. A full-scale war followed. (*Opposite*) The plan of an attack on the Pequot stockade near West Mystic, Connecticut, 26 May 1637. The attack was led by Captain John Underhill and Captain John Mason. In the war, the settlers were supported by warriors from the Mohican and Narragansett tribes. The few Pequot left were sold into slavery and the Pequot nation was declared dissolved.

Many of the early settlers of the north east were Puritans (*below, right*), who had come to the New World to escape the religious persecution of the Old. But persecution followed some of them even across the Atlantic. Roger Williams was a Puritan who questioned the settlers' practice of appropriating native land without compensation. He was banished from the colony of Massachusetts but managed to buy land from the Narragansett people (*above*) on which he established the town of Providence, Rhode Island. Perhaps the Dutch obtained the best bargain. In 1626 Peter Minuit bought Manhattan Island from the Algonquin for the princely sum of $24 (*opposite*).

John Harvard (*opposite*) was born in Southwark, London, in 1607. He studied at Emmanuel College, Cambridge, and at the age of thirty sailed to Charlestown, Massachusetts. Here he spent a few months preaching, before dying of consumption. He left his fortune (£779 and a library of more than three hundred books) to the newly founded college at nearby Cambridge (*above*) that was later to bear his name.

4

A HOME FROM HOME 1650–1750

Years passed. The land that the early colonists had sweated to clear, to plant and to protect brought forth bigger and better harvests. Country that had seemed hostile and unmanageable became sweet to own and to tend. A class system arose. At the top were hard-working landowners, for America was not yet ready to support the idle rich. In the middle were the yeomen – those who had arrived poor and stayed to thrive. At the bottom were indentured servants. Adam Thoroughgood landed in America with nothing but the clothes on his back. Fifteen years later he owned 5,350 acres. The American Dream was beginning to take shape. (*Left*) A colonial farm in the 17th century.

Introduction

Wherever people go, they take their joys and sorrows with them. The early American colonists set about recreating the lives they had left behind. The Spanish sought to make America a province of Spain, faithful to the Catholic Church, owing allegiance to the Spanish King, and sending its wealth back to the coffers and estates of Old Castile. The French fought their way through the forest wilderness in the name of *le Roi Soleil*, the British in the name of King Charles (literally in the case of Carolina) and King George (literally in the case of Georgia).

The Puritans were no different. They had come to America to escape religious persecution, but this did not mean that they wished to practise religious toleration. In the second half of the 17th century, New England was on an equal footing with Old England in its bigotry and bitterness. The walls of many a clapboard house in Massachusetts and elsewhere were lined with familiar stern texts which had a new resonance in a new land: 'make with thine own hands all the things that thou needest', 'sow the good seed and the Lord will furnish the good harvest'. And when things went wrong and the Lord failed to provide, the old suspects were rounded up. The mere accusation of witchcraft was enough to send to the gallows many a non-conformist, and the term covered anyone from Baptist and Quaker to the outright godless.

It was no paradise. There was plenty of hard work to be done, little time for recreation (even where it was permitted), and punishments were harsh for those who offended. Prison awaited drunkards and layabouts, death for those guilty of adultery or fornication. It was a home from home.

For others, the phrase would have had a more ironic meaning. By the mid-17th century there were already thousands of black slaves toiling on the plantations of Virginia. This was to be the new home for them and their descendants for the next two hundred years. For the tribes who had settled east of the Appalachian and Allegheny mountains, or in Florida, Louisiana or Texas, there was also a need to find a home from home. Slowly and inexorably, they were pushed westwards. If they were lucky, they were forced to sell their land – usually, they were simply driven from it. But the 10,000 Native Americans of Florida who died of the measles Europeans brought with them in 1659 never left home.

By the mid-17th century colonial life was organised along European patterns in much of America. On Manhattan Island the Dutch colony of New Amsterdam boasted a windmill, a fort and a cluster of large houses, with a regular coming and going of ships in the harbour (*opposite, above*). Settlements were no longer isolated. Post riders ensured communication between towns and villages (*above*). Law and order was enforced with all the rigour of European notions of justice. Executions were public spectacles (*opposite, below*), and the death penalty awaited thieves and adulterers as well as murderers.

Jacques Marquette was a French explorer who was sent to America in 1666. With Louis Joliet, he discovered and charted the upper reaches of the Mississippi River in 1673 (*above*). Marquette was also a missionary, who brought Christianity to the Ottawa people around Lake Superior (*left*).

Nine years after Marquette's pioneer expedition, the French explorer René Robert Cavelier, Lord of La Salle, sailed down the length of the Mississippi to the Gulf of Mexico and claimed the whole of Louisiana for France. His second expedition, however, ended in disaster: La Salle lost his bearings, and was murdered by his own men (*right*).

As their position became stronger, many Puritans sought to convert Indians to Christianity. By 1675 there were thousands of 'praying Indians' in New England, though relations between whites and Indians remained strained. When a praying Indian was murdered, the Plymouth colony tried and executed three members of the Wampanoag tribe. This sparked off King Philip's war, named after the chief of the Wampanoag (*left*).

Fighting was bitter and frequent (*opposite, below*), and other tribes were sucked into the war (*above, right*). Eventually King Philip was killed, and his wife and children were sold into slavery. But the whites had been frightened by the scale of the fighting, and a group of rebels, led by Nathaniel Bacon, set fire to Jamestown in protest at the lack of protection they were receiving from Governor William Berkeley (*below, right*).

In 1661 a young Englishman named William Penn received a grant of land in America from Charles II (*above, left*). The grant was to pay off a debt that Charles owed Penn's father. Penn was a Quaker. 'God took me by the hand and led me out of the pleasures, vanities and hopes of the world.' God also led him to a land that was fertile and rich in minerals, where Penn founded the colony of Pennsylvania (*below, left*).

Penn recruited settlers from all over Europe. Religious dissenters were especially attracted to the new colony – Quakers, Mennonites, Amish, Moravians and Baptists – for Pennsylvania was situated well away from Puritan New England and the Anglican conformity of the South. Pennsylvania also had the advantage of good relations with the Indians, for Penn had made a point of buying land titles from the Native Americans. (*Above*) Moravian settlers on the banks of the Delaware River in Pennsylvania.

In 1692 a group of young women in Salem, Massachusetts, started exhibiting signs of strange behaviour – barking, grovelling and twitching. They claimed they had been bewitched. It was the beginning of the Salem witch-hunt. Within a few months more than a hundred people had been identified as being possessed by Satan. (*Left*) A young woman defends herself against the charge of witchcraft while her accuser writhes on the ground. (*Below, left*) The trial of George Jacobs, accused of witchcraft, at the Essex Institute in Salem.

The Puritan community was quick to believe the young women. Hysteria gripped the town. It was said that some of the accused had called on Satan to save them (*above, right*). Nineteen people were hanged. When Giles Corey refused to plead 'guilty' or 'not guilty' to the accusation *(below, right*), he was pressed to death between heavy stones. Most of the accused were women, many of whom were financially independent. They may well have died simply for being out of step with contemporary prejudice.

Numb. XL.

THE

Pennſylvania *GAZETTE.*

Containing the freſheſt Advices Foreign and Domeſtick.

From Thurſday, September 25. to Thurſday, October 2. 1729.

THE Pennſylvania Gazette *being now to be carry'd on by other Hands, the Reader may expect ſome Account of the Method we deſign to proceed in.*

Upon a View of Chambers's *great Dictionaries, from whence were taken the Materials of the* Univerſal Inſtructor in all Arts and Sciences, *which uſually made the Firſt Part of this Paper, we find that beſides their containing many Things abſtruſe or inſignificant to us, it will probably be fifty Years before the Whole can be gone thro' in this Manner of Publication. There are likewiſe in thoſe Books continual References from Things under one Letter of the Alphabet to thoſe under another, which relate to the ſame Subject, and are neceſſary to explain and compleat it; theſe taken in their Turn may perhaps be Ten Years diſtant; and ſince it is likely that they who deſire to acquaint themſelves with any particular Art or Science, would gladly have the whole before them in a much leſs Time, we believe our Readers will not think ſuch a Method of communicating Knowledge to be a proper One.*

However, tho' we do not intend to continue the Publication of thoſe Dictionaries in a regular Alphabetical Method, as has hitherto been done; yet as ſeveral Things exhibited from them in the Courſe of theſe Papers, have been entertaining to ſuch of the Curious, who never had and cannot have the Advantage of good Libraries; and as there are many Things ſtill behind, which being in this Manner made generally known, may perhaps become of conſiderable Uſe, by giving ſuch Hints to the excellent natural Genius's of our Country, as may contribute either to the Improvement of our preſent Manufactures, or towards the Invention of new Ones; we propoſe from Time to Time to communicate ſuch particular Parts as appear to be of the moſt general Conſequence.

As to the Religious Courtſhip, *Part of which has been retal'd to the Publick in theſe Papers, the Reader may be inform'd, that the whole Book will probably in a little Time be printed and bound up by it ſelf; and thoſe who approve of it, will doubtleſs be better pleas'd to have it entire, than in this broken interrupted Manner.*

There are many who have long deſired to ſee a good News-Paper in Pennſylvania; *and we hope thoſe Gentlemen who are able, will contribute towards the making This ſuch. We ask Aſſiſtance, becauſe we are fully ſenſible, that to publiſh a good News-Paper is not ſo eaſy an Undertaking, as many People imagine it to be. The Author of a* Gazette *(in the Opinion of the Learned) ought to be qualified with an extenſive Acquaintance with Languages, a great Eaſineſs and Command of Writing and Relating Things cleanly and intelligibly, and in few Words; he ſhould be able to ſpeak of War both by Land and Sea; be well acquainted with Geography, with the Hiſtory of the Time, with the ſeveral Intereſts of Princes and States, the Secrets of Courts, and the Manners and Cuſtoms of all Nations. Men thus accompliſh'd are very rare in this remote Part of the World; and it would be well if the Writer of theſe Papers could make up among his Friends what is wanting in himſelf.*

Upon the Whole, we may aſſure the Publick, that as far as the Encouragement we meet with will enable us, no Care and Pains ſhall be omitted, that may make the Pennſylvania Gazette *as agreeable and uſeful an Entertainment as the Nature of the Thing will allow.*

The Following is the laſt Meſſage ſent by his Excellency Governour *Burnet*, to the Houſe of Repreſentatives in *Boſton*.

Gentlemen of the Houſe of Repreſentatives,

IT is not with ſo vain a Hope as to convince you, that I take the Trouble to anſwer your Meſſages, but, if poſſible, to open the Eyes of the deluded People whom you repreſent, and whom you are at ſo much Pains to keep in Ignorance of the true State of their Affairs. I need not go further for an undeniable Proof of this Endeavour to blind them, than your ordering the Letter of Meſſieurs *Wilks* and *Belcher* of the 7th of *June* laſt to your Speaker to be publiſhed. This Letter is ſaid (in *Page* 1. of your Votes) *to incloſe a Copy of the Report of the Lords of the Committee of His Majeſty's Privy Council, with his Majeſty's Approbation and Order thereon in Council*; Yet theſe Gentlemen had at the ſame time the unparallell'd Preſumption to write to the Speaker in this Manner; *You'll obſerve by the Concluſion, what is propoſed to be the Conſequence of your not complying with His Majeſty's Inſtruction (the whole Matter to be laid*

It was not long before an established colony produced its own newspaper. Americans were hungry for news of what was happening in Europe as well as local news. Daily papers were rare – most were published weekly or even monthly. The *Pennsylvania Gazette* (*left*) boasted on its front page that it contained '...the freshest Advices Foreign and Domestick...'

The *New-York Weekly Journal* also claimed to contain the latest news. In its edition for 14 October 1734 (*right*) the paper reported on events in Danzig and Hamburg. The editorial by John Peter Zenger might well have been of more interest to New Englanders, however, as it posed the question of the legitimacy of colonial and English courts of law.

THE

New-York Weekly JOURNAL.

Containing the freſheſt Advices, Foreign, and Domeſtick.

MUNDAY October 14*th*, 1734.

Mr. *Zenger*;

I Have been Reading, the arguments of Mr. *Smith*, and *Murray*, with Regard to the Courts, and there is one Thing, I can't comprehend, *viz.* If it is the ſame Court, I take it, that all the Writs ought to be taken out in *England*, and teſted by the Judges there; if they are taken out here, the ſame Judges ought to teſt them here. If it is a like Court, it is not the ſame; and if not the ſame, it is not that fundamental Court which is eſtabliſhed by immemorial Cuſtom. I would be glad ſome of your Correſpondents would clear up this Point; becauſe in my poor Oppinion, if the Exchequer Court here is not the ſame identical Court as the Exchequer Court in *England*, it is without Lawful Authority.

FOREIGN AFFAIRS.

Dantzick, Auguſt 4.

Yeſterday the Biſhop of Cracow, in the King's Name, received Homage of this City, and the Ceremony was very magnificent. His Majeſty, before his Departure, iſſued the Univerſalia for holding of the Petty-Dyets in the Provinces. Thoſe in Poliſh Pruſſia, will be held in 15 Days. The Ruſſian and Saxon Troops will march ſuddenly to the Places where the Provincial Aſſemblies are to be opened; and the reſt are to go and poſt themſelves in Great Poland. M. Rewuſki, the Crown Carver, is declared Regimentary, and is to command a Body of Troops, conſiſting of 2000 Ruſſian Dragoons, 11000 Coſſacks, and the Regiment Guards formerly in the Service of King Staniſlaus.

Bruſſels, Auguſt 6.

Letters from Rome of the 17*th* paſt adviſe. That they had Advice there that the Siege of Gaeta was not yet formed, altho' the Spaniards had there 70 Cannon, and Mortars, and were working on Batteries, but that all they raiſed in the Night was beat down next Morning by the Cannon of the Palace; and that the Heats being already Exceſſive, the Spaniards were in Fear of looſing a vaſt Number of Men in the Reduction of that Fortreſs.

Hamburg, Auguſt 10.

According to Letters from the Camp before Dantzick, the Veſſels there were taken up by Order of the Generals in Chief, to ſerve for carrying the heavy Artillery and Baggage by Water to Thorn and Warſaw.

We have certain Advice, that King, Staniſlaus was departed from Brandenburg Pruſſia, and arrived ſafe in the Crown Army, under the Command of M. Kiowſki, near Peterkow the 24*th* paſt, and immediately afterwards held a Council of War, wherein it was reſolved to draw all the diſperſed Troops into a Body, and march directly to Volhinia in Podolia.

Amſt.

(*Opposite*) General James Edward Oglethorpe, c. 1750. Oglethorpe obtained a charter for the settlement of Georgia as a refuge for paupers in 1732. The following year he founded the city of Savannah (*left*). (*Below, left*) Felling trees on Yamacraw Bluff, 1733. The timber was used for Savannah's houses.

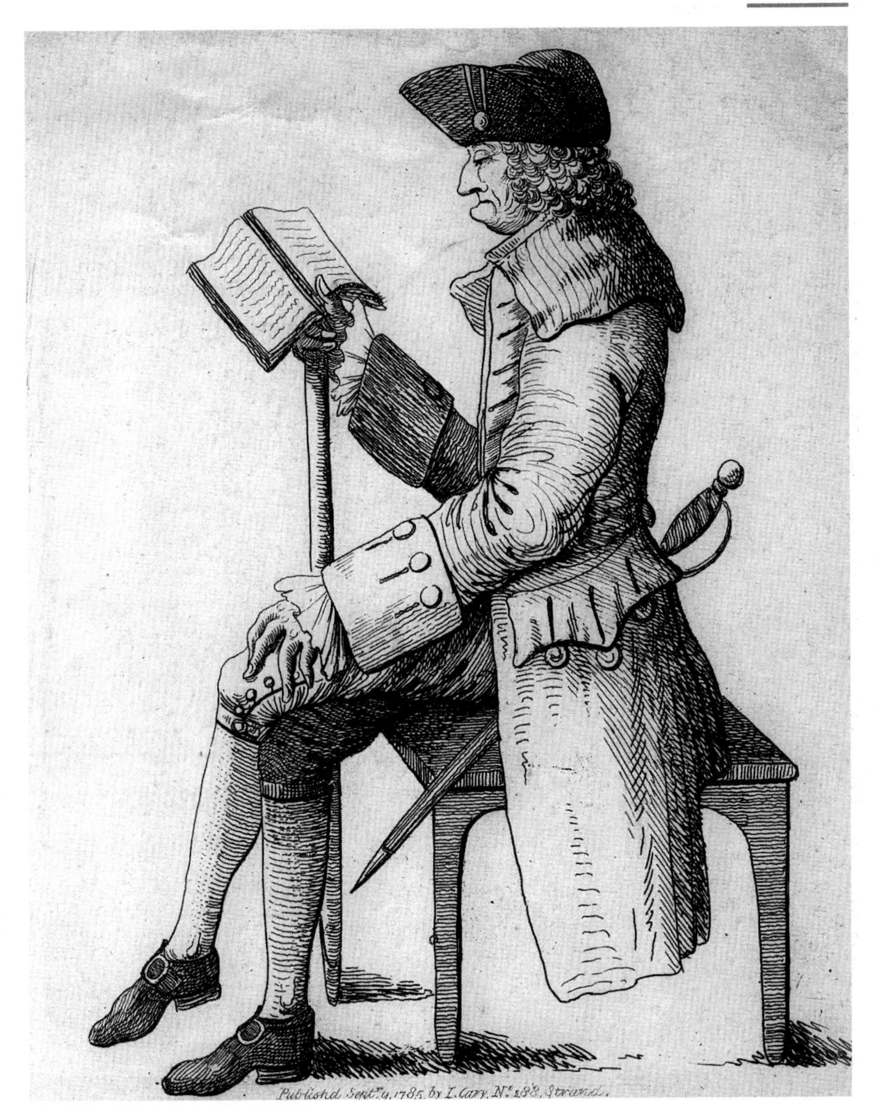
Publishd Sept.r 9. 1785. by I. Cary. N.o 188. Strand.

In the 1640s the Iroquois had gone to war with neighbouring tribes to protect their beaver hunting grounds, although they then hunted the animal to extinction in that region. (*Left*) Native Americans using muskets and bows on a beaver hunt in Ohio, c. 1750. The animals' valuable pelts were later exchanged with British or French traders for guns and tools (*opposite, below*).

(*Above*) The trading post of Grand Portage on Lake Superior, Minnesota, in the mid-18th century. The post housed the headquarters of a profitable fur trading company run by Simon McTavish and partners. Indians trapped the beavers, French-Canadians transported the pelts, and the British exported them.

5
COLONIAL BATTLEGROUND 1750–1770

(*Right*) Boston, Massachusetts, from Bunker Hill. In New England, the British colonists were bound together by language, culture and a shared mistrust of the French and their Indian allies. While the French threat remained, the colonists were also bound to Britain, for they relied largely on British troops to protect them. In the 1750s and 1760s, however, that threat was gradually removed in what became known as the French and Indian Wars, the longest and costliest struggle between rival European powers in the New World.

Introduction

It was not long before the New World became a battleground for the Old World. Within a little over one hundred years the French and the Spanish, the Dutch and the British, and, especially, the French and the British had somehow managed to bump into one another, making it appear that there really wasn't room for everyone in this enormous land. That being so, it was essential to discover whose might gave them the right to stay.

The squabbles turned into bitter fights, and produced some of the earliest of American heroes. George Washington stepped on to the historical stage as a twenty-year-old militia leader in the brief war of 1754 between the British and the French. His first command ended in defeat and he surrendered to the French at Fort Necessity in 1754. Nevertheless, Washington seems to have enjoyed his first taste of warfare.

'I have heard the bullets whistle,' he wrote, 'and believe me, there is something charming in the sound.'

Two years later the French and British clashed again at Fort Duquesne, where the wagoners attached to General Braddock's expeditionary force included the earliest 'big shot' of the West, Daniel Boone. Boone was the typical frontiersman, believing in three necessities for survival – 'a good gun, a good horse and a good wife'. He was one of the first to push westward through the Appalachian Mountains, following in the footsteps of Thomas Walker. Walker was an English doctor who named the pass he discovered 'Cumberland Gap', in honour of the Duke of Cumberland who had butchered the Jacobites at Culloden Moor in 1746. Boone and the Cumberland Gap both passed into legend and song. America was beginning to amass a written history.

In 1756 the French and British fought out a more protracted war. The French and Indian War, as it came to be called, lasted seven years. South of the Canadian border, the focal point was once again Fort Duquesne, renamed Fort Pitt by the British, who saw off their Delaware besiegers by presenting them with blankets that were infected with smallpox. Thousands died and the siege was lifted.

What neither Washington nor the British realised was that the removal of the French military threat from New England strengthened the gathering resolve of many Americans to take responsibility for their own lives. The next (and last) time New England became a colonial battleground, Washington and the British were on opposite sides, and American colonial history came to an end.

In 1755 General Edward Braddock of the Coldstream Guards, commander-in-chief of the British forces in North America, hacked his way for several hundred miles through the mountain wilderness (*left*) to attack the French at Fort Duquesne. With him was the young lieutenant colonel of militia, George Washington (*below, left*, on horseback).

Unknown to the British, the French had recently been joined by reinforcements, and were far stronger in numbers than Braddock anticipated. Not only that – thanks to their Indian scouts, the French were well aware of Braddock's approach. The British troops were ambushed and routed. Nine hundred of them were killed. Braddock himself was mortally wounded in the battle, and was carried, dying, on a gun limber during the retreat (*above*). When news of the defeat reached London, the British Government realised it had a full-scale war on its hands.

The French and Indian War of 1754–63 was the last major showdown between the British and the French in north-east America. For some two hundred years settlers and traders from the two European nations had managed to avoid each other. As their populations increased and they pushed further and further inland, however, tension rapidly developed. The French relied on a string of forts built along the major rivers to secure their domination of the area. British troops marching to relieve their beleaguered forces were often ambushed by the French and Indians (*above*).

Both European powers had Native American allies. The Hurons and the Mohawks sided with the British. (*Above, left*) Thayendanega, a Mohawk chief who received a British education, adopted the name Joseph Brant. He remained loyal to the British throughout the French and Indian War, the Pontiac Wars and the American War of Independence. (*Above, right*) Pontiac, chief of the Ottawa tribe and leader of a federation of Native Americans against settlers. He became one of the leading allies of the French during the war of 1754–63.

During the night of 12–13 September 1759, British troops under the command of General James Wolfe rowed up the St Lawrence River above Quebec, while their commander recited verses from Gray's *Elegy, Written in a Country Churchyard.* Their objective was the Heights of Abraham, at the top of the cliffs overlooking the city (*opposite*). When the morning mists cleared, the British army was lined up for battle and the French had been caught off guard.

The French hurried out of the city. It was an old-fashioned, European-style battle. The French advanced to within a musket shot of the British troops, and were decimated by two devastating volleys. Wolfe was killed (*opposite*), though he managed to live long enough to know that the French had been defeated and their power in North America totally destroyed. What neither Wolfe nor the British Government realised was that, with this success, a new era in colonial politics was to open.

The commander of the French troops at the battle for Quebec was Louis Joseph, Marquis de Montcalm (*opposite, left and right*). Montcalm was forty-seven, but had already been a soldier for more than thirty years. He was an able general. In 1756 he captured the British posts of Oswego and Fort William Henry. In 1758, with only a small force, he successfully defended Ticonderoga, but, after the loss of Louisburg and Fort Duquesne, he was forced to retire to Quebec.

Although the French troops defending the city outnumbered Wolfe's force by two to one, their retreat from the Heights of Abraham rapidly turned into a rout. Montcalm tried to rally his forces, but the task was impossible as he was borne back towards Quebec in the headlong rush. He was wounded (*opposite*) and died the following morning.

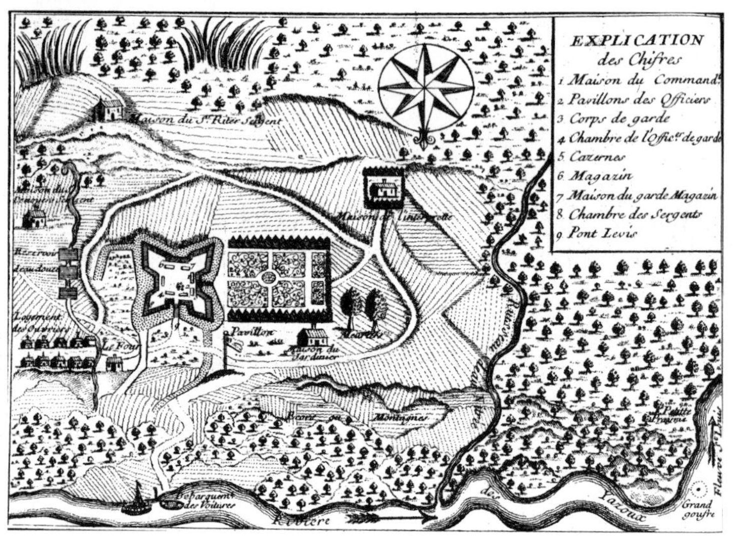

(*Below, left*) A plan of the French fort of St Pierre on the Yazoo River, Mississippi, prior to the French and Indian War. (*Above, left*) The Battle of Lake George, 8 September 1755. General William Johnson exhorts the British soldiers and settlers to attack their French and Indian enemies. After his victory in the battle he was appointed Superintendent of Indian Affairs. (*Opposite, below*) General William Pepperell rides in triumph after the British capture the French town of Louisburg, June 1745. (*Opposite, above*) The French attempt to retake Louisburg, November 1758.

(*Left and below*) Chief Pontiac of the federation of Native Americans greets Major Rogers and his British troops, 1766. Rogers later gained a celluloid immortality when portrayed by a deerskin-clad Spencer Tracy in the film *Northwest Passage.* (*Opposite*) Two years earlier, Pontiac had signed a peace treaty with Colonel Henry Bouquet (left foreground) and became a staunch ally of the British.

At the age of twenty-seven, George Washington married a wealthy widow named Martha Custis. Her estate and his own home at Mount Vernon (*left*) made Washington one of the richest men in the land. Martha's dowry also included one hundred and fifty slaves, whose condition is said to have embarrassed Washington (*below*).

Washington was no emancipator, however, and the slaves were employed on his plantation (*above*). Washington was not a cruel man, but possessed little charm or jollity. He was a man who preferred to remain aloof, to stand on ceremony, and who did not like to be touched. In 1775, at the age of forty-three, both George and Martha expected that he would spend the rest of his life running his plantation. They were wrong.

Boston (*above*) was the centre of opposition to the British. Here Samuel Adams addressed Patriots in the Old South Meeting House, urging them to direct action in what became known as the Boston Tea Party. Here the radical underground regularly met, to discuss the latest injustices and ways in which the colony was being exploited. (*Right*) Faneuil Hall, Dock Square, Boston, known as 'the Cradle of Liberty' and another meeting place for revolutionaries.

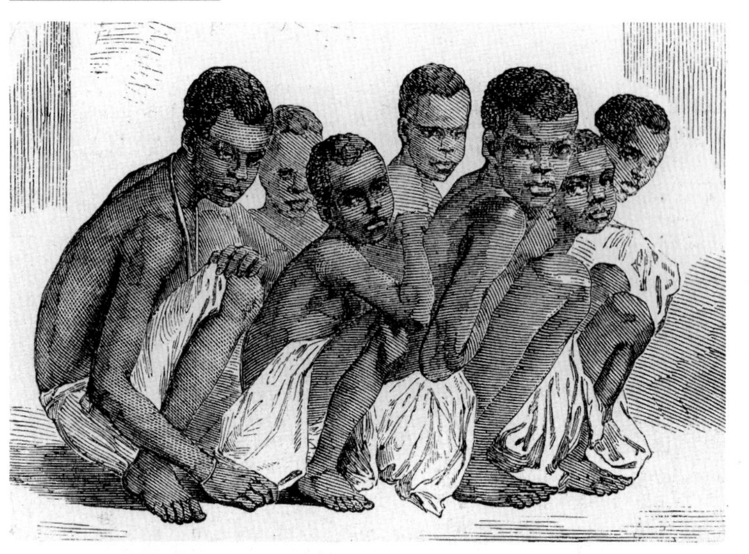

Slaves (*left*) were brought to the American colonies in crowded ships from the earliest days. The ship *Brookes* (*opposite*) was a slaver which carried two hundred and ninety-two slaves on the lower deck, with another one hundred and thirty on shelving round the sides of the hold. (*Below*) Iron masks worn by slaves to prevent them eating sugar cane, collars and shackles to prevent them running away.

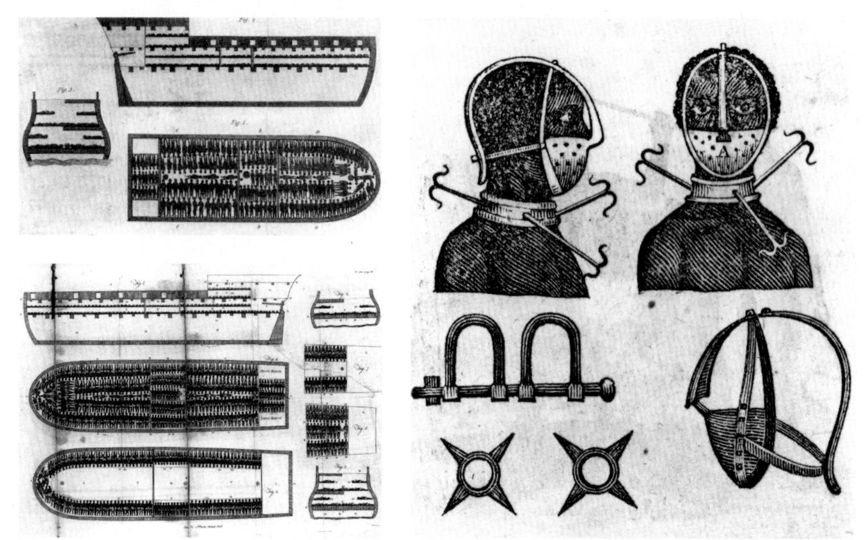

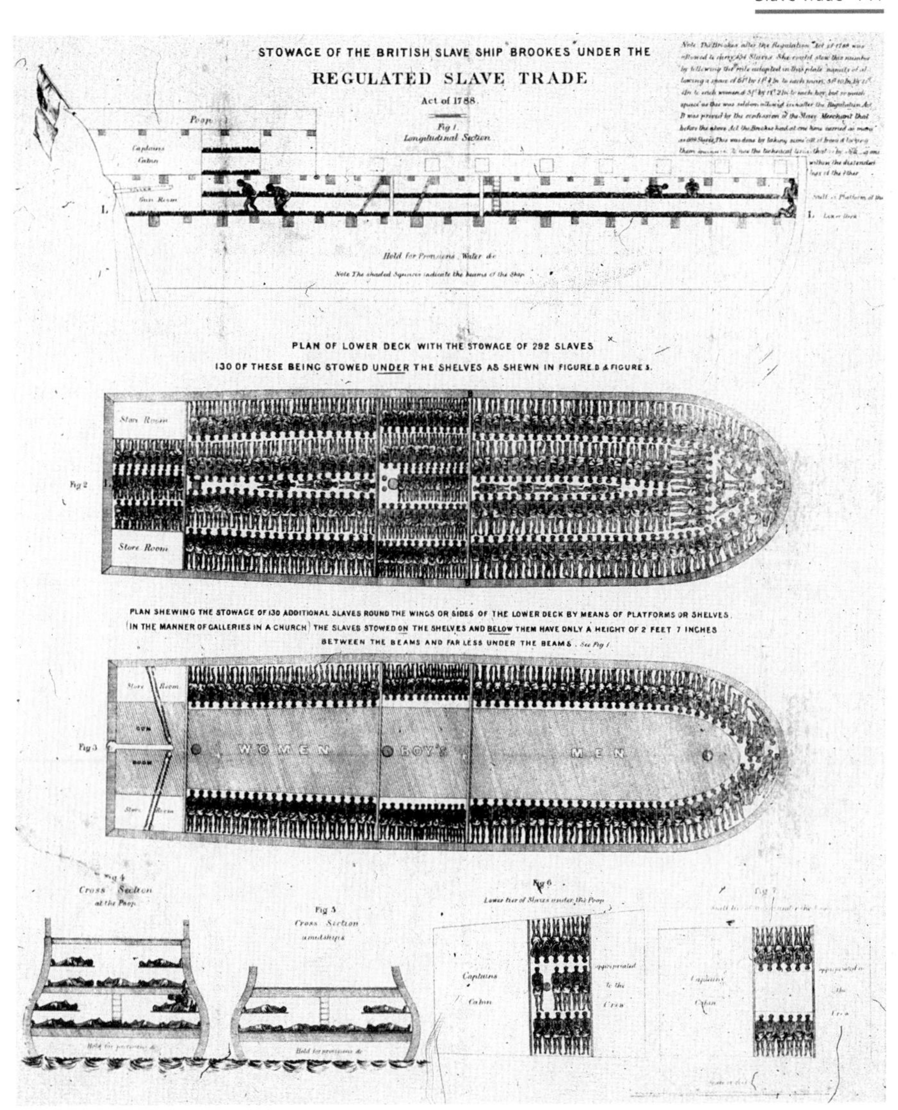
STOWAGE OF THE BRITISH SLAVE SHIP BROOKES UNDER THE
REGULATED SLAVE TRADE
Act of 1788.
Fig 1.
Longitudinal Section
Poop
Captains Cabin
Gun Room
Hold for Provisions Water &c
Note The shaded Squares indicate the beams of the Ship
PLAN OF LOWER DECK WITH THE STOWAGE OF 292 SLAVES
130 OF THESE BEING STOWED UNDER THE SHELVES AS SHEWN IN FIGURE 6 & FIGURE 5.
Fig 2
Store Room
Store Room
PLAN SHEWING THE STOWAGE OF 130 ADDITIONAL SLAVES ROUND THE WINGS OR SIDES OF THE LOWER DECK BY MEANS OF PLATFORMS OR SHELVES
(IN THE MANNER OF GALLERIES IN A CHURCH) THE SLAVES STOWED ON THE SHELVES AND BELOW THEM HAVE ONLY A HEIGHT OF 2 FEET 7 INCHES
BETWEEN THE BEAMS AND FAR LESS UNDER THE BEAMS. See Fig 1.
Fig 3
Store Room
GUN
ROOM
Store Room
WOMEN
BOY'S
MEN
Fig 4
Cross Section
at the Poop
Fig 5
Cross Section
amidships
Hold for provisions &c
Fig 6
Lower tier of Slaves under the Poop
Captains
Cabin
appropriated
to the
Crew
Fig 7
Captains
Cabin
appropriated to
the
Crew

6
THE WORLD TURNED UPSIDE DOWN 1770–1783

(*Left*) Independence Hall, Boston, formerly the Pennsylvania State House. It was here that the Declaration of Independence was first read and the Constitution of the United States was drafted. Fifty-five men met to construct the American Constitution, though in the eyes of Thomas Jefferson they were 'demi-gods'. They were professional men, and men of business, some of them with experience of government. They sat together for seventeen weeks, arguing and contesting just how this new country should be run. And, at the end, they managed to persuade the thirteen states to accept the principles that they wished to establish.

Introduction

Books, poems, films, paintings, postage stamps, monuments, songs and annual re-enactments keep alive the memory of the set pieces of the American Revolution. More than two hundred years after the events took place, every schoolchild is introduced to Betsy Ross, leaning from her upstairs window and defiantly urging the British redcoats to 'shoot if you will this old grey head, but spare our country's flag'; to Paul Revere galloping through the night from Boston to Lexington and on to Lincoln, warning the people of Massachusetts that the British army is on the move; to George Washington, standing in the prow of a small boat, as his heroic army crosses the icy waters of the Delaware. Dotted about New England are the carefully preserved sites of every battle and skirmish of the war, shrines to those that fought and died to give their country independence.

It was an odd mixture of civil war, guerrilla war, Indian war and formal 18th-century war.

The British never came to terms with a new method of fighting, where the enemy unexpectedly emerged from the landscape, fired a few rounds of devastating accuracy from their German rifles, so vastly superior to the British muskets, and immediately vanished. Washington's army was largely made up of part-time soldiers, who fought their battles at Lexington and Saratoga, Concord and Bunker Hill, and then returned to their farms and families. They were fighting for a cause in which they passionately believed – freedom. To many, that meant the right to pursue their way of life without interference from a meddling government over 3,000 miles away. To a far-sighted few, it meant the opportunity to create a new type of nation, one that held '...that all Men are created equal, that they are endowed by their Creator with certain unalienable rights, that among these are Life, Liberty and the pursuit of Happiness...'

When Lord Cornwallis, as exhausted and bewildered as the rest of his troops, finally surrendered at Yorktown on 19 October 1781, the band played *The World Turned Upside Down.* The tune was appropriate, for the event was to prove one of the most influential in all history. Modern democracy was born, with all its strengths and weaknesses, faults and benefits, hopes and disappointments. The British had been beaten in the field, and at the peace treaty in Paris in 1783 they signed away all the outposts and ports that they still held. The other European powers subsequently sold up and crept away.

THE

RIGHTS

OF

COLONIES

EXAMINED.

Stephen Hopkins

PUBLISHED BY AUTHORITY.

PROVIDENCE:
PRINTED BY *WILLIAM GODDARD.*
M.DCC.LXV.

One of the least sensible deeds of the British Government was to pass the Stamp Act in 1765. This imposed a tax on most documents. Reaction was swift and strong. (*Opposite, below, left*) Patrick Henry delivers a passionate speech against the Act in the Virginia House of Burgesses. (*Opposite, above left and below right*) Protesters hurl documents bearing the 'stamp' onto street bonfires. (*Opposite, above, centre*) *The Rights of the Colonies Examined* – a pamphlet by Stephen Hopkins of Rhode Island, exposing the injustices of the Act. (*Above and opposite, above right*) Rioting against the Act in the streets of New York.

By the summer of 1776 New York had joined Boston as one of the flashpoints of the American Revolution. On 2 July, while the new Congress voted for independence, British redcoats landed on Staten Island. By mid-August, General William Howe had assembled a force of 32,000 men. Long Island became the battleground. The Americans were driven from Brooklyn Heights and Washington was forced to retreat. For the rest of the war, New York remained in British occupation. (*Right*) A part of New York City is destroyed by fire, 19 September 1776.

(*Left*) Paul Revere's engraving of the Boston Massacre of 5 March 1770. On that day, an angry crowd gathered near the Customs House, throwing snowballs and oyster shells at a British sentry. The soldier called for help. In the ensuing scuffle one of the soldiers was knocked to the ground. He then fired into the crowd. Other shots were fired. Five people were killed, eight more wounded. The Revolution had its first martyrs.

Three years later the British Government gave permission for the East India Company to sell tea in America through its own agents, rather than through colonial retailers. Bostonians were enraged by this plan, and at the duty they would have to pay on the tea. On the night of 16 December 1773, a group of patriots, disguised as Mohawk Indians, boarded the tea ships, and tipped the chests of tea into the harbour (*right and opposite, below*).

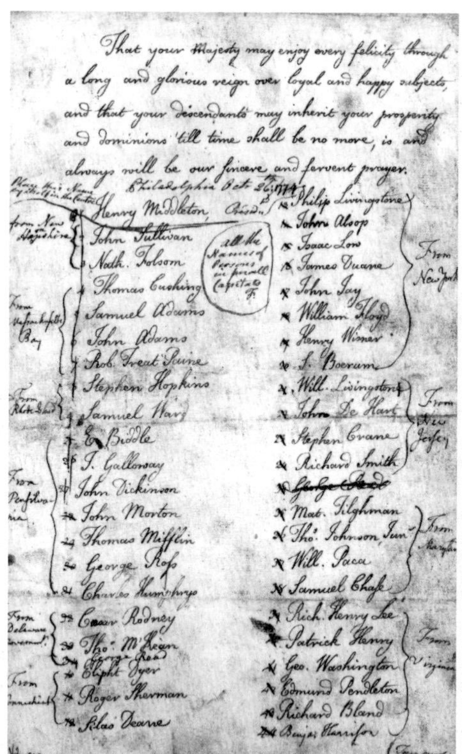

That your Majesty may enjoy every felicity through a long and glorious reign over loyal and happy subjects, and that your descendants may inherit your prosperity and dominions 'till time shall be no more, is and always will be our sincere and fervent prayer.

Philadelphia Oct 26th 1774

Henry Middleton
John Sullivan
Nath. Folsom
Thomas Cushing
Samuel Adams
John Adams
Rob. Treat Paine
Stephen Hopkins
Samuel Ward
E. Biddle
J. Galloway
John Dickinson
John Morton
Thomas Mifflin
George Ross
Charles Humphreys
Cæsar Rodney
Tho. M'Kean
George Read
Eliphalet Dyer
Roger Sherman
Silas Deane

Philip Livingstone
John Alsop
Isaac Low
James Duane
John Jay
William Floyd
Henry Wisner
S. Boerum
Will. Livingston
John De Hart
Stephen Crane
Richard Smith
Mat. Tilghman
Tho. Johnson Jun.
Will. Paca
Samuel Chase
Rich. Henry Lee
Patrick Henry
Geo. Washington
Edmund Pendleton
Richard Bland
Benja. Harrison

George Washington (*above, left*) was John Adams' choice as commander-in-chief of the American army, for Adams wanted a Virginian general, to persuade the southern colonies that they had common cause with those of the north. In 1774, Washington was one of the fifty-five delegates to the First Continental Congress, held in Philadelphia. As well as adopting the Declaration of Rights, the Congress also drafted a petition listing their grievances (*above, right*) which they sent to George III.

The first battles of the war took place in the spring of 1775, and on 23 June, at Cambridge, Massachusetts, Washington officially assumed command of the American troops (*above*). For all his reserve and lack of charm, Washington had several qualities that made him the best man for the job he had been given. He was totally honest, he had a highly developed sense of responsibility, and he was a remarkably shrewd tactician.

On 18 April 1775, British troops marched to Concord to destroy the supply depot of the local militia. Their plan was discovered and the Boston Committee of Safety ordered Paul Revere (*above*) and William Dawes to ride from village to village, spreading the alarm. When the British reached Lexington, they found some seventy militiamen opposing them (*opposite, above*). Someone fired a shot. The British then charged the militia (*opposite, below*), killing eight and wounding ten.

On 17 June 1775, British and American troops met in the first major battle of the war, at Bunker Hill on the Charlestown peninsula (*above, left*). The Bostonians had been reinforced by militiamen from Rhode Island, Connecticut and New Hampshire, and were spoiling for a fight. Joseph Warren declared: 'The British say we won't fight; by heavens, I hope I shall die up to my knees in blood!' (*Below, left*) The death of Joseph Warren at Bunker Hill.

More than 2,000 British troops advanced through the tall grass. The militiamen held their fire until the redcoats were only twenty paces away. Twice their volleys of musket fire drove the British back (*right*). When the British charged a third time, the militiamen had run out of ammunition and were forced off the hill. But the British victory had cost over 1,000 casualties.

In December 1776, as was the accepted military custom, General Howe settled his British troops in New York for the winter, convinced that Washington would make no move against him until the spring. Paying no heed to military custom, Washington crossed the icy Delaware River with 2,400 men. The next day they surprised a garrison of Hessian mercenaries, killing 1,000 out of 1,500 men, and a week later they repelled three regiments of the British army. Washington's militiamen had become a formidable enemy.

Betsy Griscom was born on 1 January 1752. At the age of twenty-one she eloped with John Ross, an upholsterer. Together they set up business, for Betsy was an accomplished needlewoman. Not long after the war started, John Ross was killed in a munitions explosion: Betsy went back to Philadelphia. In the early summer of 1776 she received a visit from the Committee of Three – George Washington, Robert Morris and George Ross. Washington showed Betsy the design for a new American flag, with thirteen stars and thirteen stripes, representing a new 'constellation'. When the Committee returned a few days later, Betsy presented them with the first American flag (*right*).

(*Above, left*) 8 July 1776 – the Declaration of Independence has been read in Independence Hall and the Liberty Bell rings out over the streets of Philadelphia from the tower that Betsy Ross' father had helped to build. The British were on the run and the old order was being replaced. In a representation of growing independence (*below, left*), the American horse throws its British master, whose whip is tipped with swords and axes.

As the redcoats retreated, symbols of British rule were destroyed. There was to be no more taxation without representation, no more kowtowing to London, no more colonial servitude. And there were to be no more kings, not even as statues. (*Right*) A group of American patriots removes a statue of George III.

In the summer of 1777, General Burgoyne, with his mistress and an army of 7,000 British troops, moved south from Lake Champlain to Saratoga. Here he was surrounded by American forces under General Horatio Gates. On 17 October, Burgoyne – in his splendid scarlet, gold and white uniform – surrendered to the blue-coated Gates (*below, left*). For the British, the war was as good as lost.

But fighting dragged on for another four years (*right, above and below*). Lord North, the British Prime Minister, wished to sue for peace, but King George III refused to accept that the Americans had won. There was hope that British resistance would win support in the south, and that New York could be held as a base from which to launch a counter attack. As British troops withdrew towards New York, however, Washington attacked them at Monmouth Court House (*opposite, above*).

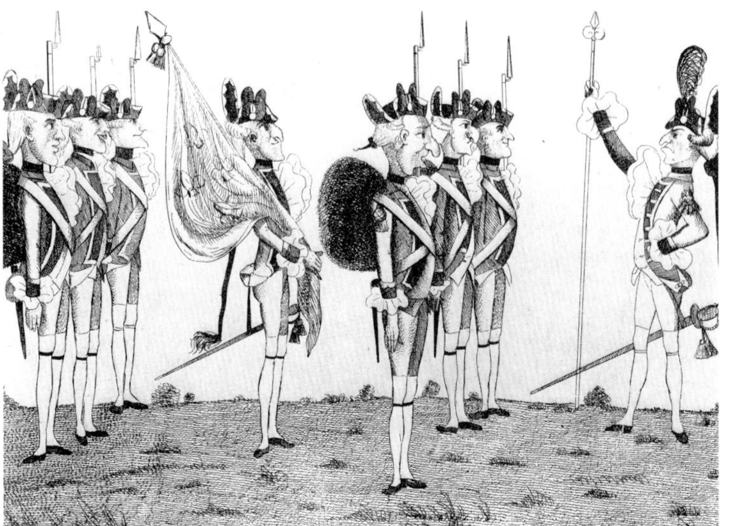

The end came in 1781 when Washington's army joined up with French troops under the command of Jean-Baptiste Donatien de Vimeur, Comte de Rochambeau (*left*, with plumed hat), general in charge of French land forces in America. With the help of the French fleet they completed the encirclement of Yorktown (*above*).

The siege began on 28 September. Nineteen days later, a British drummer boy climbed to the top of a Yorktown parapet and began beating the call for a truce. The British army marched out. The band played *The World Turned Upside Down*, and Lord Cornwallis surrendered his sword (*right*).

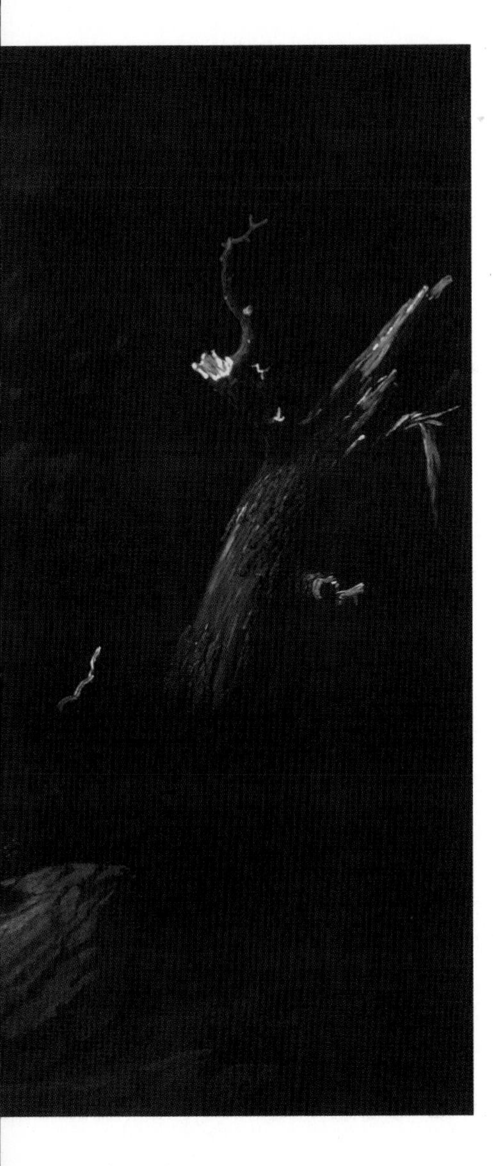

7

A NEW NATION 1783–1810

(*Left*) Daniel Boone leads a group of settlers through the wilds of Kentucky, 1773. Boone was a veteran of the French and Indian Wars who guided many travellers through the Appalachian Mountains via the Cumberland Gap, discovered by Thomas Walker in 1750. To many, Boone was the first real 'Westerner', a man who was hunter, guide, crackshot, wagoner, explorer and surveyor. From time to time, he disappeared into the wilderness for up to two years at a stretch. Others disappeared forever, giving rise to the expression 'Gone West' as a euphemism for dying.

Introduction

The founding fathers of the United States had freed their land of British military occupation and British colonial rule. They had brought together thirteen colonies and joined them in a solid union – though it was later to prove as brittle as iron rather than as strong as steel. They had drafted a Constitution that was revolutionary in its desire to protect its citizens from the tyranny of central government. It was an astonishing and awe-inspiring achievement. But it was not enough for those whose vision encompassed a nation ten times the size.

In 1787, one year after the Russians had begun their conquest of Alaska, Congress passed the Northwest Ordinance. Like the Declaration of Independence, it was one of the most ambitious and generous political documents in history. Unlike all other empires at the time, the original United States were happy to allow their neighbouring territories to gain statehood by peaceful and legitimate means. This was no exclusive club.

Further, the Ordinance appeared to safeguard the wellbeing of America's original inhabitants: 'Their lands and property shall never be taken from them without their consent.' It was a bold promise that subsequent generations of US politicians found impossible to keep.

And so the United States grew. In 1791 Vermont was admitted as a state, a year later Kentucky. In 1796 Tennessee joined, and in 1803 Napoleon Bonaparte sold the vast swath of French possessions to the United States. Thomas Jefferson had offered him $10 million in exchange. France needed the money for the war in Europe, however, and Bonaparte was astute enough to push the price up to $15 million. Nevertheless, the Louisiana Purchase was the real estate bargain of all time.

Within a year of the purchase, Meriwether Lewis and William Clark set out from St Louis, Missouri, to explore a territory that stretched from New Orleans to the Canadian border, from Kentucky to the Rocky Mountains. Two years later they returned to St Louis, bringing with them seeds, plants, animals, birds and – most important of all – a series of maps.

It did not take long for modern America to take shape. Alexander Hamilton and Thomas Jefferson compromised on the site of government, and Washington, DC, was created on land donated by Maryland and Virginia. West Point Military Academy was founded in good time to provide well-trained officers for the war against Britain of 1812–15. The White House, originally called the President's Palace, was built in 1792. One of its first occupants was Abigail Adams, wife of John Adams, the second president. She complained that the building was too cold and damp to air clothes adequately. Other than that, things seemed to be progressing most satisfactorily.

(*Left*) Richard Henry Lee, the American statesman who moved the resolution in favour of American Independence. Richard Henry and his brother, Francis Lightfoot Lee, were among the fifty-six men who signed the Declaration of Independence. Lee was an anti-federalist and an egalitarian, a descendant of Richard Lee of Shropshire, England, who emigrated to Virginia in the mid-17th century, and an ancestor of another famous Virginian, Robert E. Lee, commander of the Confederate army in the Civil War.

(*Above*) Benjamin Franklin arrives in Paris as the new Minister to France, 1778. Franklin was a man of many talents: he organised the first American volunteer fire brigade. He founded the first free public library. He was the first person to wear bi-focal glasses. (*Right*) George Washington (with sword) is inaugurated as the first President of the United States, 1789. (From left) Alexander Hamilton, Robert R. Livingston, Roger Sherman, James Otis, Vice President John Adams, Baron von Steuben and General Henry Knox.

A new nation needed a new presidential mansion. The White House was designed by an Irish-born architect who had emigrated to America after the War of Independence. His name was James Hoban, and he was paid $500 for his work. Building began in 1793, and the White House was completed by 1801. When it was gutted by British troops eleven years later, Hoban also supervised the restoration work.

(*Above, left*) Zebulon Montgomery Pike, army officer and explorer. He was the first to map the mountains to the west of Colorado Springs, and the 14,000 foot (4,300 metre) high Pike's Peak is named after him. The view from the summit inspired Katharine Lee Bates to write the words to *America the Beautiful*. (*Opposite, above*) Pike on an expedition to determine the US boundary with Mexico. (*Above, right*) Daniel Boone, known to the Shawnee as Sheltowee, or 'Big Turtle'. (*Opposite, below*) Boone rescues his daughter Jemima, and Betsey and Frances Callaway from the Shawnee.

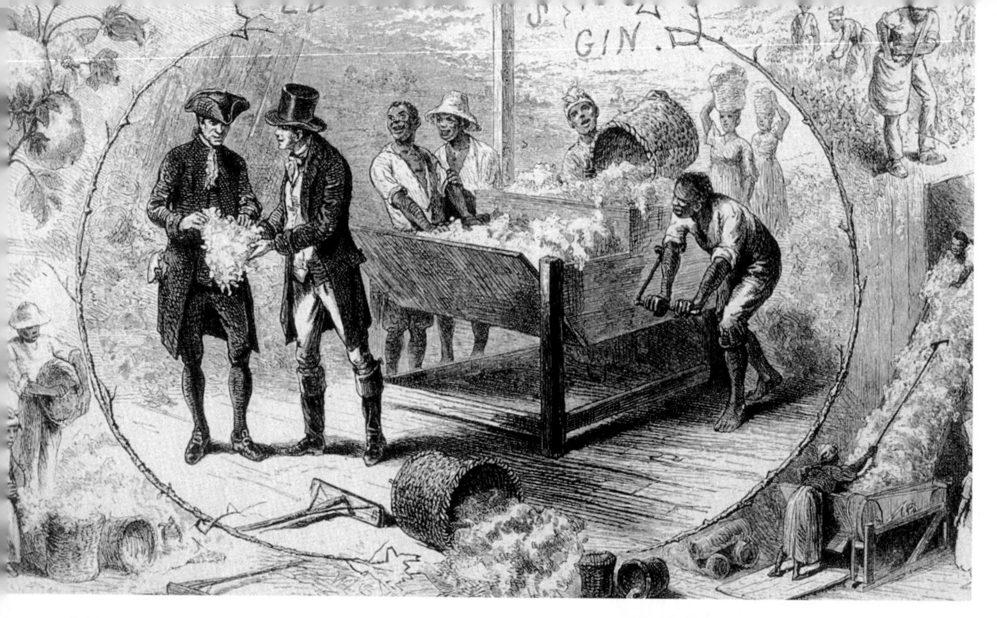

It took a slave a whole day to pick and clean a pound of cotton. Eli Whitney put his mind to designing a machine that would do the work. Watching a cat clawing the feathers off a passing chicken gave him the idea for his cotton gin (*above*).

Robert Fulton (*opposite, below*) was a painter and inventor who experimented with early steam boats while in France. By 1807 he had perfected a steam-driven paddle wheel (*above*), which successfully powered the *Clermont* (*right*) one hundred and fifty miles up the Hudson River in thirty-two hours.

JOURNAL

OF THE

VOYAGES AND TRAVELS

OF

A CORPS OF DISCOVERY,

Under the command of Capt. Lewis and Capt. Clarke of the army of the United States,

FROM THE MOUTH OF THE RIVER MISSOURI THROUGH THE INTERIOR PARTS OF NORTH AMERICA TO THE PACIFIC OCEAN,

During the Years 1804, 1805, and 1806.

CONTAINING

An authentic relation of the most interesting transactions during the expedition; a description of the country; and an account of its inhabitants, soil, climate, curiosities, and vegetable and animal productions.

BY PATRICK GASS,

One of the persons employed in the expedition.

WITH GEOGRAPHICAL AND EXPLANATORY NOTES.

THIRD EDITION—WITH SIX ENGRAVINGS.

[Copy-right secured according to Law.]

PRINTED FOR MATHEW CAREY,
NO. 122 MARKET STREET,
PHILADELPHIA.

1811.

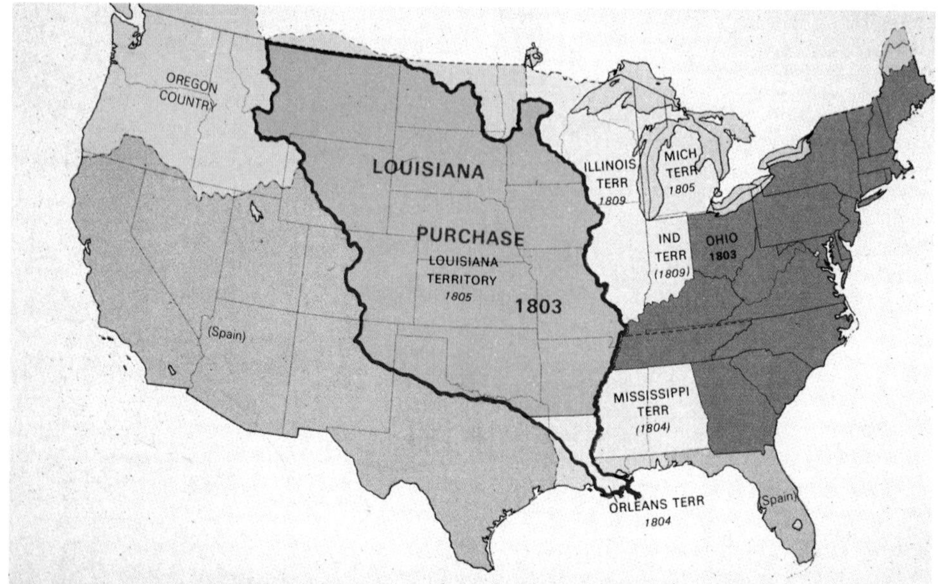

In 1803 Robert Livingston, the US Minister to France, completed the Louisiana Purchase – 400 million acres at 4 cents an acre (*opposite, below left*). The following year, Meriwether Lewis and William Clark (*opposite, above right)* set off to explore this vast new land. Lewis and Clark journeyed to the mouth of the Columbia River (*above, right*), and through the forests and waterways of Oregon (*below, right*), where their Indian guide Sacajawea (in bows of boat) acted as interpreter with the Chinooks. On their return, Lewis and Clark published a book of their adventures (*opposite, above left*).

Lewis and Clark kept careful records of all their adventures on their epic voyage of exploration. Later these were published in a copiously illustrated book. (*Left, top*) The US Corps of Discovery, as the expedition was officially known, almost comes to grief when the canoe in which they are travelling capsizes. (*Left, centre*) Members of the expedition build a semi-permanent camp. (*Left, below*) One of the many brushes with Native Americans.

In many ways, Lewis and Clark's expedition was as bold a journey as space exploration two centuries later, for they covered thousands of square miles of territory that no white American had ever seen before. (*Right, top*) Hunting for food – the expedition had to be self-sufficient in this respect. (*Right, centre*) Negotiating with Native Americans. Thanks to Sacajawea, their guide, Lewis and Clark were able to establish good relations with most of the tribes they met. (*Right, below*) 'Discretion is the better part of valour' – an encounter with a bear.

(*Left*) Thomas Jefferson, the moving spirit of the Declaration of Independence and third President of the United States. Jefferson was a gentleman – upper class, scholarly and, to a degree, eccentric. After the War of Independence, he toured Europe, noting down whatever he felt the new Republic should avoid: 'No public statues...no titles of nobility...no wigs on judges...' He was also against the British system of pounds, shillings and pence, favouring a decimal currency for America.

(*Right, above and below*) Thomas Jefferson's country estate at Monticello, Charlottesville, Virginia, around the year 1810. It was built to Jefferson's own design and incorporated many unusual features that he had invented. The house contained a twenty-four-hour clock, a revolving chair so that he could sit with the light always over his shoulder, and a four-sided music stand so that a string quartet could play closely together.

The founding fathers of America were all of European descent, and they rejected the European systems of government – of kings, princes and emperors. The new nation could only be a republic, and that had resonances of the government of Ancient Greece. There were echoes of Greece in the architecture that they chose for their seat of government, the Capitol in Washington, DC (*left*). George Washington himself (in Masonic robes) laid the corner-stone in 1793, and from then on the grand halls and splendid chambers grew in step with the power of the nation.

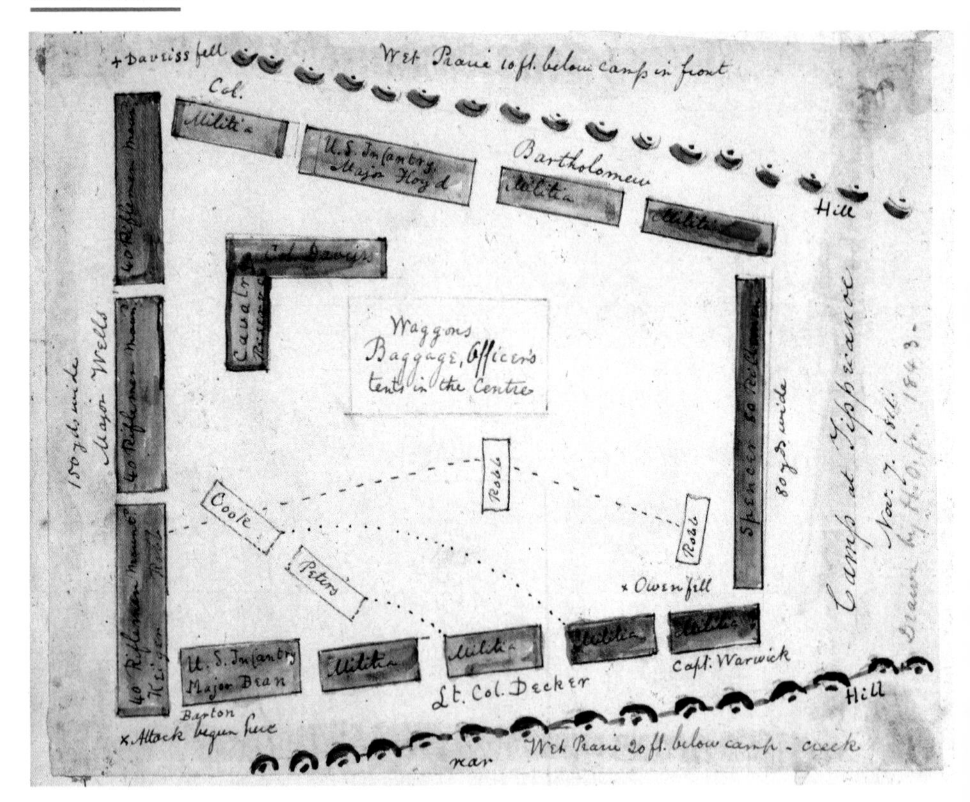

In 1810 the Shawnee nation was led by a new chief, Tecumseh. He dreamed of a federation of tribes that would drive the whites back from the traditional lands of the Shawnees, Creeks, Cherokees, Choctaws and Chickasaws. 'The white race is a wicked race,' Tecumseh declared. 'They seize your land; they corrupt your women.' Faced with this threat, General William Henry Harrison, governor of Indian Territory, gathered a thousand men on the banks of the Tippecanoe River, near Tecumseh's camp. (*Above*) The whites' camp at Tippecanoe.

The Shawnees attacked the camp in Tecumseh's absence and were defeated, though they inflicted heavy casualties on the whites. Tecumseh fled to Canada, to seek British protection. After Tippecanoe, the Shawnees had to rely on negotiation to protect their rights. Paytakootha (Flying Clouds) (*above, right*) was a wandering arbitrator between Native Americans and white settlers in the early 19th century. (*Above, left*) The Shawnee chief and warrior, Kish-Kal-Wa.

8
GROWING PAINS 1810–1845

The War of 1812 against the British was fought on several fronts. In Congress there were plenty of 'war hawks' who were eager to see the British routed in the west, in revenge for the attacks on Washington itself. William Henry Harrison, who had defeated the Shawnees at Tippecanoe in 1811, was placed in charge of an expeditionary force aimed at the conquest of Canada. After initial failure, Harrison drove the British out of the north west at the Battle of the Thames on 5 October 1813. In the battle, the Shawnee chief Tecumseh fell, shot by Colonel Richard Mentor Johnson (*left*). The dream of Indian unity and federation died with him.

Introduction

Like Topsy in Harriet Beecher Stowe's *Uncle Tom's Cabin*, the United States grew and grew. Within a decade six new states were admitted to the Union: Louisiana (1812), Indiana (1816), Mississippi (1817), Alabama (1819), Maine (1820) and Missouri (1821). Others were soon to follow, for Spain ceded Florida to the United States in 1820, and Texas seceded from Mexico in 1836.

The United States went to war for the first time as an independent nation in 1812, against the old enemy, Britain. Some have called the war 'foolish and unnecessary'. To the major protagonists it was neither of these. Tecumseh, chief of the Shawnees and ally of the British, saw the war as the last hope for Indian claims to the interior. Governors Harrison of Indiana and Henry Clay of Kentucky saw it as the means of ejecting the British, Spanish and Indians from lands to the south and west of the existing United States, essential for future expansion. Andrew Jackson, of the Tennessee State Militia, saw it as an opportunity to avenge the wrongs done by the British to his mother, father and brothers.

The war ended with the American victory at the Battle of New Orleans in 1815, with yet another song of legend to celebrate the event. But, in general, the United States wished to keep out of wars. In 1823 President Monroe published his famous doctrine, closing 'the American continents to colonial settlements by non-American powers' and excluding 'the European powers from all interference in the political affairs of the American republics'.

For there was much to do in this new and vast land. It had to be put to work. The Great Plains were broken by the plough, and the harvests they produced were gathered by Cyrus Hall McCormick's new mechanical reaper. It had to be crisscrossed by systems of communication. Samuel Morse invented his code in 1832, and strings of telegraph wires dotted and dashed news from New York to Denver, from New Orleans to Detroit. Large chunks of it still had to be explored and exploited – hence the Yellowstone Expedition of 1819–20, Brigham Young's march with the Mormons to Salt Lake City in the 1840s, and the forced removal of the Five Civilised Tribes (the Cherokee, Choctaw, Chickasee, Creek and Seminole) along the Trail of Tears in the 1830s. Paddle steamers moved ponderously up and down the Mississippi. The first railroad – the Baltimore and Ohio – opened in 1830. James Fenimore Cooper wrote *The Last of the Mohicans* in 1826. Andrew Jackson became the first American president to be photographed in 1845.

And down in Texas in 1836 a small band of heroes fought their way to glory at a mission called the Alamo.

For several years American shipping had been caught in the crossfire between Britain and France during the Napoleonic Wars. The *Philadelphia* (*above, left*) was one of many frigates built as the United States drifted towards war with Britain. When President Madison finally declared war on 18 June 1812, the United States navy was a force to be reckoned with. (*Below, left*) The US frigate *United States* captures HMS *Macedonian* off Madeira Island, 25 October 1812.

Accustomed to ruling the seas, the British fleet was surprised and shaken by a series of American successes. (*Top, right*) Commander Perry defeats the British at Put-In-Bay on Lake Erie, 10 September 1812. (*Centre, right*) The American frigate *Constitution*, better known as 'Old Ironsides', captures the British vessels *Cyane* and *Levant*, 20 February 1815. (*Bottom, right*) The American privateer *General Armstrong* repulses a British attack at Fayal harbour in the Azores, 26 October 1814.

On 24 August 1814, a British army marched unopposed into Washington, DC. A group of officers went straight to the White House (*right*), where they ate a meal that had been prepared for the President and Mrs Madison. In an act of wanton destruction, they then set fire to the building, leaving it gutted. Both the White House and the Capitol would have been more seriously damaged if a thunderstorm had not extinguished the flames. The English press condemned the action: 'The Cossacks spared Paris,' wrote one editor, 'but we spared not the Capital of America.'

While Harrison fought the Shawnees in the north west, war flared up in the south. On 30 August 1813 the Creeks attacked Fort Mims, near Mobile, killing half the inhabitants. Andrew Jackson, later to be President but then a major-general in the Tennessee militia, raised 2,000 men and set out for revenge. With him was Chief William McIntosh (*above, left*), a part-Scot, part-Creek fighter.

Revenge came at the Battle of Horseshoe Bend on 27 March 1814. The Creeks were utterly destroyed. Only a handful of warriors survived, among them Menawa (Crazy War Hunter) (*opposite, above right*). After the battle, William Weatherford (also known as Chief Red Eagle) surrendered to Andrew Jackson in his tent (*above*). The Creeks ceded two thirds of their lands to the United States, including part of Georgia and most of Alabama.

The fiercest battle of the War of 1812 was that fought at New Orleans on 8 January 1815. The defence of the city was organised by Andrew Jackson (*above*, on horseback, pointing with telescope), a man who regarded the British as responsible for the deaths of his father, mother and brothers. The British army of 8,000 troops was commanded by Sir Edward Pakenham, a veteran of the wars against Napoleon. Pakenham waited too long before launching his attack, giving Jackson time to secure his position with earthworks and a wall of cotton bales.

Pakenham also made the mistake of underestimating the fighting ability of Jackson's motley army, which was composed of frontier militiamen, Creole aristocrats, pirates and free blacks (*above*). The redcoats emerged out of the morning fog and were met by murderous fire from the defenders of the city. A quarter of the British troops were killed or wounded, among them Pakenham, whose body was pickled in a barrel of rum and sent to the boat in the harbour on which his wife was awaiting news of the battle.

American trappers, hunters and settlers pushed further and further west in the early 19th century. Fur traders were especially interested in the headwaters of the Missouri River in Nebraska Territory, an area already explored by William Clark in 1806. By the 1830s several major routes from east to west had been established: the Oregon Trail, from Independence, Missouri, to Oregon City; the Mormon Trail, from Nauvoo, Illinois, to Salt Lake City; and the California Trail. By the mid-1820s, the 'rendezvous system' was well-established – regular meetings at designated places where whites and Native Americans traded.

Gradually, however, the tribes were pushed further and further west. The Pawnee were originally from the central American plains. By 1820 they were concentrated in parts of what would later become the state of Nebraska. (*Above*) Major Stephen H. Long speaks with representatives of the Pawnee tribe during his Yellowstone Expedition of 1819. (*Opposite*) Peskelechaco, a Pawnee warrior, 1821.

A temporary Choctaw encampment, by Karl Bodmer, 1833 (*right*). One of the 'Five Civilised Tribes', the Choctaw were one of the first southern tribes to suffer the effects of the Indian Removal Act of 1830. The Cherokee suffered in equal measure. In 1838, aggressive claims by white settlers forced the Cherokee leader Major Ridge (*opposite, above*) to sign the Treaty of New Echota. The Cherokee were dispossessed of their land. Of the 14,000 who set out on the Trail of Tears to Oklahoma, 4,000 died. In their fury at this tragedy, members of the tribe dragged Ridge's son John (*opposite, below*) from his home and stabbed him to death in front of his wife and children.

TO BE SOLD & LET

BY PUBLIC AUCTION,

On MONDAY the 18th of MAY, 1829,

UNDER THE TREES.

FOR SALE,

THE THREE FOLLOWING

SLAVES,

VIZ.

HANNIBAL, about 30 Years old, an excellent House Servant, of Good Character.
WILLIAM, about 35 Years old, a Labourer.
NANCY, an excellent House Servant and Nurse.

The MEN belonging to "LEECH'S" Estate, and the WOMAN to Mrs. D. SMIT

TO BE LET,

On the usual conditions of the Hirer finding them in Food, Clot[illegible] and Medical [illegible]ance,

THE FOLLOWING

MALE and FEMALE

SLAVES,

OF GOOD CHARACTERS,

ROBERT BAGLEY, about 20 Years old, a good House Servant.
WILLIAM BAGLEY, about 18 Years old, a Labourer.
JOHN ARMS, about 18 Years old.
JACK ANTONIA, about 40 Years old, a Labourer.
PHILIP, an Excellent Fisherman.
HARRY, about 27 Years old, a good House Servant.
LUCY, a Young Woman of good Character, used to House Work and the Nursery.
ELIZA, an Excellent Washerwoman.
CLARA, an Excellent Washerwoman.
FANNY, about 14 Years old, House Servant.
SARAH, about 14 Years old, House Servant.

Also for Sale, at Eleven o'Clock,

Fine Rice, Gram, Paddy, Books, Muslins, Needles, Pins, Ribbons, &c. &c.

AT ONE O'CLOCK, THAT CELEBRATED ENGLISH HORSE

BLUCHER,

The economy of the South was based on the plantation system, where black slaves harvested cotton (*right*) or tobacco for white landowners. Slaves were regularly sold at auction (*opposite*). (*Below*) A plantation house in Convent, Louisiana, built in the 1830s.

In 1834 General Santa Anna of Mexico dissolved the national congress of Texas. The American population rose in revolt. Santa Anna attacked Texan and American volunteer forces at the Alamo mission (*top*) in 1836. The defenders included the legendary heroes Jim Bowie (*opposite, below left)* and Davy Crockett (*opposite, above,* with his famous rifle, Old Betsy, raised above his head, *and above)*. The final assault came on 23 February (*right*) when the entire garrison was slaughtered. It was left to Sam Houston (*opposite, below right*) to avenge the defeat at the Battle of San Jacinto.

The Smithsonian Institution (*left*) was established in 1846 'for the increase and diffusion of knowledge among men'. Its founding figure was James Louis Macie Smithson, bastard son of the first Duke of Northumberland, a man who never set foot in the United States. His action was prompted by pique when the British Royal Society rejected a scientific paper he wished to present to them. The Smithsonian now holds a unique collection of historical artefacts and fine art and has been given the somewhat derogatory title of 'the nation's attic'.

One thing the new republic did not lack was space. There was plenty of land, but not enough hands to farm it – until the coming of the agricultural machine. One of the earliest was Obed Hussey's reaper (*opposite, below*) of 1831. A year later, Robert and Cyrus McCormick produced their own reaping machine (*opposite, centre*). (*Left, top*) An early iron turbine wind engine. (*Left, centre*) A Broadcast grain sower, planter and guano distributor.

Many of these machines were based on the reaper designed by the Scotsman Patrick Bell (*right, top*). The market for such machines was enormous and between them they brought about a revolution in agriculture. (*Opposite, below left*) The sophisticated McCormick binding reaper of 1878. (*Opposite, below right*) The Seymour cotton planter.

THE BASE BALL QUADRILLE
FOUL
CHAMPION
BALL

Abner Doubleday is credited as the inventor of baseball, and it was first played in New York in 1839. It was an immediate success. By 1865 Frank Leslie's *Illustrated Newspaper* included pictures from the leading baseball clubs of New York, Brooklyn and Newark (*Above, right*). (*Below, right*) *The Second Great Match for the Championship* in Philadelphia, October 1866. The Philadelphia Athletics beat the Brooklyn Athletics 31-12. (*Opposite*) An early musical tribute to America's national game.

Introduction to Period 3 – 1825–2000

At the beginning of the year 2000, the United States stood unrivalled as the richest and most powerful nation in the world. No other country had the resources to stand against the military, industrial and commercial might of Uncle Sam. For much of the 20th century the Soviet Union was seen as posing a threat, but the collapse of what President Reagan had dubbed 'the Evil Empire' left the United States in a league on its own.

The rise and rise of the United States took the rest of the world by surprise. No one had really bothered to keep tabs on what was happening in that Wild West continent. Even as late as the early 19th century, Europeans saw America as a land of opportunity, but of opportunity for Europeans rather than Americans. Few had the foresight to see that the president of what still seemed a fledgling state would one day become Csar of All the Americas, holding sway over an empire that was twice the size of Europe and free from the enmities and rivalries that crippled the Old World.

Many Americans viewed their land (some still

do) as the last chance on earth to create God's Own Country, Utopia, Paradise, or at least a land in which their own individual dreams could come true. The pioneers who joined the wagon train as it shuffled westwards were single-minded people. Nothing and no one was to get in their way – especially not those who were there before them, or those who came after them. It was not the law of the jungle, but it was certainly the survival of the fittest that dictated how the great American interior should be run.

These hardy souls built their homes of timber when they could get it, of sods of earth when they could not. They raised their families – as many children as possible, for there were no doctors within hundreds of miles to tend the sick, and the land was as dangerous as it was rich. They planted their crops and hunted. They raised cattle. In their wake came trades-people, carpenters, tinkers, shopkeepers, clergymen, prostitutes, railwaymen and all that were needed to build and maintain the little towns that took precarious hold along the pioneer trails.

The names that have survived are those of the misfits – outlaws and gunmen, like Jesse James, Wild Bill Hickok, Calamity Jane, the Younger brothers and Billy the Kid. There are no names commemorating those who built the United States from the inside, save those of the few that prospered. There was Joseph McCoy, who recruited cowboys from Texas to drive his herds along the Chisholm Trail, and whose name lives on in the expression 'the real McCoy'. There was John Deere from Vermont, who invented a plough with a revolving blade and a steel mouldboard that cut the earth and turned it over – 'the plough that broke the Plains', they called it, and a hundred years later it was celebrated in the music of Aaron Copland.

There was Joseph Smith, who marched with his Mormon followers from New York to Ohio, and on into Missouri (where they were beaten and imprisoned), to Illinois (where they were hounded as adulterers and where Smith was murdered). Brigham Young took over, and the march went on. They were seeking a place to build the holy city 'up in the mountains where the devil cannot dig us out...where we can live...as we have a mind to'. And they would not be denied. They walked to and through Nebraska, to Wyoming and at last into Utah, where Young announced: 'This is the place.'

To outsiders, the Mormons were strange, even demented people, who practised a strange form of Christianity that allowed polygamy. What the Mormons also practised, and what makes them especially American, was sound economics. They were astute bankers, and their church became very rich. This was what lay at the heart of the development of the United States in the 19th and 20th centuries – the ability to turn a profit.

Here was a land and a time when fortunes could be made on an unprecedented scale. Rockefeller, Vanderbilt, Mellon, Carnegie – their names became synonymous with wealth. Some were generous – Andrew Carnegie donated more than $350 million to good causes in his life. Some were mean – the Rockefeller family paid to have a photograph suppressed that showed John D. Rockefeller refusing to give money to a beggar. All were well aware of how to make money, and what it could and could not do. John Pierpont Morgan was once asked how much it cost to run a luxury yacht. 'If you have to ask,' he said, 'you can't afford it.'

It was a typical American remark, similar to that given many years later by the pianist Fats Waller when asked what 'jazz' was. 'If you got to ask,' he replied, 'you'll never know.' But a great many Americans did know – about jazz and cinema and vaudeville and beauty contests and drum majorettes and Oscar ceremonies and all the other razzmatazz with which they have enlivened the world.

Above all America has known about popular music. The legacy of Irving Berlin, Jerome Kern, Rodgers and Hart, the Gershwin brothers, Cole Porter, Harold Arlen and a hundred others is wealth of a different kind from that of Rockefeller and company. The whole history of the United States is there, and a well-voiced professor could sing his or her way through the 20th century to let students know what it was all about. There were songs about the First World War, the early motor car, the Depression, clothes, radio, love and courtship 20th-century style, baseball, the happy days that were here again, the Second World War, consumer durables, advertising, Ike, television and every other joy and sorrow.

In the last fifty years of the millennium, the dream became more than a little tarnished, the songs went into a minor key. Power remained, wealth remained, but the United States lost a sizeable chunk of its glamour and its popularity. The Vietnam War destroyed much of America's self-confidence, and also exposed the dangers that accompany even the best-intentioned attempts to act as the world's police force. Across the planet people love Elvis and Disneyland, McDonald's and Coca-Cola. But not all the world loves where they come from.

9
QUICKENING PULSE 1840–1860

Essex, one of the early giants of the Great Western Railway of Canada, forerunner of the Canadian Pacific, photographed at its Clifton depot, near Niagara Falls, in 1859. Another twenty-six years were to pass before the railway straddled the entire width of Canada. As well as being there to remove cows, the 'cowcatchers' at the front of locomotives on both Canadian and United States railroads were needed to shunt fallen timber from tracks that ran for hundreds of miles through pine forests.

Introduction

Just how big was this rapidly growing nation going to be? There were still plenty of territories waiting to be accepted as fully-fledged members of the Union. Iowa became a state in 1846, California in 1850, Minnesota in 1858 and Oregon in 1859. After the war with Mexico of 1848, the United States acquired New Mexico, Texas, California, Nevada, Utah, Arizona and parts of Wyoming and Colorado. The Webster–Ashburton Treaty of 1842 defined the border between the USA and Canada.

And as the Union grew, so did the problem of communication. It was one thing to send a letter from New York to Boston, quite another to send orders from Washington, DC, to San Francisco. One short-lived but romantic experiment was the Pony Express, a string of expert riders who defied landscape and hostile tribes to deliver mail from St Joseph, Missouri, to Sacramento, California. It was a financial disaster wrapped in a cloud of heroic dust.

The Mississippi riverboats offered a more comfortable way of appreciating the enormity of the brash young country, but the greatest travelling luxury was to be had in the special railcars of George Mortimer Pullman. And, as the railroad inched its way across the continent, the day was not so far away when it would be possible to take a train from coast to coast.

One small discovery made many an American ever more impatient to head westwards as fast as possible. On the morning of 24 January 1848 a Southern carpenter named James Wilson Marshall was clearing out the tailrace of a sawmill. In it he found some unusual matter, roughly the size of small peas. Marshall later said it made him 'think mighty hard'. He took the peas to his boss, John Sutter. They locked the doors of Sutter's office before carrying out some tests, and discovered that the peas were gold of rare purity.

Sutter did all he could to register a claim, but California was not yet US territory – he was eleven days too early for that. The result was a gold rush of unparalleled mania, with the greedy and the desperate trekking to California any way they could – from Peru, China, Chile, New York, Europe, Canada and even Hawaii.

For a long while the nation was gripped by gold fever. No matter how many sad souls were ruined in the search, there were always others eager to take their place. But on 16 October 1859, another event took place that was to change American history far more profoundly, and far more tragically. A zealous anti-slavery preacher named John Brown gathered together a group of like-minded men and raided Harper's Ferry.

Though it had started life in 1670 as a British enterprise in Canada, by the 1840s the Hudson's Bay Company had extended its fur-trading business well into the north-western corner of the United States. The man who ruled the 'unimaginable wastelands of the west' for the Company was John McLoughlin (*above, left*), later to become known as the Father of Oregon. (*Left*) The coat-of-arms of the Hudson's Bay Company.

The Company continued to expand. In 1800 its headquarters on Vancouver Island (*right*) was a modest enough affair, but, sixty years later (*above*), it had greatly expanded. The Company played an important part in supporting American settlers throughout the winter months, thus consolidating the United States' claim to this part of America.

George Catlin was a Pennsylvania artist who spent the years from 1832 to 1840 painting the illustrations for his two-volume *Manners of the North American Indians.* He travelled all over the west of the United States, drawing portraits (*left and far left*), and making detailed pictures of the Indian way of life.

(*Opposite, below*) A hunting party of Plains Indians attack and kill a 'grizzly' bear. (*Above*) Catlin's drawing of a Plains Indian village. (*Right*) A group of Indians perform a traditional Bear Dance, to invoke the aid and protection of the bear spirit.

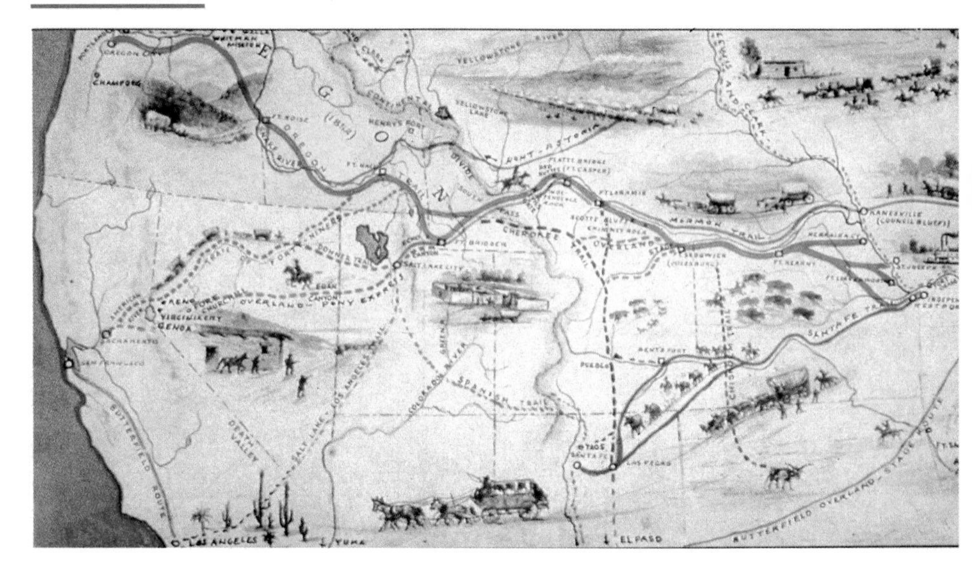

Well before 1849, the leading press agent for California was John Charles Frémont – the Pathfinder (*opposite, above right*). Frémont was an energetic and courageous explorer, who later founded the Republican Party. Between 1842 and 1844 he mapped the Oregon Trail (*above*) and traversed the Rocky Mountains (*opposite, above left*), making sure he gained plenty of publicity.

Frémont's reports on these expeditions whetted the appetite of many Americans in the east. And then, on the morning of 24 January 1848, a Scottish carpenter named James Marshall found some strange particles in the tailrace of a sawmill. Within weeks the California gold rush was at its height (*right and opposite, below*).

On the banks of the river, by Sutter's Mill (*above*), Marshall sat down and, in his own words, began to 'think mighty hard'. Having done that, he took the glittering particles to his employer, John Sutter (*left*).

Sutter and Marshall tested the small lumps of ore, and discovered they were gold of a rare purity. Over the next few years, fortune hunters poured into Sacramento (*above*), a town nicknamed the 'Emigrant's Hope'. The hills and valleys round Sutter's Mill filled with shacks, tents, huts, and mere holes in the ground (*right*). Gamblers, politicians, salesmen, desperadoes fought for any scrap of land in their hunger for gold.

The Church of the Latter-Day Saints was founded by Joseph Smith Jnr in 1820 at the age of fourteen. Early Mormon life was not easy, and in the late 1830s the Mormons began their epic journey to Salt Lake City. Smith never got there. He was shot by a lynch mob in Nauvoo, Illinois.

His place was taken by Brigham Young (*opposite, below left*). (*Opposite, below right*) Young (second from left) ruled with a group of elders. The journey to Utah was recorded in a series of watercolours (*right, below right and opposite, above*) by W. H. Jackson.

PONY EXPRESS!

CHANGE OF TIME! REDUCED RATES!

10 Days to San Francisco!

LETTERS

WILL BE RECEIVED AT THE

OFFICE, 84 BROADWAY,

NEW YORK,

Up to 4 P. M. every TUESDAY,

AND

Up to 2½ P. M. every SATURDAY,

Which will be forwarded to connect with the PONY EXPRESS leaving ST. JOSEPH, Missouri,

Every WEDNESDAY and SATURDAY at 11 P. M.

TELEGRAMS

Sent to Fort Kearney on the mornings of MONDAY and FRIDAY, will connect with PONY leaving St. Joseph, WEDNESDAYS and SATURDAYS.

EXPRESS CHARGES.

LETTERS weighing half ounce or under $1 00
For every additional half ounce or fraction of an ounce 1 00
In all cases to be enclosed in 10 cent Government Stamped Envelopes,

And all Express CHARGES Pre-paid.

☞ PONY EXPRESS ENVELOPES For Sale at our Office.

WELLS, FARGO & CO., Ag'ts.

New York, July 1, 1861.

The Pony Express was inaugurated in 1860, a mail service operated by a relay system of riders from St Joseph, Missouri, to Sacramento, California – a distance of some 2,000 miles. The first rider left on 3 April 1860 (*opposite, above*). The journey took eight days, but a letter from New York took only two days longer (*right*) as the first part of the journey was by rail. It was a lonely and dangerous business (*opposite, below left, and above*), for the route crossed territory where whites and Indians were at war. (*Opposite, below right)* A poster advertising the Pony Express. By 1861 it had been replaced by the telegraph.

The American novel flourished in the mid-19th century. Harriet Beecher Stowe *(below, left)* wrote *Uncle Tom's Cabin* as anti-slavery propaganda, the friendship between Eva and Topsy (*left*) condemning racism. Just as powerful were the novels of Herman Melville (*below, right)* whose most famous work was *Moby Dick*.

Nathaniel Hawthorne (*below, left*) completed *The Scarlet Letter* in 1850, a disturbing novel that examined the hypocrisy of New England Puritanism in the 17th century. On the lighter side, Mark Twain (*below, right*) delighted millions of readers with his *Adventures of Tom Sawyer,* published in 1876. (*Right*) The clapboard house, with the wooden fence that Tom was ordered to whitewash by his aunt.

(*Left*) *The Last of England* by Ford Madox Brown, 1852. There was mass emigration from England and Ireland in the 1840s and 1850s. In 1847 alone, nearly 214,000 Irish sailed across the Atlantic looking for a new life. The first port of call was the emigration agent's office, such as this one in Cork (*below*). The next was the Government Medical Inspector's Office (*opposite, above*).

Those who could afford the fare and were passed fit then waited for a passage. The White Star Line ran ships every Thursday from Liverpool to New York (*below, right*), and there were sailings from Cardigan in Wales and from Queenstown in Ireland. A third of those that sailed died en route, and for those who survived there were the slums of Boston and New York, and 'No Irish Need Apply' signs hung out by American employers. The brave new world was yet to come.

In 1853 Commander Matthew Perry (*left*) arrived at Yedo Bay, Uraga, Japan (*opposite, above*). His mission was to open up trade and to seek freedom for the ship-wrecked American sailors who had been refused permission to leave. Perry sought to impress – and intimidate – the Japanese with American technology. He presented them with cannon, pistols, rifles and a miniature working locomotive.

At first the Japanese declined Perry's offer. A contemporary cartoon *(right)* shows an ill-drawn Japanese saying: 'We won't have free trade. Our ports are closed and shall remain so.' The American replies: 'Then we will open our [gun] ports, and convince you that you're wrong.'

Even before the Civil War there was bitter fighting between abolitionists and pro-slavery irregulars. On 19 May 1858, five Kansas 'freesoilers' were murdered by Missouri irregulars at Marais des Cygnes (*below*). On 21 August 1863, Bill Quantrill's Confederate guerrillas killed one hundred and eighty-two men and boys in Lawrence, Kansas (*left*).

John Brown (*above*) had a commitment to abolish 'the wicked curse of slavery'. On 16 October 1859, his force of twenty men raided Harper's Ferry, seeking to spark a slave uprising. The next day a squad of marines stormed the engine house (*right*) and captured Brown. He was hanged a few days later, and passed into legend. (*Above, right*) John Brown on his way to the scaffold.

Charles Blondin, whose real name was Jean-François Gravelet, came to America in 1859 at the age of thirty-five. He was an acrobat and showman with a genius for pulling in the crowds. Blondin chose Niagara Falls as the site for one of his most daring stunts. Here the Niagara River suddenly drops dramatically into one of the largest waterfalls in the world, and in this spot Blondin set up his tightrope (*above*).

It was a hot summer day. A large crowd gathered on the banks above the Falls (*above*). Blondin stepped on to the rope and made his way slowly across. The height and the setting lent drama to the performance, but to Blondin it was all in a day's work. Later he was to repeat the feat, with variations – once blindfold, once pushing a wheelbarrow, once carrying a man on his back, and once on stilts.

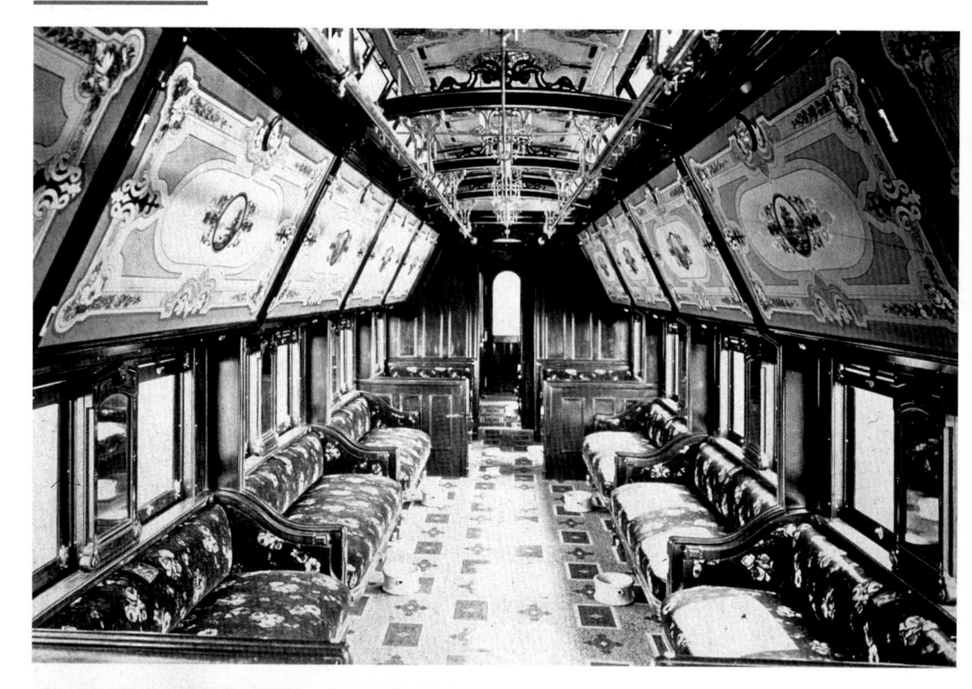

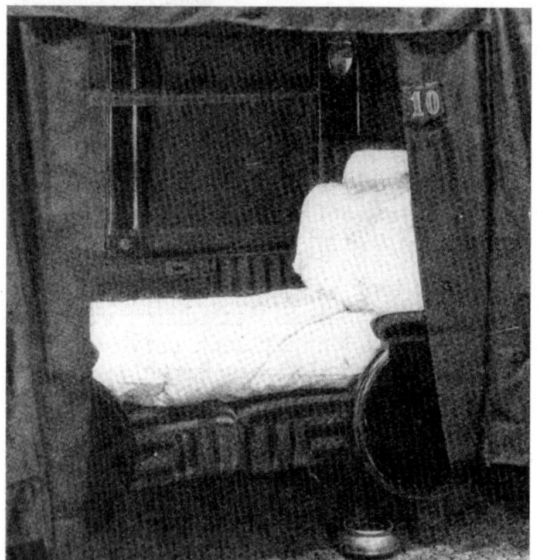

George Mortimer Pullman (*opposite*) was born in Brocton, New York, in 1831. He was a cabinet-maker and a storekeeper, but he made his fortune with one simple idea. Since it took several days to cross the United States by rail, why not make the journey as comfortable as possible? Why not equip carriages with fine furniture, good windows, carpets and decorative panels (*above*)? Why not even provide travellers with special sleeping-cars? (*left*).

Pullman designed and patented the railroad sleeping-car in 1865, and founded the Pullman Palace Car Company two years later. In 1868 he introduced the first of his dining-cars. Travel by railroad was revolutionised, and Pullman's fortune was made. With it he built Pullman City for his workers, in what is now a suburb of Chicago.

Allan Pinkerton was born in Glasgow in 1819. He emigrated to the United States in 1842, for political reasons, and settled in West Dundee, Illinois, where he became a detective. After capturing a gang of counterfeiters, he was elected county sheriff. In 1850 he set up Pinkerton's National Detective Agency, establishing agents across the States. His agents (*above*) successfully ran down a number of train robbers, and both Pinkerton and the Agency came to the notice of Abraham Lincoln.

Pinkerton was appointed personal bodyguard to Lincoln as the President journeyed to his inauguration in Washington, DC. During the journey, Pinkerton foiled a plot to assassinate Lincoln when the train stopped in Baltimore. He was later employed by Lincoln to establish the secret service of the Union army. (*Above*) Pinkerton (left) with Lincoln and General J. A. McClernand at an army camp early in the Civil War.

Edwin Drake was a railroad conductor and amateur prospector of Titusville, Pennsylvania. He was hired by the owner of a tract of land at Oil Creek to dig for 'black glue', as petroleum was locally known. Drake (*opposite, left*, in top hat) in turn hired Uncle Billy Smith and his two sons (right, in background by wooden derrick) to sink a 70 foot (20 metre) shaft. They were almost drowned when an underground spring gushed out (*opposite, below right*), but with it came a flood of black glue.

Uncle Billy rode his mule into Titusville, proclaiming he had 'Struck oil!' The rush was on (*top, right*). Within a few years, Oil Creek became a mass of shanty towns. By 1865 there were oilfields at nearby Franklin (*opposite, above*) and over seventy production rigs at Pioneer Run (*opposite, below*). By the end of the century, Oil Creek was producing more than thirty-one million barrels of oil in a single year. Drake failed to protect his interests, and died a poor man in 1880.

Amelia Jenks (*above, left*) was an early champion of women's rights and dress reform. She was born in New York, where she married a lawyer named Bloomer (*left*), and founded and edited a feminist paper called *The Lily* from 1849 to 1855. In her pursuit of dress equality, she designed trousers for women, which became popularly known as 'bloomers' (*opposite*). For a short while bloomers were highly fashionable among the young (*above*), but Amelia and her trousers were subjected to a prolonged campaign of ridicule. 'Bloomerism' produced jokes and cartoons about strong-minded American women. 'Where would it end?' asked the cynics. Would women soon be seen smoking cigars, asking men to dance, and seeking their father's permission to marry?

10
BLUE AND GREY
1860–1865

(*Right*) A battery of Union artillery during the Civil War, 1861–5. The War between the States was in many ways the first truly modern war. It was fought by massed armies divided into three disciplines – cavalry, infantry and artillery. Though cavalry still provided much of the 'dash' of warfare, and was capable of delivering a crushing blow, the power of the artillery increasingly decided the outcome of a battle.

Introduction

The War between the States was the worst trauma in American history. States, communities and even families were torn asunder. Brother fought brother, father fought son. Mrs Lincoln, loyal wife of the Union President, mourned the deaths of her three brothers, all killed fighting for the Confederate cause.

Losses were appalling on both sides. More American soldiers died in this one war than in all subsequent wars involving US troops. Fever killed many of them, bullets and gangrene did for the rest. Wise-minded military heads learnt the gruesome lesson that modern weapons necessitated a rethinking of tactics, but there were many unwise military heads.

South Carolina precipitated the split between the states by seceding from the Union in 1860, within a few weeks of the election of Abraham Lincoln as President. The following year, eleven Southern states banded together in a Confederacy under their own President, Jefferson Davis. The first shots of the war were fired at Fort Sumter, where Confederate troops captured a Union outpost on a spit of sand in the mouth of Charleston harbour.

It was an ill-matched contest. Twenty-two million Northerners faced eight million Southerners. The North had steel, armaments, and a cause that appealed to the wider world – the abolition of slavery. They also had a navy strong enough to blockade every Southern port. The South had cotton, sugar and resolute loyalty to a system that was feudal and often cruel. They also had incredible courage, and at first more than held their own, winning the first Battle of Bull Run in July 1861 and the Battle of Chancellorville in 1863.

The turning point was Gettysburg. After three days of fighting both sides were exhausted and the field was littered with the dead and dying in blue and grey. But the North had reserves to call upon, and the South did not. General Sherman drove a blazing wedge through Georgia. Savannah, Atlanta and Richmond fell. The Confederacy had been brought to its knees. On 9 April 1865 General Robert E. Lee surrendered at Appomattox Court House, and the war was over.

Five days later, at Ford's Theatre in Washington, DC, Lincoln was assassinated by a deranged Southern patriot named John Wilkes Booth. All along, the President had sought to heal the rift between North and South, to build for a better future, 'that this nation, under God, shall have a new birth of freedom'.

The fear was that more foolish counsels would now prevail.

(*Above*) In 1922 a picture researcher came across this hitherto forgotten photograph of the second inauguration of President Lincoln in Washington, DC, in March 1865. It was one of Lincoln's last public appearances; he was shot two weeks later. (*Opposite*) John Breckinridge, vice-president to James Buchanan and Democrat and pro-slavery opponent of Lincoln in the 1860 presidential election. Following his defeat in the election, the South seceded from the Union. Breckinridge became a general in the Confederate army. He escaped to Europe at the end of the war, but returned to the United States, where he died in 1875.

JCBRECKIN
5568

(*Above*) William England's photograph for the London Stereoscopic Company of the rebuilding of the Capitol in Washington, DC, 1859. The original building on Capitol Hill had been one of the few imposing structures above a swampy wilderness, though not ready in time for Jefferson's inauguration in 1801. By the 1850s, the entire complex had to be enlarged, for the business of government had greatly increased.

The major development in the mid-19th century was the work on the rotunda. This was enlarged and raised in height, giving the building a more graceful appearance (*above, left*), though when it rained, there were times when the swamp threatened to re-establish itself (*above, right*).

(*Left*) The barrel machine room on the first floor of the Remington arms factory, c.1860. The slaughter that took place on the battlefields of the Civil War would not have been possible without the weapons that poured forth from armament factories. One of the biggest was that founded by Eliphalet Remington in the early 19th century. It was later managed by his son Philo, who in 1860 perfected the Remington breech-loading rifle, a weapon that was to play its part in the eventual victory of the Union.

Samuel Colt (*left*) was an American inventor from Hartford, Connecticut. He first took out a patent for his famous revolver *(opposite, above)* in 1836. Twelve years later it was adopted as standard issue by the US army. Colt also worked on submarine mines and a submarine telegraph, and spent over $2.5 million on his immense armaments factory at Hartford (*opposite, below*)

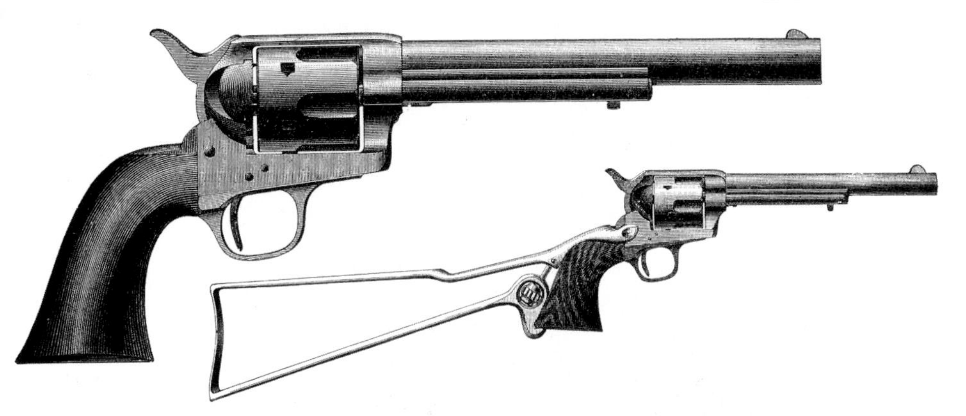

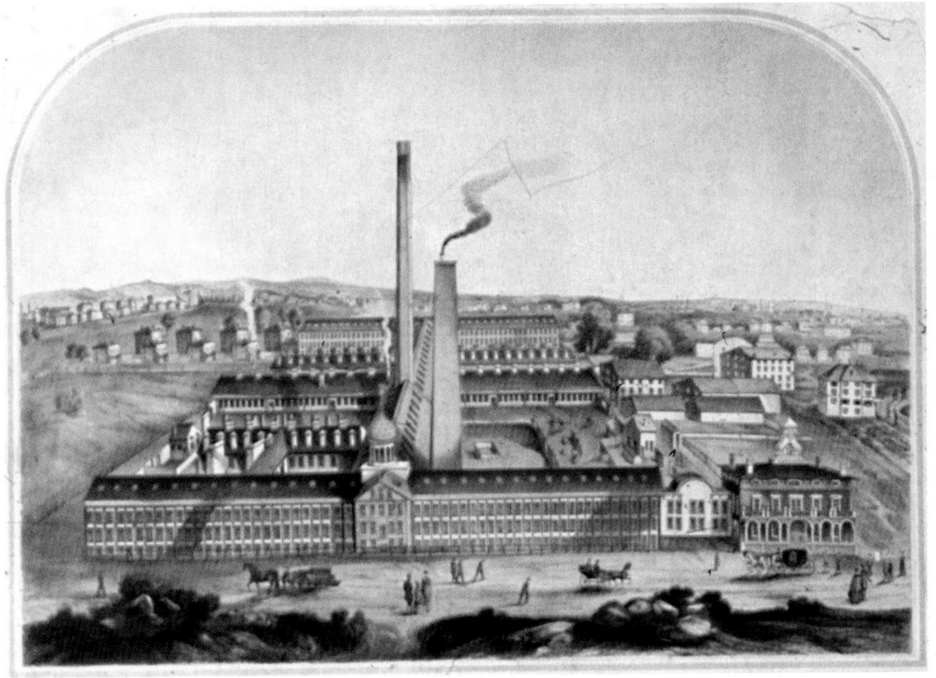

Jefferson Davis (*left*) was the first and last President of the Confederate States of America, the man directly opposed to Lincoln. The split between the two became war on 12 April 1861. Confederate batteries shelled Fort Sumter (*opposite, above*). The Union garrison held out while they had ammunition, but were forced to surrender the following day (*opposite, below*).

The early battles of 1862 were indecisive. Lincoln replaced McClellan with Ambrose E. Burnside, the man whose whiskers became famous as 'sideburns'. On 13 December, Burnside sent his men across the icy Rappahannock River to face Lee's forces at Fredericksburg. Six times the Union troops attacked the Confederate positions, and six times they were driven back, with murderous losses. The Union suffered 12,000 losses, the Confederates 6,000. (*Left*) Matthew Brady's chilling picture of a dead Confederate soldier on the field of Fredericksburg.

The Union army and the Confederates had already met once to fight by the meandering stream known as Bull Run, back in July 1861, the first real battle of the war. On 30 August 1862 they met again (*above*). The Union troops, led by the bombastic John Pope, were taken by surprise. 'Jeb' Stuart's Confederate cavalry raided Pope's headquarters, capturing Pope's dress uniform, and, more importantly, his strategy book, which contained information about the position of his units. Pope, meanwhile, was wasting time and energy trying to find 'Stonewall' Jackson and the Confederate infantry.

By the time he found them, they had been joined by the army of Robert E. Lee. Pope blundered into a trap. Thirty thousand Confederates, screaming 'like demons emerging from the earth', drove the Union forces from the field (*above*). One New York regiment lost one hundred and twenty-four of its four hundred and ninety men, and the Union army retreated to Washington. Pope was sent to Minnesota, to fight in the Indian Wars. But the Confederates had no reserves to follow up their victory.

The South was more vulnerable by sea than by land. Jefferson Davis had few ships with which to oppose the Northern fleet that sailed to the Gulf of Mexico, seeking to force open the lower Mississippi. In the spring of 1862 Flag Officer (later Admiral) David Farragut *(left)* attacked New Orleans (*above*). The city surrendered on 1 May. Farragut went on to attack the forts along the Mississippi *(opposite, below)*. A year later, as admiral, Farragut returned to attack the Confederate batteries at Port Hudson, Louisiana (*opposite, above*).

In September 1862, Lee hoped to move the war into the north and to gain foreign recognition for the Confederacy. His strategy was discovered when a Union soldier picked up a bundle of cigars and found Lee's secret orders wrapped round them. McClellan, the Union commander, delayed acting on this information, giving Lee time to reform, near the town of Sharpsburg – seen here (*above*) shortly before the battle. The battle itself was horrendous. Antietam was the bloodiest single day in the entire war (*opposite*).

Between 2 and 4 July 1863, 50,000 Americans were killed at the Battle of Gettysburg, more than have died in any other battle in the history of the United States. The worst day was 3 July, depicted in this diorama of the battle (*right*). That afternoon, at about 2 p.m., Pickett's 15,000 Confederate troops emerged from the woods west of Cemetery Ridge and began their suicidal advance through the wheatfields. Seeing the carnage, Lee muttered 'All this has been my fault'.

It became the most famous battle of the Civil War, though neither side had planned to fight at Gettysburg. A Confederate foraging party entered the town on 1 July 1863 and was surprised to meet units of Union cavalry – and so began the three-day battle. (*Above*) Confederate troops move up towards Gettysburg. They were outnumbered by two to one.

The flashpoint of the battle was the attack on Cemetery Ridge by 15,000 Confederate soldiers under General George Pickett. The attack failed, and only half of Pickett's troops returned. This was slaughter on an unprecedented scale, a bitter foretaste of what was to come in the First World War. Timothy O'Sullivan's camera captured the field strewn with dead (*right, and opposite, below*). As Lee's exhausted remnants of an army retreated, rain washed the blood from the grass.

General William Tecumseh Sherman (*above, and left*, with his staff) is remembered for two great deeds of destruction in the Civil War – the burning of Atlanta, and the famous 'march to the sea'. Sherman encircled Atlanta in August 1864. Three times John B. Hood led brave Confederate attacks from within the city. It was no use. Sherman destroyed the rail lines and Hood was forced to retreat. Atlanta surrendered on 1 September.

Before he left the city, to make 'all Georgia howl', Sherman made sure that the rail depot was totally destroyed (*opposite, below, and right, top, centre and bottom*). There was to be no chance that a Southern army could regroup, be supplied by rail, and set off to pursue him. That done, Sherman set out to 'whip the rebels, to humble their pride, to follow them into their inmost recesses, and to make them fear and dread us'.

By early 1865 the South had been brought almost to its knees. Sherman had burnt his way to Savannah, and Grant's army was about to isolate Richmond, the capital of the Confederacy. In the city, President Davis gathered his papers and escaped by train. The Confederate army then set fire to everything of military or industrial value (*opposite, above left*). By the time the Union army, accompanied by Lincoln, entered the city, it was a mass of smouldering ruins (*opposite, below left, and above and below, right*). The end was mercifully near.

When war broke out, the North established an early and commanding control of the sea. In five years the Union navy grew from ninety ships to six hundred and fifty, blockading Confederate ports from the Gulf of Mexico to Chesapeake Bay. Their boats were steam-powered, lightly armed and more than a match for most of the cargo vessels and blockade runners on which the South relied. (*Right*) The New York ferryboat *Hunchback* towards the end of the war. This photograph was taken on the James River some time between May 1864 and February 1865.

A halfway house between the redoubts of the Crimean War of the 1850s and the trenches of the First World War – Fort Sedgwick, photographed by Timothy O'Sullivan in May 1865 (*below, right*). (*Opposite, below*) A burial party on the battlefield of Cold Harbor, Virginia, 1864. Here, on 1 June, 7,000 Union troops were killed or wounded in twenty minutes of slaughter. (*Right*) A column of Confederate prisoners. Those who survived the battles and were taken prisoner were usually treated well, though disease was common in the overcrowded camps.

(*Left*) Matthew Brady's portrait of General Robert E. Lee, taken in Richmond, just eleven days after Lee's surrender to Grant (*above*). When the end came, it was swift. Some Confederates urged Lee to take to the woods and continue the fight, but Lee knew the war was lost and that further killing and devastation was pointless. On Palm Sunday, 9 April 1865, Lee put on a crisp dress uniform and rode to the McLean home at Appomattox (*opposite, above*).

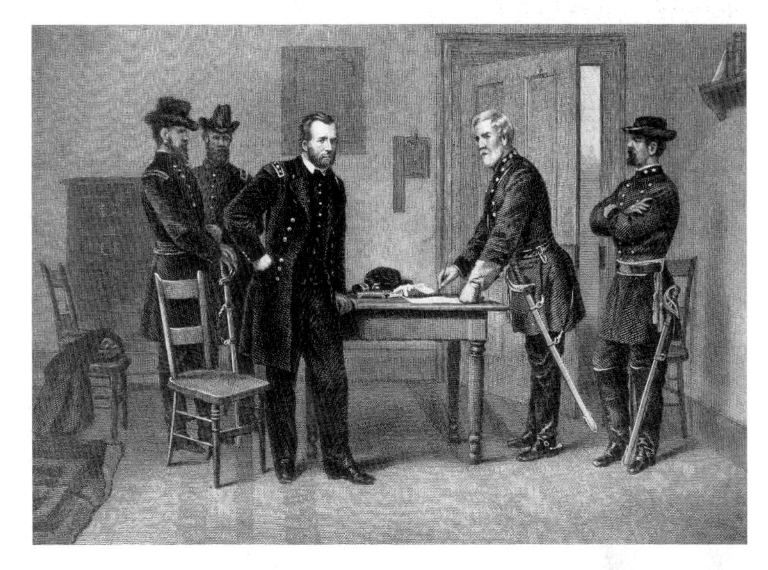

In the parlour (*right*) Lee met a mud-spattered Grant, and tendered his surrender. At Lee's request, Grant allowed the Confederate officers to keep their sidearms. Three days later, the formal surrender took place in 'an awed stillness...as if it were the passing of the dead'.

(*Left*) A picture researcher holds the glass negative of one of Matthew Brady's portraits of Abraham Lincoln. Brady was born near Lake George, New York, in 1823. From 1844 until the outbreak of war, he operated a daguerrotype portrait studio, but then left New York to join the Union armies. His team of photographers and helpers travelled from battlefield to battlefield, capturing war on an unprecedented scale, but the effort ruined him financially, and he died in poverty in a New York almshouse.

It was more than four months after the battle that Lincoln visited Gettysburg (*left*). The dead had long been buried, and the field of carnage had already become a shrine. And here, on 19 November 1863, Lincoln delivered what was to become his most famous speech – the Gettysburg Address. It was not a long speech, just over two hundred and seventy words, and it took Lincoln two minutes to deliver it. Moreover, it followed a two-hour peroration by Edward Everett, the best-known orator of the time. Nobody recalls what Everett said. Generations have committed Lincoln's speech to memory.

Viscount Palmerston, Prime Minister of Britain at the time of the Civil War, claimed that Lincoln undertook 'to abolish slavery where he was without power to do so, while protecting it where he had power to destroy it'. Emancipation was to be granted to all slaves in the South – once the war had been won. There was no promise to abolish slavery in the border states. Nevertheless, Lincoln has gone down in history as the president who freed the slaves (*opposite, below*). (*Left*) A group of escaped slaves outside a cabin, 1861. Their status was still unsure, and some regarded them as contraband property. (*Opposite, above)* A Currier and Ives print of a freed slave, 1868.

The last photograph of Lincoln *(above)* was taken only days before his assassination at Ford's Theatre, New York (*above, right*) on 14 April 1865. Lincoln had spent the day working on a reconstruction programme that would include 'no persecution, no bloody work'. He went to the theatre with his wife, and was shot by a crazed Southern bigot named John Wilkes Booth. Booth broke his leg leaping on to the stage, but made his escape, with a reward of $100,000 offered for his capture (*opposite, above left*). (*Right*) Lincoln's funeral train, and (*opposite, below*) the box at Ford's Theatre, draped in mourning for Lincoln.

Booth was trapped a few days later and shot. Four of his accomplices – Mary Surratt, Lewis Payne, George Atzerott and David Harold – were hanged on 7 July (*above, right*). The doctor who set Booth's broken leg was sentenced to life imprisonment, giving rise to a new expression in the English language, for his name was Mudd.

11
GO WEST, YOUNG MAN 1865–1880

(*Right*) *The Oregon Trail Beyond Devil's Gate*, by W. H. Jackson, c. 1865. The Oregon Trail was originally mapped by John Charles Frémont in the 1840s. Once news of Oregon's fertile soil, temperate climate and magnificent forests reached the eastern states, the trickle of emigrants became a flood. By the 1850s and 1860s 'Oregon Fever' led thousands of would-be settlers to sell up and head west in slow-moving wagon trains.

Introduction

There were many reasons why the young, the bold, God-fearing idealists and sundry fugitives should head west across the wild interior of the United States in the late 19th century. There was still the hope of finding nuggets of gold in California. There were tens of thousands of buffalo to slaughter for their meat and hides. There was good land in plenty. Technically, much of it belonged to the Indians, but it was not difficult to invent legal fictions to sweep that problem aside. And there was also little chance that lovers, creditors or anyone from the past could find you.

The journey had already been made by a few. Joseph Smith and Brigham Young led their persecuted Mormons to the City of the Saints – Salt Lake City – back in the 1830s. John Charles Frémont crossed the Rocky Mountains in 1842. Buffalo Bill (William S. Cody), Pony Bob Haslam and other Pony Express riders rode hell-for-leather across Kansas and Colorado in the 1850s.

Now – from 1869 – there was the Union Pacific Railroad, an iron road running right across the continent, with frequent jumping-off points into the wilderness. In the spring of 1867, Joseph McCoy took the train from Illinois to Abilene, Kansas. There it occurred to him that, if you grazed cattle on the lush grass of Kansas, you could ship them by rail to the stockyards of Chicago. It was the beginning of a vast new empire. But there were problems – rustling, encroaching, trespassing. Range wars began, but order, of a rough and ready sort, was established by Joseph Glidden's ingenious invention – barbed wire. Then came combine harvesters and twine-binding machines, seed drills and straddle row cultivators, and the heartland's of America became the world's granary as well as its abattoir.

Back east inventions were noisier but more civilised. In 1868 C.L. Sholes invented the typewriter, and handwriting was never the same again. Eight years later Alexander Graham Bell produced the telephone, and privacy was never the same. An uneducated genius named Thomas Alva Edison invented the telegraph, an electric vote-recording machine, and the paper ticker-tape automatic repeater for stock exchange prices – just three ideas from the mind of the world's most prolific inventor.

There was plenty for everyone. Unlike European powers, the United States had little need to scour the world for raw materials. Almost everything was to hand – oil, land, manpower, invention, hunger and greed – the last exemplified by George Armstrong Custer, whose greed for glory cost the lives of all his command at the Little Big Horn in 1876.

WORLD
OF
CARE
AND
RESPONSIBILITY
TAXATION.
DUTIES.
CUSTOM HOUSE
FRAUDS.
HARD TIMES
FINANCIAL CRISIS
INDIAN TROUBLES.
INDIAN RINGS
K.K.
GOV. MOSES
ARKANSAS TROUBLES
FOOLISH THIRD TERM RESOLUTIONS
THE KELLOGG (MIS) GOVERNMENT
CORRUPT "CARPET BAGGER" STATE DEBTS.
CIVIL RIGHTS
WHAT CONGRESS DOES AND DOES NOT

C. SCHURZ
CARPET-BAG
FROM WISCONSIN
TO
MISSOURI
CARPET BAGGER
SOUTH

With the death of Lincoln, Ulysses Simpson Grant (*opposite, left*) became President of the United States. His government was beset by corruption (*opposite, above right*), but Grant's troubles were nothing compared with those of the South. After the Confederate defeat carpetbaggers (*opposite, below right*) moved in to exploit the poverty and desperation of the survivors. The Ku Klux Klan (*right*) was a bitter white backlash that started life as a social club in Pulaski, Tennessee, in 1866.

The exhortation 'Go West, young man, and grow up with the country' was the creation of Horace Greeley, founding editor of the *New York Tribune*, and a man who seldom moved further west than Eleventh Avenue. But many answered his call, farmers, prospectors, gamblers, tradesmen, and soldiers among them. After the Civil War there were many veterans of both sides who believed the army offered them as good and exciting a way of life as they were likely to get.

The backbone of the US army on both sides of the Mississippi was the cavalry. Dotted across the harsh country were military strongholds, many of them named after famous officers – Fort Kearney, Fort Sedgwick, Fort Myers, Fort Smith and, later, Fort Custer (*above*). Here the pony soldiers (as they were called by the Indians) drilled, drank and dreamed. Life was often boring, and it probably came as a relief when hostilities flared and Death or Glory might lie round any bluff.

The Great Sioux War began in 1875 and lasted for fifteen months. It was caused by gold seekers who were allowed to invade the Black Hills of Dakota, territory sacred to the Sioux, despite promises that the army would keep them out. The war was one of movement, with fifteen battles fought across Wyoming, Montana, Nebraska and South Dakota.

The most famous battle was that of the Little Big Horn (*opposite, below*), where two hundred and ten troopers (estimations vary) of the US 7th Cavalry under General George Armstrong Custer (*above, right*) were annihilated by 2,500 Sioux, Cheyenne and Arapaho warriors under Tatanka Yotaka (Sitting Bull) (*above, left*). (*Opposite, above*) A painting by White Bird of the Northern Cheyenne depicting the retreat of Major Marcus Reno during the battle, 25 June 1876.

The building of the transcontinental railroad (*opposite, below and above, left and right*) was the work of two companies – the Central Pacific and the Union Pacific. The two lines met on 10 May 1869 at Promontory Point, Utah (*right and above, left*). Towns along the route were soon crowded with travellers (*above, right*).

The construction of the railroad was an amazing feat of engineering skill and endurance. Track laying crews of up to 10,000 men needed 400 tons of rail, timber and other materials to lay a single mile of track, more when there were gullies and canyons to cross (*left, above and below*).

To the north was another transcontinental line – the Canadian Pacific. Though sparse by modern standards, travel on both lines was infinitely swifter, more reliable and more comfortable than on the old stagecoaches. (*Above, right*) A third-class sleeping-car on the CPR, c. 1880. (*Below, right*) A tourist sleeping-car in the 1870s.

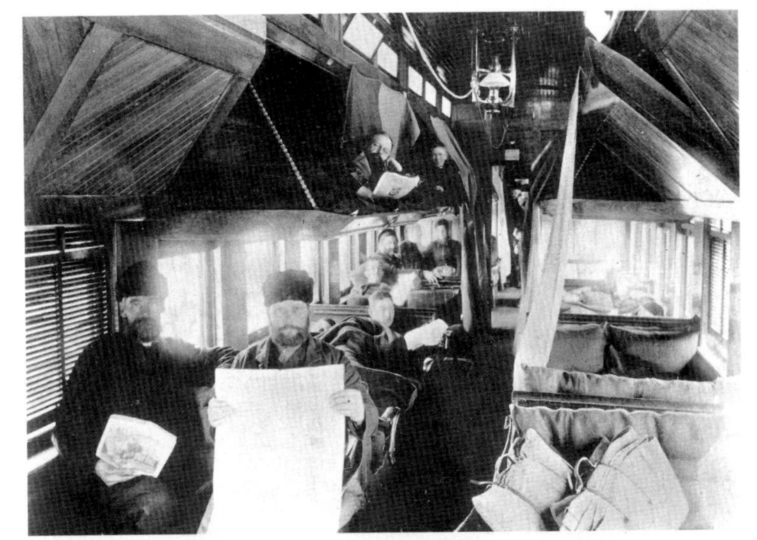

The human mind poured forth a multitude of inventions. Communications in the 1870s entered a new age with the phonograph of Thomas Edison (*opposite*), the telephone of Alexander Graham Bell (*above, right*), and the 'Perfected Machine' – the typewriter of C.L. Sholes (*below, right*).

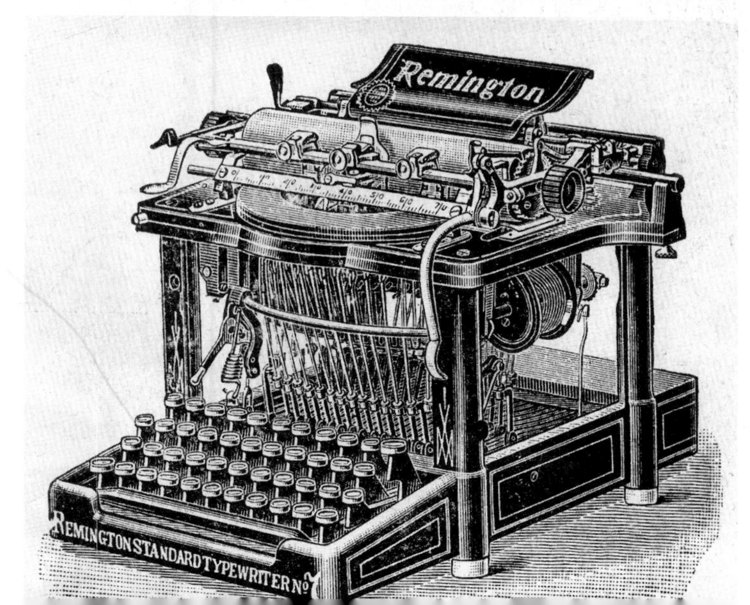

From 1841 until it was destroyed by fire in 1865, crowds flocked to Barnum's American Museum in New York (*left*). Barnum was the ultimate showman – a man who believed in giving the public what he thought it ought to want.

The collection of curios in the museum was highly eclectic. As well as the Siamese twins (*above, left*), there was General Tom Thumb (George Sherwood Stratton) (*above, right*). Jumbo the elephant (*right*) was one of the favourites of the circus that Barnum later ran with his partner, James Bailey.

In 1852, at the age of twenty-four, the English photographer Eadweard Muybridge emigrated to California. He became the chief photographer to the United States Government, and in 1877 he captured the city of San Francisco in a unique eleven-frame panorama (eight of which are shown on this and the following spread). The city had been created almost overnight following the 1849 gold rush, and, by the time the transcontinental railroad had been completed in 1869, it had become a lawless boomtown of bordellos and drinking dens.

But the city was cleared up within a very short time, and, when Muybridge took the pictures (*opposite and above, and on the following spread*), an imposing mixture of high civic architecture and bay-windowed suburban buildings, with libraries and cathedrals, had replaced the old shanty town. Visitors came by rail and by ship from all over the world to join the 300,000-strong population. In 1872 gold fever was temporarily replaced by 'diamond frenzy' after two strangers deposited a huge cache of stones in a San Francisco bank.

After a long and frightening journey across America by rail, the Viscountess Avonmore arrived in San Francisco a couple of years before Muybridge climbed Nob Hill to take his photographs. The Viscountess was delighted with Mr Sharon's world-famous Palace Hotel, which offered a choice of 'European or American accommodation' and arranged conducted tours to nearby Yosemite Valley.

Another great admirer of San Francisco at this time was the writer Robert Louis Stevenson. 'From Nob Hill,' he wrote, 'looking down upon the business wards of the city, we can decry a building with a little belfry, and that is the stock exchange, the heart of San Francisco; a great pump we might call it, continually pumping up the savings of the lower quarter to the pockets of the millionaires on the hill.'

By the late 19th century the trains and tramcars had invaded American city centres. In Chicago the steam-operated elevated track ran along Market Street, near Lake Street (*above, left*). (*Below, left*) A cable car enters the tunnel under the river, La Salle Street, Chicago, 30 June 1895.

In 1867 Charles T. Harvey built the West Side and Yonkers Patent Elevated Railway, which tiptoed through the city, supported on single columns. Seven years later came the larger, stronger New York Elevated Railroad (*above, right*), with its famous 'Big S' (*below, right*). Strangely, the tramway, which ran beneath the 'El', began to pay its way only after the railway opened.

America's first subway was built by the Beach Pneumatic Transit Company, and was inaugurated on 26 February 1870 (*above, left*). Initially, it was experimental, simply running under the length of Broadway, but it was soon extended. It was designed as a simple tube (*below, left*), and became one of the many wonders of the city.

The first pneumatically powered railway had been built three years earlier as part of the Exhibition of the American Institute at the Armory, New York City. The tube ran across the exhibition building from gallery to gallery, supported by iron hoops attached to the roof (*above, right*). Alfred E. Beach, founder of the New York subway, also proposed a pneumatic mail dispatch system (*below, right*).

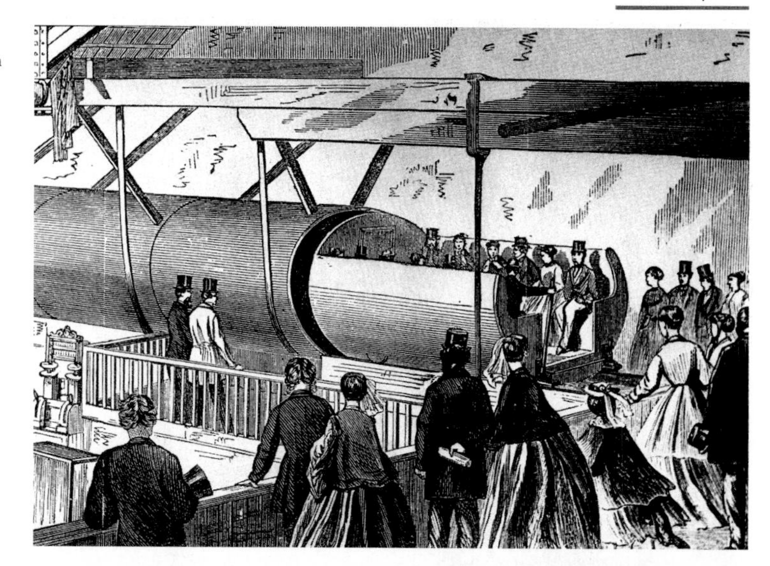

COPPERTONE

Atlantic City (*opposite*) rapidly developed on Absecon Island, New Jersey, after 1854, when Philadelphia speculators made it the rail terminus. It boasted the nation's first boardwalk (opened in 1870), first colour postcards (1893), and the world's first big wheel (1869). An early edition of the Baedeker guide recorded, 'there is something colossal about its vulgarity'. Vulgar or not, it had immense appeal. Women paraded on the sands (*above*), or sat with their beaux under the pavilions of the boardwalk. And there was always the fun of paddling in the sea (*right*).

12
MAKING A FORTUNE
1870–1890

If you wanted to make a fortune in late 19th century America, all you had to do was decide 'how' – steel, lumber, railroads, banking, housing – there were plenty of different ways. One of the best was oil. The black glue discovered by Edwin L. Drake back in 1859 was still bubbling and gushing up through the fields of Pennsylvania (*right*). In neighbouring Ohio it had made John Davison Rockefeller one of the richest men in the world. And there was plenty more of it...

Introduction

The story begins a little earlier – in 1859. The owner of a strip of land near Oil Creek in western Pennsylvania asked Edwin L. Drake to search for oil. For well over a hundred years petroleum, or 'black glue' as it was known, had been bottled and sold as a cure for asthma, rheumatism, gout, tuberculosis, cancer, constipation and fallen arches. Drake, and the owner of the land, knew it had a more profitable use – as the distilled fuel, kerosene.

Drake noticed that oil oozed out of the land to form a dark scum on the water of the creek. He dug down, deep into the land, helped by the local blacksmith. On a hot August afternoon the black glue bubbled to the surface. The first petroleum well had been drilled. A year later John Davison Rockefeller was sent from Cleveland to examine the potential of the new industry. He was not impressed and reported that there was no commercial future for oil. Whether he genuinely believed this, we shall never know. But nine years later he founded the Standard Oil Company and bought thirty-five refineries.

Other big players entered the arena. Henry Ford was apprenticed to a machinist in Detroit in 1878. It took him fifteen years to produce his first petrol-driven motor car. John Pierpont Morgan built on his father's early success, and by the 1890s was in charge of the most powerful private banking house in the United States. Andrew Carnegie invested in oil and made his fortune in iron and steel.

And a name that was to outlast all others first appeared in 1888. It was Coca-Cola, and it was the invention of a poor Georgia farmboy named Asa G.Candler, who started making and bottling his fizzy beverage in a small shed. The same year Henry J. Heinz, with his brother and his cousin, reorganised the family business to form H.J. Heinz and Company.

The pace of life and leisure quickened. Vaudeville theatres opened. Broadway blazed as a ribbon of light and magic across Manhattan. Coney Island was built to entertain the incoming thousands to New York. The world's first motor race careered crazily from Green Bay to Madison, Wisconsin. American football stamped its foot on the gridiron. Buffalo Bill took his Wild West show to the Wild East and beyond. John L. Sullivan and Gentleman Jim Corbett punched their way to befuddled glory.

And the hungry masses began to pack the jetties of Europe, begging and borrowing for the price of a ticket to this wonderful new land of opportunity.

Bureal of the Dead
at the Battle of Wounded Knee S.D.
North Western Photo Co
Chadron Neb

Accounts vary as to what happened at Wounded Knee on 29 December 1890. Frederic Remington's illustration (*opposite, above left*) suggests it was a battle; the contemporary wooden sign on the site (*right*) states that it was a massacre. (*Opposite, above right*) Lieutenant Cloman, First Infantry, surveys the carnage; (*opposite, below*) the burial of some of the dead in a mass grave. (*Above*) Buffalo Bill Cody in the company of General Nelson Miles a few days after the massacre.

87784

By the 1880s few tribes still had the will to resist the white man. Under Goyathlay (Geronimo) Chiricahua Apache renegades *(above*, with Geronimo on the extreme right) held out for a while longer in the Sierra Madre mountains. Geronimo was captured by General George Crook in March 1886. For three days in the Canyon de los Embudos, Crook tried to persuade the Apache leader to resign himself to life on a reservation *(opposite, above)*. Geronimo slipped away, only to surrender later and to end his days as a farmer in Indian Territory (later Oklahoma). (*Opposite, below*) Camillus S. Fry's photograph of Geronimo with his warriors in March 1886.

The fate of the old Chiracahua Apaches was to die in poverty on reservations; the fate of the young was to be sent to American-style schools run by the Bureau of Indian Affairs, to be integrated into the ways of the whites. John N. Choate was a photographer who charted the progress of these children. They arrived at Carlisle School, Pennsylvania, dressed in the clothes their parents would have worn (*above*). Within a few days, they were wearing the uniform of the school (*opposite*).

Life was harsh at such schools – for example, the children were beaten if they spoke their own language. Daily routines were rigidly regimented. Perhaps the cruellest irony was that life was frequently short, for the children were infected with diseases they had hitherto not encountered. In the grounds of such schools you can still see the rows of headstones, as though in a military cemetery. Many of them are labelled 'unknown', for the identity of the children mattered little to those who ran the schools. Carlisle School closed in 1918.

After his scouting days for the US army were over, Buffalo Bill Cody ran his Wild West Show (*left*), a travelling extravaganza that included mock battles between himself and Sitting Bull *(below, left)*. (*Below, right*) Buffalo Bill (centre), with Ned Buntline (left) and Texas Jack, in costume for 'Scouts of the Prairie'.

Though tending to be a little generous with the truth, posters advertising Buffalo Bill's Wild West *(top)* gave at least a promise of things to come. As well as the mock battles, there were parades, races, stagecoaches chased round the ring by whooping Indians, and displays of sharp-shooting. Buffalo Bill (*above, left*) is credited with extending the myth of the West. Among his co-stars were Annie Oakley (*above, centre*) and Wild Bill Hickok (*above, right*), who was later murdered in a saloon in Deadwood.

One way to make a fortune was to have a bright idea. Joseph McCoy was a twenty-nine-year-old livestock trader from Chicago when he bought the town of Abilene and instituted the Chisholm Trail, bringing cattle from Texas to the railhead.

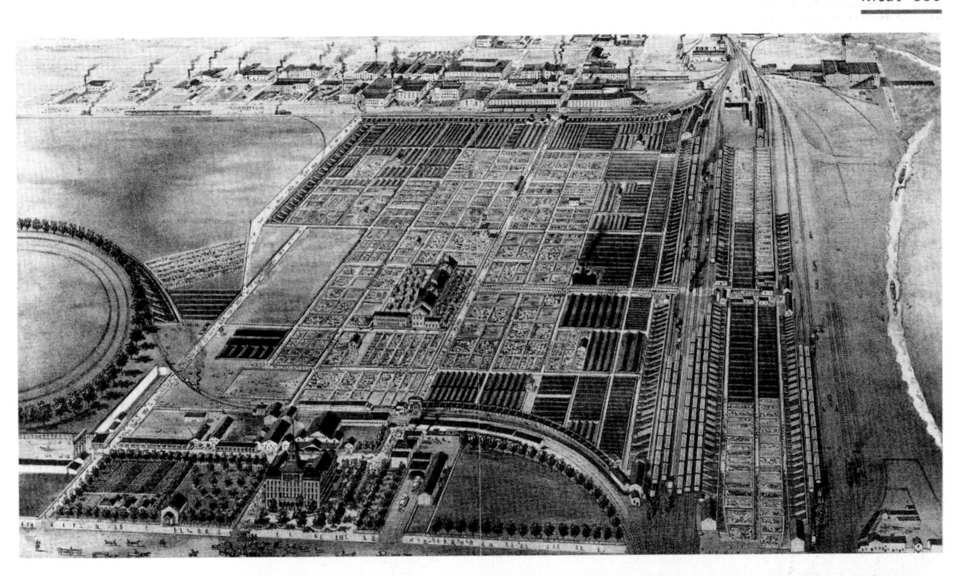

The Texas longhorns (*opposite, above*) were driven to the depot of the Kansas Pacific Railroad and there loaded into freight cars (*opposite, below*). From Abilene they were taken to the largest livestock market in the world, the Great Union Stockyard in Chicago (*above*), and slaughtered (*right*).

For some blacks, life slowly improved in the decades following the Civil War. Booker Taliaferro Washington (*left*) was an ex-slave from Franklin County, Virginia, who became a teacher and a writer, and also the founder of the Tuskegee Institute for black students in Alabama (*opposite, above*). There were those who saw Washington as too moderate in his views, and were unhappy with some of the views he expressed. Others believed he did more to help the cause of the American Negro than any other person.

'No race can prosper till it learns that there is as much dignity in tilling a field as in writing a poem,' wrote Washington. 'It is at the bottom of our life that we must begin, not at the top. Nor should we permit our grievances to overshadow our opportunities.' (*Below, right*) The American scientist George Washington Carver, son of a Missouri slave, at work in the laboratory at the Tuskegee Institute, 1896.

On the evening of 8 October 1871 a small fire started on the suburban outskirts of Chicago. It was fanned by unusually strong winds and its progress was accelerated by previous weeks of drought. It quickly consumed the wooden houses and timber yards, and reached the commercial centre of the city (*below*).

Firemen did what they could (*opposite, above right*), but the fire raged through the night, destroying all the old landmarks – Crosby's Opera House, McVicker's Theatre, the central depot, hotels, churches and banks. At its height, the blaze created panic, and desperate crowds swarmed over the Randolph Street Bridge (*right*). The following morning newspapers all over the country reported the dreadful news (*opposite, above left*). Two hundred and fifty people died. The cost of the damage was estimated at $200 million.

It was the heyday of New York City's most famous street. Broadway – the Great White Way – was booming in the 1890s (*above*). Stars of vaudeville, theatre, the Follies and burlesque all congregated on the strip of starlight that ran diagonally across Manhattan.

Its rise had been meteoric. Just thirty years earlier, when it was photographed by William England (*above*), Broadway had been busy but demure, an avenue of horse carts and small-time traders

Work began on Brooklyn Bridge in 1870 (*left*), though John Augustus Roebling, its designer, died before the first stone was laid. By September 1872 the towers at either end of the bridge had reached almost half their eventual height (*below*).

In 1877 it was possible for those brave enough to walk from the shore to the tower top on a ladder of suspension wires (*above, right*). Roebling's son Washington supervised the completion of the project, and the bridge was opened in triumph in 1883. The finished bridge shimmered in the brilliance of electric light and became one of the earliest landmarks of the modern New York City skyline. It also brought new prosperity to Brooklyn

Cornelius Vanderbilt (1794–1877) – steamships and railroads.

Jay Gould (1836–92) – lumber, railroads and banking.

Andrew Carnegie (1835–1918) – oil, iron and steel.

John Pierpont Morgan (1837–1913) – banking, railroads and steel.

John D. Rockefeller (1839–1937) – oil.

Andrew Mellon (1855–1937) – banking.

Frank Winfield Woolworth (1852–1919) – retail stores.

C.M. Schwab (1862 – 1939) – steel and banking.

One of the newly arrived immigrants to New York in the 1880s was a Danish photographer named Jacob Riis. He became the police reporter for the *Daily Tribune*, and took hundreds of pictures of life and death in the slums of the city. *(Left)* Riis's portrait of 'Bandits' Roost', off Mulberry Street in New York City, 1887. (*Below, right*) A squalid room, and (*below, left*) a beggar's home in the cellar of 11 Ludlow Street.

(*Above, right*) Young children saying their prayers in Five Points House, 1887. The area was one of the most notorious slums in the city, and was likened to the Black Hole of Calcutta by the English novelist Charles Dickens. (*Below, right*) A family of Jewish tailors in New York. The picture was one used by Riis as a magic lantern slide to illustrate his lecture 'The Other Half, How it Lives and Dies in New York'. Riis himself later became a social reformer.

John Lawrence Sullivan (*left*) was born in Roxbury, Massachusetts, in 1856. In February 1882 he became the last bare-knuckle heavyweight champion of the world when he beat Paddy Ryan in nine rounds. Seven years later Sullivan was the victor in the last bare-knuckle title fight of all time. It took him seventy-five rounds (two hours and fifteen minutes) to fight off the challenge of Jake Kilrain. Both men were later prosecuted for breaking the Mississippi state laws, which forbade such fights.

James John Corbett (*right*) was known as 'Gentleman Jim'. He was a dapper dresser and a handsome man, who started adult life as a bank clerk, and who went on to appear in films after giving up boxing. In September 1892 he challenged Sullivan for the world heavyweight championship (with gloves). Corbett's style was fast and scientific: Sullivan still relied on wild round arm swings. The fight lasted twenty-one rounds before Sullivan was defeated. It was the end of an era.

In the 1890s the six-mile long beach of Coney Island was the most exciting – and perhaps the roughest – playground in the world. In the morning, the resort slept. In the afternoon, thousands walked on the sands and paddled in the sea.

In the evening, the entire boardwalk came to life. There were parades (*above*) through the amusement parks, of which the greatest was Luna Park (*opposite, above and below*). Lights glittered on every building, every lamppost, every bar and café. There were rides, side shows, sleazy cabarets, hot dog stalls, roller coasters, gin palaces, and brothels. If you were lucky, no one stole your wallet and you could go home penniless, having spent all your money on Coney Island.

13
SEND ME YOUR POOR 1890–1900

(*Right*) High above the waterfront of New York City, a construction worker is hauled to his working eyrie – photograph by Henry Guttmann. Emotionally and commercially, the United States was better prepared than any other nation for the 20th century. In a way, the new century was a purely American invention – busy, hungry, brash and resourceful – and reaching for heaven like the skyscrapers that were only a couple of years away. What the country needed was more workers, and they were on their way from corners of Europe that had barely limped into the 19th century.

Introduction

Nature and nurture were between them creating the American personality – energetic, brilliant and competitive. Mrs Howard Vincent, an experienced traveller, noted her impressions of three great cities: 'In Boston they ask you what you know, in Philadelphia who you are. And in New York they ask you what you have.'

The American spirit was personified by Teddy Roosevelt, whose Rough Riders battled their way through the Spanish American War that William Randolph Hearst had promised he would supply.

For the most part, it was more of the same. The rich got richer and the poor barely got a living wage. Opulence was the order of the day for those who made their fortune. William K. Vanderbilt's 'cottage' at Newport, Rhode Island, cost $11 million to build and furnish. It was a Renaissance palace, the dream house of a shrewd operator who read little, could barely write, but was able to leave $94 million to his son.

Those seeking a less permanent home could always book into the new Waldorf Astoria in New York, with its bathrooms and electric lights, its rented luxury and its wealthy clientele. Modern Manhattan was beginning to rise. The steel frame of the Flatiron Building, twenty storeys high, created unusual wind currents at ground level, so that policemen had to be posted around it to prevent crowds of men gathering in the hope that a gust would raise women's skirts on nearby 23rd Street. This was the origin of the cry '23 Skidoo', which joined the rest of America's colourful new language.

John Philip Sousa created a bandbox full of American marches. John Harvey Kellogg developed a process of cooking, rolling and toasting wheat and corn into flakes that have filled a million bowls since. Flo Ziegfeld brought his Follies to Broadway. Oscar Wilde came and went, declaring his genius to bewildered Customs' officials.

Down on Ellis Island, others came and went – Poles, Russians, Germans, Swedes, Italians, Irish and Jews. The healthy and the lucky stayed to learn the language, salute the flag, jostle each other for jobs and take up the American way of life. The fortunate few found themselves free of persecution, charmed players in a game of chance where Lady Luck smiled down on them. The majority sweated in garrets and basements, making money for others, and praying that their sons and daughters would succeed where they had failed.

(*Left*) The last President of the United States to campaign from his own porch – William McKinley in the summer of 1896. McKinley's foreign policy was driven by 'bullish' elements in the United States who felt it was time the US asserted itself around the world. (*Above*) Uncle Sam peruses a menu that includes Cuba Steak, Porto Rico Pig, Philippine Floating Islands and Sandwich Islands. The waiter is McKinley. (*Opposite*) McKinley's campaigning *Republican Two Step and March.*

MOST RESPECTFULLY DEDICATED TO
OUR CANDIDATE
PATRIOTISM PROSPERITY PROTECTION
THE REPUBLICAN
TWO STEP AND MARCH
COMPOSED BY
ION ARNOLD
FULL ORCHESTRA $1.00
FULL BAND .75
PIANO SOLO .50
Maj. William McKinley.
PUBLISHED BY
EMPIRE MUSIC CO.
1424 BROADWAY NEW YORK.
COPYRIGHT 1896 BY ION ARNOLD

In 1895 Theodore Roosevelt wrote in a letter to a friend: 'This country needs a war.' Three years later he got one. American newspapers printed graphic reports of the suffering of the Cubans under Spanish rule, and of the courage of the rebel fighters (*above, right*). When the war came it was not confined to Cuba. US troops were also sent to the Philippines. (*Above, left*) American soldiers near Manila, 1898.

Roosevelt himself could hardly wait to join the fray in one theatre or another. He ordered a tailor-made uniform from Brooks Brothers and hurried to Cuba with his Rough Riders, a mixture of Ivy League athletes, ex-convicts and sharpshooters. Their day of glory came on 1 July 1898, when the Rough Riders charged to the top of San Juan Hill (*above*), a minor action in a larger battle. Spain had neither the strength nor the will to hold out against the United States, and peace came soon afterwards. The following year, the Fighting Tenth and other units of the US army marched in triumph down Fifth Avenue (*opposite, below*).

The incident that did most to rally American public support for the war was the sinking of the USS *Maine* in Havana Harbour. The *Maine* had arrived in Cuba (*left, top*) to protect American interests. On the night of 15 February 1898, the ship suddenly exploded and sank with the loss of two hundred and sixty-six men (*left, centre and below*).

None of the officers was on board when the *Maine* exploded. The captain sent a telegram to Washington, stressing 'Public opinion should be suspended until further report.' This was not what Roosevelt, Randolph Hearst and others wanted. The 'yellow press' whipped up anger towards Spain, Roosevelt declaring that this had been 'an act of dirty treachery on the part of the Spaniards'. Later, the wreck of the *Maine* was raised from the bottom of Havana harbour (*right*).

Almost forty years after the California gold rush, gold was discovered in the Klondike, Yukon Territory, north-west Canada. More than 22,000 prospectors a year trudged through the snow (*left*) to seek their fortunes. In this barren landscape, they dug and scraped, crushed and sifted, desperate to extract the precious dust from the mountains of slag and shale. (*Below*) Miners pose by a slag heap near Disc Miller Creek.

The prospectors were men – loners who had left their friends and families, homes and past with the promise, or the boast, that they would make a fortune. A few, however, were accompanied by their wives (*right*). Other female company was provided by 'actresses' who braved the perils and discomforts of the journey (*below*) for a hard-earned share of the wealth.

Shanty towns sprang up along the route to the goldfields. (*Opposite*) A prospectors' camp known as *Les Chevaliers de Fortune* – the starting-point on the journey to the goldfields, which in one year yielded $22 million of gold. (*Above*) Early days at the town of Skagway – built of canvas, mud and hope. (*Right*) Children (and dogs) await a better home on the fringes of Klondyke City.

Back in the 17th century, Ellis Island (*above*) was used by the Dutch as a picnic ground. It was greatly enlarged by landfill over the next two hundred and fifty years to become the major point of entry for immigrants to the United States.

On arrival, individuals and family groups (*opposite, below*) were herded into the biggest room most of them had ever seen – the Registry Hall (*right*) – amidst what one immigrant described as 'din, confusion, bewilderment, madness'.

For the lucky ones, 'processing' on Ellis Island ended with a wait at the railroad station to proceed into the brave new land (*above, left*). But processing took a long time. For Italian families (*below, left*), for English Jews (*opposite, above left*), for Germans (*opposite, below left*) for Russians (*opposite, below right*), and for all others (*opposite, above right and centre*) there were health checks to undergo.

Doctors chalked 'H' on the clothes of any with suspected heart conditions, 'F' for facial rash (eczema), 'L' for a child's limp that revealed rickets, 'E' for the eye disease trachoma. Whatever the letter, to be so branded meant instant deportation back to Europe. Those who passed did so with glad hearts through a door marked 'PUSH TO NEW YORK'.

Once through Ellis Island, immigrants struggled to find work and somewhere to live in the big cities of America. Many got no further than New York City itself, where their daily lives were photographed by Jacob Riis. (*Above, left*) Immigrant families living in shacks, c. 1890. (*Below, left*) European immigrants in a New York slum, c. 1900.

'Crime, filth and disease make up the trio that dominates that plagued neighbourhood of newly arrived immigrants. Rancid tenements line the crowded streets. It is not uncommon to find a family of ten or more living in two tiny rooms. The dimly lit hall smells of urine or worse' – from a report on the Lower East Side, 1900. (*Above, right*) A New York family, c. 1900. (*Below, right*) A Jewish cobbler in the coal cellar in which he lives with his family.

Pennsylvania was the centre of the US steel industry and at its heart was the giant Otis Steel Works in Pittsburgh (*opposite, above*). Conditions inside the works were harsh, the furnaces (*opposite, below right*) and rollers (*opposite, below left*) roaring and rumbling all day. In July 1892 trouble flared in the steel town of Homestead. Pinkerton detectives were called in to break a strike by workers, and a pitched battle was fought (*right*).

GEARY 12 STREET.
MARKET ST. & GOLDEN GATE
12
GEARY ST. PARK & OCEAN

Away on the other side of the United States was the prosperous city of San Francisco, its business centre dominated by the Stock Exchange (*opposite, above*). Cable cars (*opposite, below*) ran up and down the hilly boulevards, through as yet open country. (*Right*) San Francisco Bay, photographed by Henry Guttmann in 1890, long before Alcatraz Island (left background) had become a prison. (*Below, right*) California Street from Sansome Street, c. 1880.

From the ashes of the Great Fire of 1871 arose a bright and bustling new Chicago. One of the first architects to design skyscrapers and massive office blocks was Louis H. Sullivan (*opposite, left*), the 'Father of Modernism'. In Chicago, Sullivan was responsible for the Carson, Pirie & Scott department store, the Gage Building, the Stock Exchange and the Masonic temple (*left*).

By the time this photograph was taken (*right*) on 2 July 1895 from the ninth storey of the Old Colony Building, the centre of Chicago had already taken on the appearance of a modern American city, and Sullivan had established its reputation as one of the finest homes of modern architecture.

By no means did New York City have a monopoly on immigrants. Irish, German and Italian refugees from poverty and exploitation in Europe also flooded into New Orleans, Louisiana. By 1890 the city was notorious as the American headquarters of the Mafia. But it was an easy-going city, slowly drifting into an economic depression caused by the decline in river traffic on the Mississippi, once the railroad took over, and the abolition of slavery after the Civil War.

The heart of the city was the French Quarter, with its overhanging balconies, stuccoed walls and cobbled courtyards. Typical of the residences here was the house of Madame John Legacy (*opposite*, on the right). Decatur Street ran from the old US Mint past Jackson Square, and was the home of the French Market (*above*), where fruit and vegetables, clothes and leather goods had been sold since the 1720s.

As well as being the home of Madame John Legacy (*opposite, above left*), the French Quarter contained Old Beauregard House (*opposite, above right*), home of the Confederate general responsible for firing the shots at Fort Sumter that started the Civil War. In the 1890s and 1900s, the levee was still the centre for the export of raw cotton (*above and opposite, below*). The cotton was brought from the plantations of the South and loaded on to paddle steamers. The steamers carried their cargo up the Mississippi to railheads, whence it was taken to the cities of the North.

P

As the mighty nation opened up, there were some with the foresight to anticipate the need to preserve some of the riches of the landscape for the benefit of future generations. In 1851 Major James Savage's Mariposa Battalion had, while trailing Indians, been the first white Americans to set foot in Yosemite Valley. Thirteen years later it became the first National Park. With the backing of President Benjamin Harrison (*opposite, above*), James Muir (*opposite, below*) founded the Sierra Club, with the express aim of preserving Yosemite. (*Left*) The Half Dome in Yosemite Valley.

Several years before the triumph of Kittyhawk, American aviators were experimenting with gliders. (*Left, and below, left*) Octave Chanute's biplane is piloted by Augustus Moor Herring at Lake Michigan, June 1896. (*Below, right*) Samuel Langley (left) and Charles Manly, the inventors of early flying machines. (*Opposite*) Orville and Wilbur Wright at Kill Devil Hills, North Carolina.

John Philip Sousa (*left*) was a composer and bandmaster from Washington, DC, who became conductor of the United States Marine Band (*opposite, below*) in 1880. The marches he wrote have a youthful exuberance and optimism that made them America's most popular and most patriotic tunes in the late 19th century.

Sousa believed that his best marches (*The Stars and Stripes Forever, El Capitan* and *The Washington Post*) 'should make a man with a wooden leg step out'. For those who did not wish to march, however, he gave many concerts (*above, right*) with his own band. He also composed ten comic operas, few of which would today make a man with a wooden leg wish to do anything.

John Harvey Kellogg and his brother, Will Keith Kellogg, were born in Tyrone and Battle Creek, Michigan, respectively. John was a physician who worked at the Battle Creek Sanitorium. Will was an industrialist. Together they formed the idea of cooking, rolling and toasting wheat and corn to make crisp flakes that would provide a nourishing breakfast for patients in the sanitorium. Within a short space of time they were selling their Toasted Flakes (*left and opposite*) by mail order across the state of Michigan.

In 1906 the W.K. Kellogg Company was founded. It was a great and typically American success – a mixture of product, presentation, advertising and marketing that resulted in a revolution in American eating habits. The brothers made a fortune, and Kellogg's breakfast cereals were soon on sale across the world. Later, in 1930, the W.K. Kellogg Foundation was established and became one of America's leading philanthropic institutions.

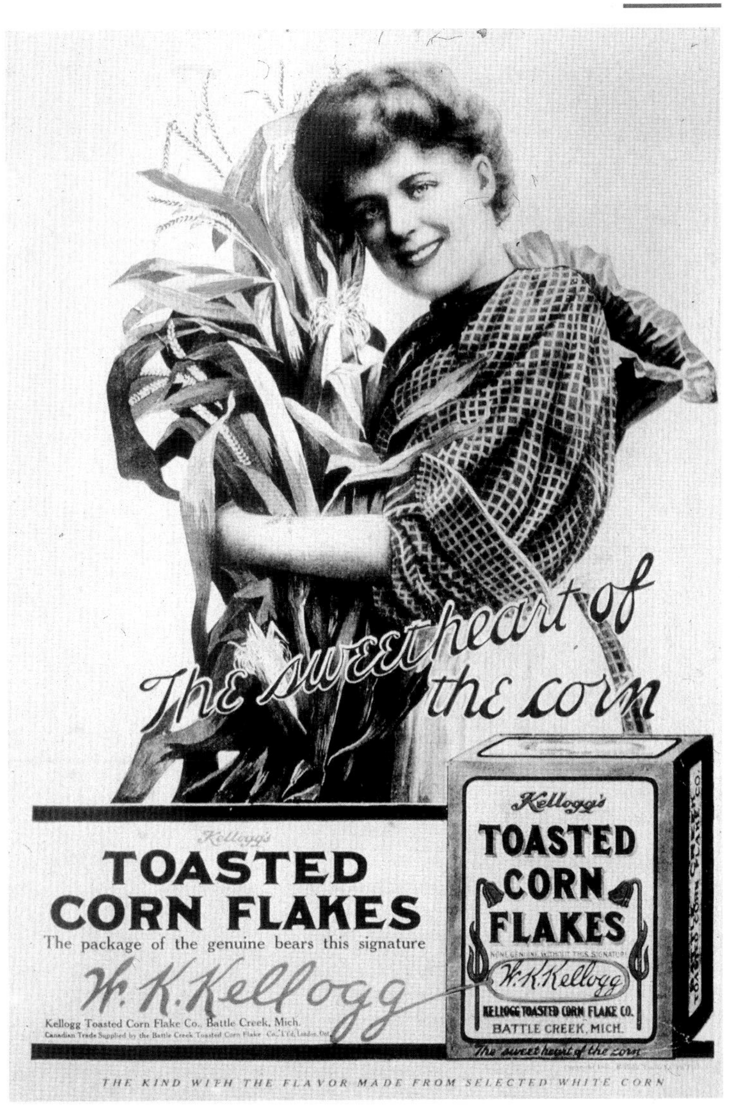

14
REACHING FOR THE SKY 1900–1917

Long before *The Jazz Singer*, Thomas Alva Edison had invented the talking picture. In his workshop and laboratory in West Orange, New Jersey, Edison had already produced the first sound-recording machine back in 1877. In 1891 he was ready to demonstrate his kinetoscope, to project motion picture images. It took him twenty-one years to marry the two processes, but by 1912 he had assembled the first talking picture machine (*right*). In due time it became one of the most powerful tools in the promotion of the American way of life.

Introduction

The United States entered the 20th century with a foreign policy that it tried unsuccessfully to maintain for the next hundred years. The basic idea was to stay out of the troubles that beset the rest of the world. If Europe, Asia or Africa wanted to scrap – well, let them. The US would not get involved.

But the world was still shrinking, and the problems of Mexico and Central America were far too close to home to be ignored. There was Panama to be considered. Here a great canal was to be dug linking the Atlantic and Pacific oceans. Its policing and protection were of vital concern to the US. Hence the Hay–Pauncefoote Treaty of 1901, by which Britain and America agreed that the canal should remain neutral and open to ships of both nations on equal terms. In January 1903 came the Hay–Herran Treaty, by which Colombia ceded the land for the canal in perpetuity.

The same year the Alaskan frontier between Canada and the United States was finally settled. Surely Americans could now get on with their own business? It seemed so, for in November 1912 Woodrow Wilson was elected President on a ticket that promised 'America first'. But in April 1914 a thousand American marines landed at Vera Cruz, to begin a complicated war with Mexico that dragged on until September. By then Europe had plunged into the worst war in history.

Still President Wilson wished to have nothing to do with it. 'There is such a thing,' he proclaimed, 'as a man being too proud to fight; there is such a thing as a nation being so right it does not need to convince others by force that it is right.' Then, in May 1915 the Cunard liner *Lusitania* was sunk by German U-boats off the coast of Ireland. Among those drowned were one hundred and twenty-four Americans. American opinion hardened.

In March 1916, General Pershing led 4,000 American soldiers into Mexico to hunt down the rebel leader Pancho Villa. It was a dress rehearsal for what was to come. A year later Wilson called on Congress to provide the means for an 'armed neutrality' against Germany, for U-boats were now patrolling in packs off the coast of New England. Finally, on 6 April 1917, Congress voted to enter the war, approving Wilson's call that 'the world must be made safe for democracy'.

It was to be a fight that lasted on and off for the rest of the century.

On 18 April 1906 an earthquake struck the city of San Francisco. A thousand people died and damage was estimated at $200 million. When the worst of the shock was over, residents climbed the hills to watch their city burning (*right*). Martial law was declared and looters were shot. Half the population slept in the public parks and open spaces, fearing more shocks and more destruction. Others crowded the railroad station and the ferry ports in a desperate attempt to get out of town.

The massive San Francisco earthquake was followed by fire and it was three days before the authorities could bring it under control. A month later the city was in ruins (*above*), a foretaste of the urban destruction that was to come later in the century. (*Opposite, below*) The ripped and buckled trolley car lines outside the main post office in San Francisco, 19 May 1906.

On 6 September 1901, President William McKinley (*above, left*) was shot by an anarchist named Leon Czolgosz. The President died eight days later. He was succeeded by Theodore Roosevelt (*top, right*) who brought a new energy to the White House.

(*Opposite, below right*) Roosevelt's successor, William Howard Taft, with his wife at a baseball game in New York, May 1910. (*Above*) Woodrow Wilson (left), with Taft, shortly after Wilson's victory over Taft in the presidential election.

Work had begun on a canal through the Isthmus of Panama back in 1881, when a French company spent $300 million and sacrificed 20,000 lives digging a channel that went only a third of the way. In 1903 the United States took over. For $10 million dollars and an annual rental of $250,000, President Roosevelt bought a Canal Zone ten miles wide 'in perpetuity'.

Most of the work was done by armies of labourers (*opposite, above*), though steam shovels were also used (*opposite, below*). Ten years later the canal was complete, and crowds gathered at the western entrance to watch the tug boat *Gatun* passing through Gatun Lock (*above*). (*Right*) Cargo ships passing through the same lock in 1915.

In the early 20th century a cartoonist and illustrator named Charles Dana Gibson drew a series of sketches for several 'society' magazines. The sketches were of full-bosomed, narrow-waisted, elegant young women. They became the prototype for the Gibson Girl, an idealised creature who combined beauty and breeding. Life copied art, and real Gibson Girls soon appeared (*above*).

One of the most noted was the Danish-born actress and musical comedy star, Camille Clifford (*left*). In many ways the Gibson Girls were seen as an antidote to the modern, sporting and increasingly militant 'independent' woman. No records exist detailing what damage the Gibson pose and corset did to the spine.

Light entertainment on the American stage mirrored the class structure of society. At the bottom were the street performers – dancers, jugglers and solo musicians who busked for a living. One step up were the burlesque artists – comedians, singers, dancers and novelty acts who played several venues a night in some of the poorest halls. The bulk of the players, however, made their living in the vaudeville houses, which could mean anything from a run-down theatre to a Broadway palace.

Yancsi and Rosie Deutsch (*opposite*) were known as the Dolly Sisters (Jenny and Rosie), a famous singing and dancing act. They were twins from Hungary who topped the bill for a number of years. Many of the vaudeville stars were also engaged in Broadway musical comedies. (*Right*) Joseph Stirling Coyne in costume as Prince Danilo for a 1907 production of Franz Lehar's *The Merry Widow.*

Some might argue that the invention of jeans did more for the notion of equality than the later Bolshevik Revolution. The trousers that 'will never wear out' became *de rigueur* for construction workers, film stars, farmers and artists. This early advertisement for jeans (*right*) borrows heavily from the silent movie serials of the age, when every episode ended with a 'cliffhanger' – perhaps a victim tied to a rail track with a train approaching at speed, spreadeagled in the path of a circular saw, or being swept downstream in a swollen river. Whatever the hazard, jeans could survive them all.

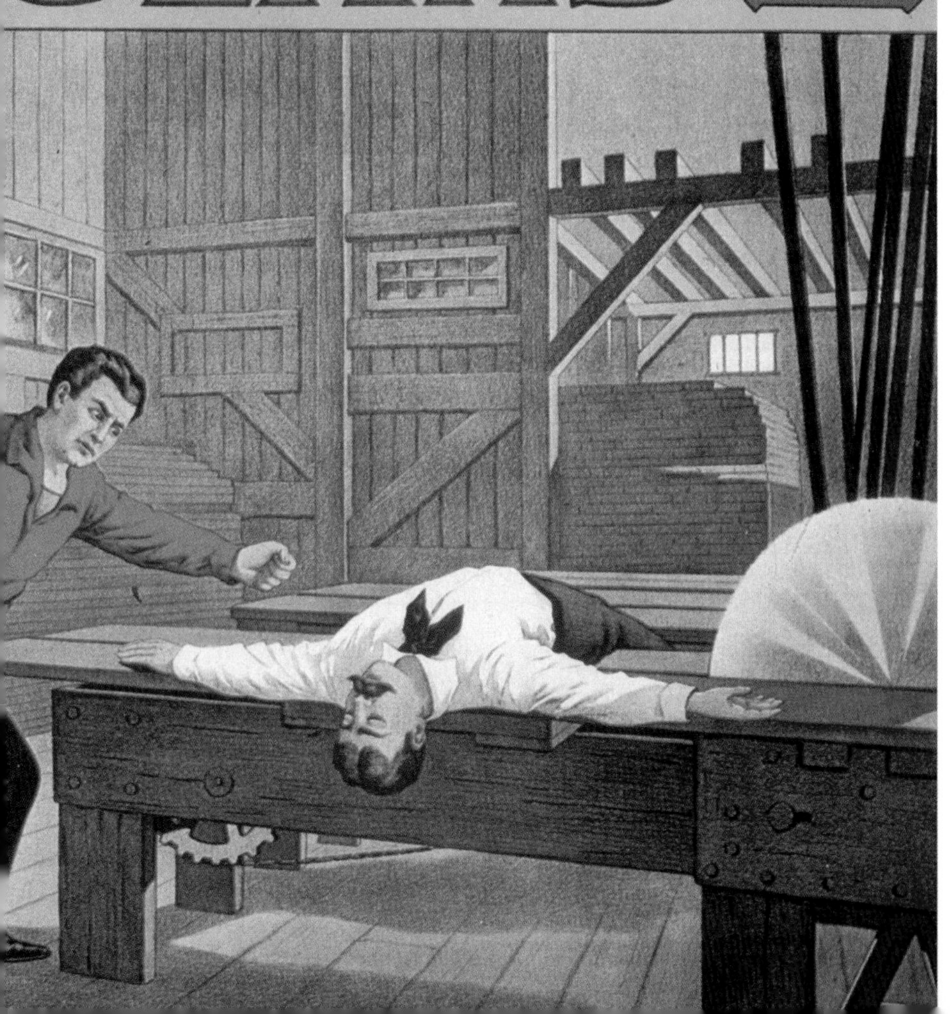
JEANS
BY JOSEPH ARTHUR
— AUTHOR OF —
"THE STILL ALARM"

(*Left*) Thomas Edison in his West Orange laboratory. Inventions poured from his brain – the incandescent electric light bulb, the modern battery, the gramophone and over a thousand others – all of which were patented. According to the poster (*below, left*) his greatest marvel was the Vitascope. 'Wonderful is the Vitascope,' proclaimed the *New York Herald* on 24 April 1896. 'Pictures life size and full of colour. Makes a thrilling show.'

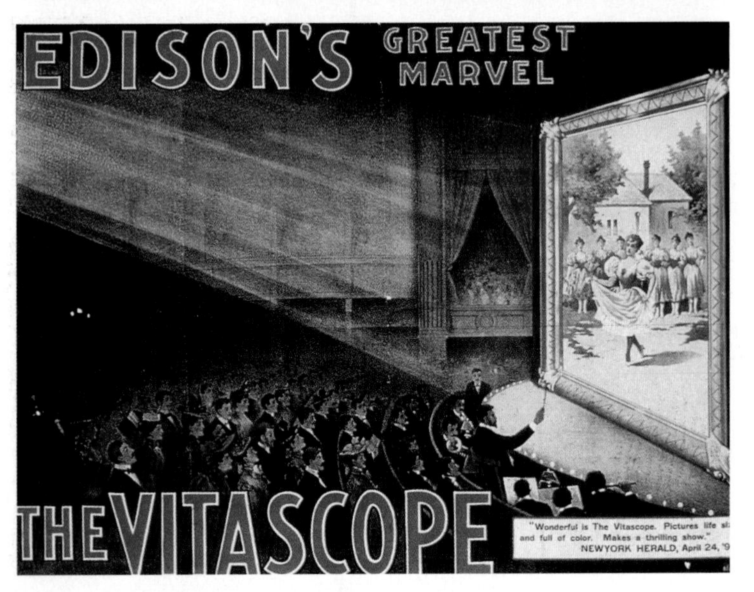

(*Above*) Edison's 'Black Maria' at West Orange, c. 1901. (*Right*) One of the first motion pictures to tell a story – a still from *The Great Train Robbery*, 1903. The film was directed by Edwin Porter and starred George Barnes. Members of early audiences fainted when Barnes pointed his gun straight at the camera and fired.

Charlie Chaplin (*opposite*) left England for Hollywood in 1914. There he created the character of the little tramp, with his moustache, walking cane, bowler hat and turned-out feet. (*Above*) The Keystone Kops, lunatic lawmen in dozens of early silent comedies. Ford Sterling is on the telephone, Roscoe 'Fatty' Arbuckle is on the extreme right. (*Right*) Syd Chaplin, Charlie's lesser known older brother, whose move to Hollywood was less successful

(*Left*) Charlie Chaplin and Pearl White on a studio lot, c. 1915. Pearl White was the star of *The Perils of Pauline* and *The Exploits of Elaine,* both of which made perhaps too much use of high melodrama, though it certainly brought in the fans. She retired from Hollywood in 1924 and spent the rest of her life in France. (*Opposite*) A still from an early screen 'shocker', *The Telegrapher's Daughter.*

Michael Sinnott (*opposite*), better known as Mack Sennett, was a Canadian who founded the Keystone Picture Company in 1912. Among his greatest stars were Charlie Chaplin and Fatty Arbuckle.

Sennett's films featured two groups of players – the Keystone Kops and (*opposite, above*) the Bathing Belles. Whereas the Kops spent most of their time in front of the camera racing, falling, fighting and bumping into each other, the Bathing Belles were required to do little more than pose on the beach (*opposite, below right*). (*Opposite, below left*) Two of Sennett's best Belles – Andrea Sayley and Margaret Oliver. It is said that in this picture they are demonstrating how to save someone from drowning.

By 1918 Chaplin was at the height of his fame and popularity. His silent two-reel comedies were shown all over the world – in cinemas, converted halls, on the walls of buildings in the open air, wherever an audience gathered. In 1916 he transferred from Essanay Pictures to Mutual for a $150,000 bonus and a salary of $10,000 a week. Eighteen months later he moved again, to First National, who paid him $150,000 a film (each film was roughly a month's work).

Chaplin's first three pictures for First National were *Shoulder Arms*, *Sunnyside* and *A Dog's Life*. The first dealt with war, the second with 'paradise', and the third (*opposite and above*) with poverty. The critic Robert Payne described these three films as 'more magical than any he composed before or afterwards...' They were enormously successful financially; Chaplin was on his way to demanding (and getting) $400,000 a film and a share in the profits.

The musical shock of the age was the coming of jazz. Its syncopated rhythms and brash sounds were labelled 'Satan music' by the publisher William Randolph Hearst – though that did not stop millions of Americans from enjoying it. Jazz was the music of black Americans, though early bands still exhibited some of the buffoonery of the old minstrel troupes (*above*). Jazz developed from the already popular ragtime compositions of pianists such as Scott Joplin (*right*), whose big hit *Maple Leaf Rag* brought him fame and relative prosperity.

Bessie Smith (*right*) was less fortunate. She was called the 'Empress of the Blues', and her magnificent voice and the passion with which she sang gained her recognition as one of the outstanding artistes of the early 20th century. No matter how great the talent, she was still black. When she was injured in a car accident in 1937, the white hospital to which she was taken refused to treat her, and she died.

Isadora Duncan (*all pictures*, in sequence) was born in San Francisco in 1878. As a dancer and dance teacher, she had an enormous influence on modern ballet. Her style was highly individual, borrowing heavily from the images of Greek art and sculpture.

At the very beginning of the 20th century, Isadora Duncan was photographed by Eadweard Muybridge, as part of his studies into the way humans and animals moved. Using a series of trip wires, Muybridge lined up a number of cameras enabling him to take a rapid sequence of photographs of Isadora in motion.

As in several other countries at the beginning of the 20th century, society in the United States was rocked by the emergence of the modern woman. Middle-class women were better educated and some were assertively independent. Many men quailed before this phenomenon – the woman who lived alone, expressed her own thoughts, pursued her own career and even smoked openly (*above, right*). Most shocking of all were Margaret Sanger (*above, left*) and other pioneers of birth control. Sanger established the first clinic in the 1910s.

Jeanette Rankin (*opposite, below left*) was one of the most successful. She was a politician who became the first woman member of the US Congress. Harriet Quimby (*right*) reached new heights as the first American woman to gain a pilot's licence. Whatever these women did, and wherever they went, they were sure to find themselves in the full glare of publicity (*above*) – some of it critical, much of it sensational.

One of the issues then haunting America was child labour. Laws had been passed to prohibit the employment of children in factories and mines, but the laws were ignored by many employers, and it was common in some states for children as young as eight to work a full shift at a cotton machine (*left*). Many of the hundred and twenty-five workers who died in the Triangle Shirtwaist Company fire in New York on 25 March 1911 were only thirteen years old.

(*Right*) Members of the 'Valiant 16' leave Newark on the first leg of their march to Washington, DC. As part of the Women's Suffrage Movement, they intended to picket the inauguration of President Woodrow Wilson. (*Below*) Wilson signs a bill outlawing the transportation of child-manufactured goods across state lines, 1916.

In 1904 the city of St Louis, Missouri, hosted a World Fair. The exhibition ground (*right*) was built on swampland and offered an exciting mixture of entertainment and education. (*Opposite*) The skeleton and cast of the biggest known whale in the world. It was caught off Newfoundland and was 75 feet (25 metres) long. (*Above, left*) The 31,500 kilowatt Bullock Generator and the 5,000 hp Allis-Chaleners engine. (*Above, right*) The biggest Ferris wheel on earth – 240 feet (75 metres) in diameter.

The movement to break up tribal reservations peaked between 1900 and 1910, when some 18 million acres of land passed into the control of white Americans. Edward S. Curtis was a photographer working at that time to collect images of fast disappearing native cultures. All the pictures on this spread were taken by Curtis. (*Opposite, clockwise from top left*) Moshe, a young Mojave girl; Show As He Goes; the Navajo wind doctor Nes-Ja-Ja-Hot-Tala; a Hopi mother with a child on her back. (*Right*) Hos-Toe-Biga, another Navajo medicine man.

(*Left*) The Fuller building, popularly known as the Flatiron building because of its unique triangular shape. It was designed by Daniel Burnham and built on a steel frame in 1902. (*Opposite*) Three times as tall as the Flatiron, and with its head peeping through the clouds, the Woolworth building was the tallest in the world when it was built on Broadway in 1913.

Railroad stations were among the glories of American architecture at the beginning of the 20th century. They were the cathedrals of the age, worshipping commerce rather than God. Union Station, Washington, DC, was one of the finest. The Waiting Room (*above*) – with its high vaulted roof, marble floor and heavy wooden benches – was the mammoth lobby through which passed millions of passengers in the last great age of the railroad.

(*Above*) The grand façade of Union Station, Washington, DC. These were the days of the private railroad car, the ultimate status symbol. The very rich had their own palaces on wheels, with gold dinner services, chefs stolen from Paris restaurants, and chilled beer piped under pressure into every compartment. Their owners paid up to $100,000 to own such a luxurious means of transport, and a great deal more to maintain it.

In 1893 Henry Ford (seated at steering tiller) produced his first petrol-driven motor car (*above*). It had been a hard struggle. Banks refused to lend him money for such a mad scheme, but Ford scraped together $28,000 and went on to sell 1,700 of the two-cylinder, eight-horse power car with chain drive. In 1909 Ford came across a piece of imported vanadium steel, the material that he used for the body on his first Model T. The first touring versions cost $850.

Fifteen years later the same car cost only $350 and Ford had produced over 1 million of them. (*Above*) A Ford Model T Couplet convertible of 1914. Elwood G. Haynes was just a few months ahead of Ford in producing the first American automobile (*right*).

In October 1902, Orville (*opposite, below left*) and Wilbur (*opposite, below right*) Wright were experimenting with gliding machines at Kill Devil Hills near Kittyhawk, North Carolina (*left, above and below*). Their ambition, however, was to build a powered flying machine. On 17 December 1903 they made the first flight in a heavier-than-air machine (*opposite, above*). It was powered by a 12hp engine and was made in their cycle repair workshop. It stayed aloft for less than ten seconds, covering some 120 feet (40 metres).

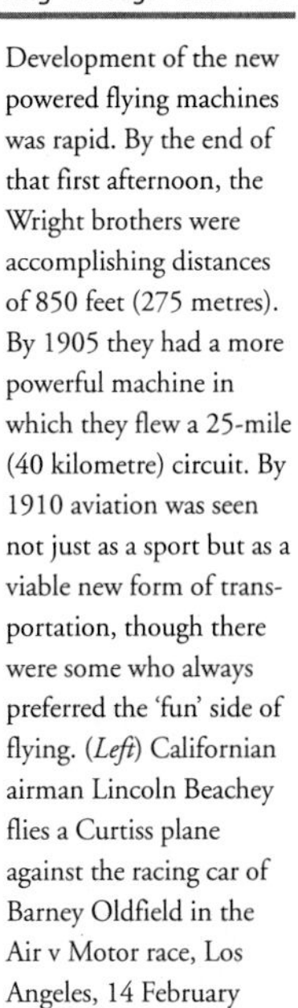

Development of the new powered flying machines was rapid. By the end of that first afternoon, the Wright brothers were accomplishing distances of 850 feet (275 metres). By 1905 they had a more powerful machine in which they flew a 25-mile (40 kilometre) circuit. By 1910 aviation was seen not just as a sport but as a viable new form of transportation, though there were some who always preferred the 'fun' side of flying. (*Left*) Californian airman Lincoln Beachey flies a Curtiss plane against the racing car of Barney Oldfield in the Air v Motor race, Los Angeles, 14 February 1914.

James Francis Thorpe (*opposite*) was an American all-round athlete of Native American extraction; he was born in Prague, Oklahoma, in 1888. In 1912 he competed in the Stockholm Olympics, winning gold medals in the Pentathlon and Decathlon (*above, left and right*). Charged with breaking the code of amateurism through having played semi-professional baseball, he was subsequently disqualified. Only after his death in 1953 were his Olympic titles restored.

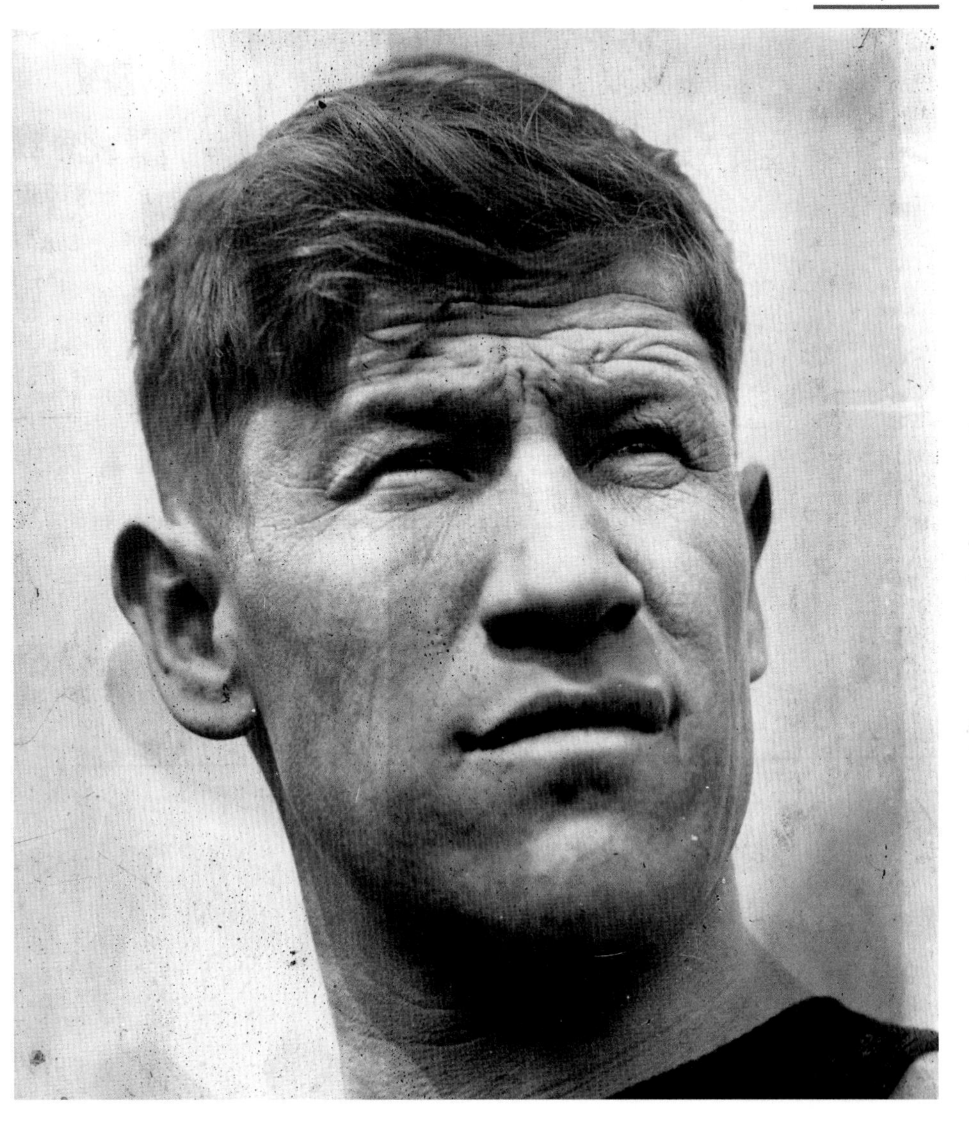

Jack Johnson (*all pictures left, and opposite, below right*) was born in Galveston, Texas, on 31 March 1878. He was 6 foot 1 inch tall, weighed between 188 and 221 lbs during his fighting career, and was the World Heavyweight Champion from 1908 to 1915. He was the first black to win the title, and his triumph was followed by a wave of lynchings and race riots. Johnson's greatest battle was to persuade white boxers to fight him, for John L. Sullivan and his successors operated a colour bar. (*Opposite, above*) French referee Georges Carpentier (himself a champion) separates Johnson and Frank Moran, Paris 1914. (*Opposite, below left*) Johnson v Jess Willard, Havana, Cuba, 5 April 1915. Willard won. Johnson later claimed he took a dive.

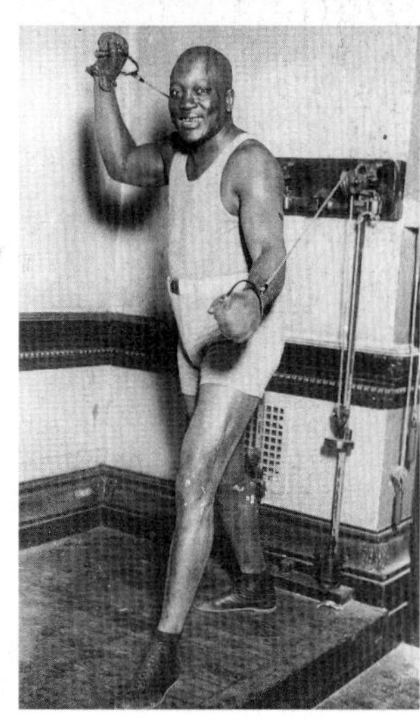

"All the News That's Fit to Print."

The New York Times.

THE WEATHER

VOL. LXIV...NO. 20,923. NEW YORK, SATURDAY, MAY 8, 1915.—TWENTY-FOUR PAGES. ONE CENT

LUSITANIA SUNK BY A SUBMARINE, PROBABLY 1,000 DEAD; TWICE TORPEDOED OFF IRISH COAST; SINKS IN 15 MINUTES; AMERICANS ABOARD INCLUDED VANDERBILT AND FROHMAN; WASHINGTON BELIEVES THAT A GRAVE CRISIS IS AT HAND

SHOCKS THE PRESIDENT

Washington Deeply Stirred by Disaster and Fears a Crisis.

BULLETINS AT WHITE HOUSE

Wilson Reads Them Closely, but Is Silent on the Nation's Course.

HINTS OF CONGRESS CALL

Loss of Lusitania Recalls Firm Tone of Our First Warning to Germany.

CAPITAL FULL OF RUMORS

Reports That Liner Was to be Sunk Were Heard Before Actual News Came.

WASHINGTON, May 7.—

SOME DEAD TAKEN ASHORE

Several Hundred Survivors at Queenstown and Kinsale.

STEWARD TELLS OF DISASTER

One Torpedo Crashes Into the Doomed Liner's Bow, Another Into the Engine Room.

SHIP LISTS OVER TO PORT

Makes It Impossible to Lower Many Boats, So Hundreds Must Have Gone Down.

ATTACKED IN BROAD DAY

Passengers at Luncheon—Warning Had Been Given by Germans Before the Ship Left New York.

LONDON, Saturday, May —The Cunard liner Lusitania which sailed out of New York

On 7 May 1915 the Cunard liner SS *Lusitania* (*above, left*) was sunk by two torpedoes ten miles off the Old Head of Kinsale on the Irish coast. It was known before the liner sailed from New York that German U-boats (*centre, left*) were hunting in packs in the Irish Sea. News of the event, and of the loss of one hundred and twenty-four American lives (*below, left*), shocked public opinion throughout the United States. Theodore Roosevelt denounced it as 'an act of piracy'. Woodrow Wilson demanded, 'in the name of humanity', that such a deed would never be repeated.

(*Above, right*) Two members of the crew who survived the sinking of the *Lusitania* arrive in Ireland. (*Below, right*) Passengers are brought ashore at Cobh, County Cork. (*Below*) A life belt from the *Lusitania* washed ashore at Philadelphia five years after the incident. The sinking of the *Lusitania* played a part in provoking Wilson to take the unthinkable step of entering the First World War.

184
220
221
244
245
273
274
275
303
304
305
306
310
311
312
333
334
335
336
363
364
365
366
367
368
369
370
371
393
394
395

15

BOOTLEG AND BOOM 1917–1929

On 4 April 1917 the United States Congress voted by a majority of three hundred and seventy-three to fifty to enter the First World War. Jeannette Rankin, the only woman member, was one of the few to vote against, declaring: 'I want to stand by my country, but I cannot vote for war.' Six weeks later, the Selective Draft Act became law. All men between the ages of twenty-one and thirty had to register for possible service in the Armed Forces. Once registered, each man was given a number. (*Left*) Secretary of War Newton D. Baker draws the number of the first man to be conscripted. A million more were to follow.

Introduction

The Dough Boys had done their bit. They had been 'Over There' and they had fought in the filth and mud of France. On the morning of the Armistice, Wilson wrote on a piece of White House stationery: 'Everything for which America has fought has been accomplished. It will now be our fortunate duty to assist by example, by sober, friendly counsel, and by material aid, in the establishment of just democracy throughout the world.'

It was a proud hope, and it died. Wilson was opposed by victor and vanquished alike in Europe, and lost popular support at home. There were other problems to engage America's attention. Bolshevism was seen as spreading like a plague from Europe. Battles were fought between organised labour and the police, or between organised labour and hired thugs whose approach was more brutal and hence more satisfactory for some employers. There were race riots in Michigan and lynchings in the Deep South.

And there were other ideals, such as the Noble Experiment of 1919, banning the sale of beer, wine and liquor. It was enforced by the national Prohibition or Volstead Act. In some states certain medicines and hair tonics were also banned. The result was a small increase in the consumption of alcohol and a vast increase in crime. In New York, Fiorello La Guardia rightly predicted that it would take another 250,000 police officers in that city alone to enforce the Act.

Meanwhile, there were other entertainments. Clara Bow, Theda Bara and Gloria Swanson paraded their beauty and their sex appeal on the still silent screen. Buster Keaton created masterpieces of comedy. King Oliver and Jelly Roll Morton stomped their way out of the brothels of New Orleans and brought jazz into the recording studio. Henry Ford sold a million Model Ts, Cadillac sold far fewer swell limousines. Babe Ruth broke all baseball records. Bonnie and Clyde robbed their way to a grisly immortality.

There were non-stop dance competitions, and pole-squatting contests that lasted for weeks. Clarence Birdseye found a way to make food last just as long, giving his name to the frozen food business he invented. Scott Fitzgerald and Dorothy Parker chronicled the tragedies, scandals and delights of the Roaring Twenties.

And the decade came to an end with murder and mayhem. On St Valentine's Day 1929, a garage in Chicago echoed with sub-machine gunfire in the most famous gangland slaughter of all time. Black Thursday hit the New York Stock Market on 24 October the same year. A week later *Variety* reported in a headline: 'WALL STREET LAYS AN EGG.'

Basic training was a hurried process. Only twelve weeks passed between the declaration of war and the arrival of the first US troops in France. There was just time for the new khaki-clad heroes to spend a furlough at home, and then bid farewell to families and loved ones. (*Left*) A bugle boy comforts the girl he leaves behind. Europe seemed very far away.

Eighteen months later, it was all over. The heroes came home, among them many black units (*above*). There were some who were against the idea of providing black Americans with military training, and some ex-soldiers were given a sour welcome when they came home. Many black families moved north during the war, finding work in the factories that were geared to war production. After 1918, they stayed on, often in what had previously been regarded as white neighbourhoods. A new and uncomfortable world was emerging.

Once in France, the Americans threw themselves into the war with an energy and commitment that brought new hope to their exhausted allies. By October 1917 they occupied front line trenches in Lorraine. (*Above, left*) American troops in a captured wireless station on the Western Front, 16 October 1917. (*Below, left*) Soldiers of the American 18th Infantry Division sprint across a road while under shell-fire in north-east France, 7 October 1917.

In the spring of 1918, trench warfare gave way to a war of movement. Ludendorff's offensive drove the French, British and American allies many miles back towards Paris. Horse-drawn artillery units struggled to keep up with the pace of the action, and there was the traditionally hot work in the batteries (*above, right*). (*Below, right*) Soldiers of the 23rd Infantry US Army firing a 37mm gun at a German position in the Argonne.

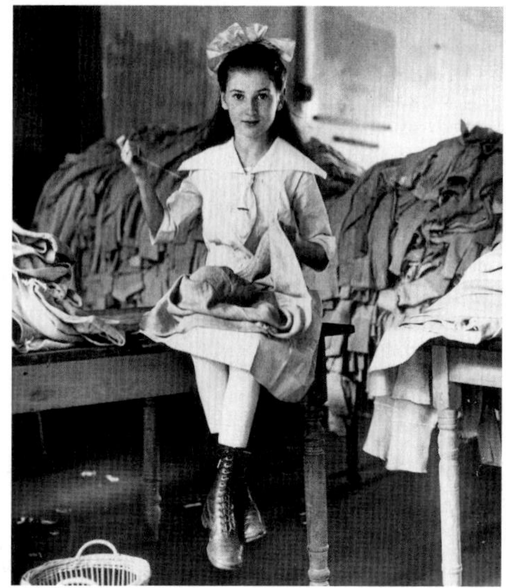

The draft led to an acute shortage of labour. Women were called upon to replace men in many occupations. Girls from Vassar (*opposite, above left*), Newton Square (*below, right*) and other colleges (*above, right*) worked on the land. Others worked on the weapons of war. (*Opposite, below*) Women sew canvas over the frame of a Boeing warplane, Seattle, 1918. (*Opposite, above right*) A young woman repairs army uniforms.

When victory came at last it was greeted by Americans at home (*left*) and on the Western Front (*opposite*) with joyful relief. Crowds gathered in the streets, crying, laughing, shouting, singing – even making love with total strangers. In Congress, President Wilson quietly announced 'The war thus comes to an end...' There was a moment's silence, then a faint clapping of hands, a few cheers and then all hell broke loose.

It took 25,000 soldiers to form this human Liberty Bell (*opposite* – with crack) in 1918. The line of men forming the beam in the background was 368 feet (120 metres) long. The total length, from beam to clapper, was 580 feet (190 metres). When news reached America of the Armistice, bells pealed throughout the country. People danced in the streets (*above, right*). Soldiers in uniform were mobbed by their grateful fellow citizens (*below, left*). (*Below, right*) Crowds cheer President Woodrow Wilson as he drives through the streets of New York on Liberty Day, October 1918. A month later, the cheers were even louder.

The Bolshevik Revolution in Russia gave hope to some, struck fear into others. By 1919 employers were demanding that troops and police rid the United States of subversives. It was a year of great industrial unrest, with a national steel strike, a national rail strike and even a police strike. There were race riots and pitched battles in the streets. The headquarters of a Russian Union was raided and ransacked (*below, left*) on 23 November. (*Above, left*) When not on strike, Boston police confiscate 'dangerous' books.

Big Bill Haywood (*right*) was the leader of the Industrial Workers of the World. He opposed America's entry into the war, and was imprisoned. Later he jumped bail and fled to Moscow where he wrote his memoirs. (*Above*) The anarchists Nicola Sacco (second from left) and Bartolomeo Vanzetti (third from left) arrive at court, July 1921. After an unfair trial, they were convicted of murdering the paymaster and guard of a shoe factory. Although innocent, they were executed seven years later.

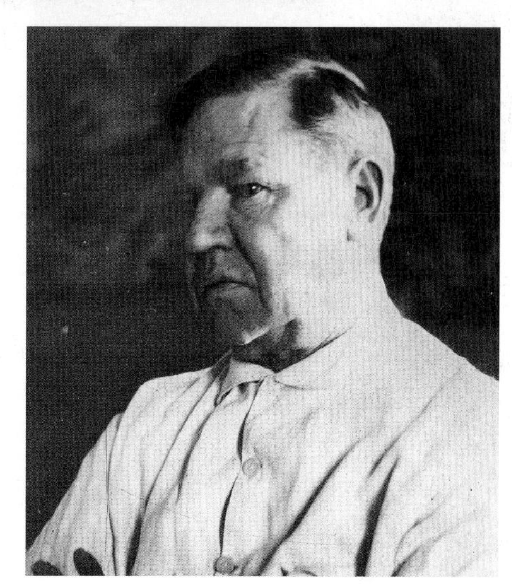

President Wilson believed he had won the fight for democracy at the Versailles Peace Conference in 1919. At home there was another battle to fight – against women's suffrage. (*Left*) Some of the 10,000 men who mobbed women's suffrage pickets at the White House in the summer of 1917. (*Below*) Police arrest members of the National Women's Party after a scuffle.

(*Above*) Society women parade with sandwich boards, advertising a meeting at Cooper Union, 1916. The meeting was to be addressed by the governors of those states that had already granted women the right to vote. (*Right*) A group of actresses campaigning for women's suffrage, 1916 – (from left to right) Fola La Follette, Virginia Kline, Madame Youska and Eleanor Lawson. The message on their banner ('To hold, as 'twere, a mirror up to nature') is a quotation from Shakespeare's *Hamlet*.

It had been coming for a long time. Before the war several states had already prohibited the sale (and consumption) of alcohol. On 16 January the Volstead Act officially banned beer, spirits and wine. America became a 'dry' country. People dodged the Act in any number of ways. There were private brewers, patients went to their doctors seeking alcohol on medical prescriptions, floating bars were moored in the harbours of major cities. The authorities would have none of it. The battle was on to keep the United States free from the demon drink.

(*Opposite*) Federal enforcement officers smash open casks of illegal beer. (*Above, right*) More than 33,000 gallons of wine are flushed into the gutter outside the North Cucamonga Winery in Los Angeles in the early days of Prohibition. (*Below, right*) Police smash beer bottles against the wall of a brewery. Republican Congressman Fiorello La Guardia predicted that it would take 250,000 extra police to enforce Prohibition in the city of New York alone. Others described the law as the Bootleggers' Charter.

Prohibition spawned several new features of American life – among them the speakeasy, the hip flask and the cocktail party. Few people gave up drink. In the north it was still easily obtainable from Canada, across the border. In the south there were plenty of smugglers bringing wine and spirits from Europe, the Caribbean and South America. But distribution was a problem, and this was where the mobsters came in. The most famous among them was 'Scarface' Al Capone (*left*). In 1927 alone, Capone made $60 million from gambling, prostitution and bootlegging.

One of Capone's rival gang leaders was George 'Bugs' Moran. Between them the two men practically ruled Chicago, but neither felt there was room for the other. On 14 February 1929, seven members of Moran's gang were machine-gunned to death in a garage. The slaying became known as the St Valentine's Day Massacre (*right*). Police suspected Capone of ordering the killings, but no evidence could be found to implicate him. Eventually Capone was tried (*below, right*) and convicted – of tax evasion.

After the initial shock of a slump that lasted from 1919 to 1922, the American economy boomed in the 1920s. Stocks and shares soared in value...until the market crashed on Black Thursday, 24 October 1929. Within a couple of weeks, billions of dollars had been wiped off the value of the Market. (*Opposite*) Crowds running through Wall Street, following news of the Crash. (*Above, right*) Investors and stockbrokers meet in panic outside the Sub-Treasury Building, Wall Street. (*Below, right*) The New York Stock Exchange, a week after Black Thursday.

Every New Yorker has his or her favourite Manhattan building. To many the supreme skyscraper is the Chrysler building, on Third Avenue (*left and opposite*). It was the brainchild of Walter Percy Chrysler (*above*). Chrysler began his working life as an apprentice engineer with the Union Pacific Railroad, but switched to automobiles in 1912. By 1925 he was president of his own Chrysler Corporation.

For a short while in the early 1930s, before the completion of the Empire State building, the Chrysler building was the tallest in the world. It was an Art Deco monument, with friezes that celebrated the automobile, gargoyles, and its glorious arched stainless steel pinnacle. When it opened, visitors were left breathless by the glories of the foyer – marble walls, opulent elevators and murals that paid homage to the men who had constructed this wonderful tower.

Henry Ford revolutionised production in American industry. He paid his workers well and worked them hard. He established the assembly line as the most efficient way to produce the goods that he sold. (*Above*) The assembly line at the Ford Motor Company factory at Dearborn, Michigan, March 1928. (*Opposite, below*) 'Customers can have any colour, so long as it's black.' (*Opposite, above*) The 15th million Model T is ready to leave the factory, 26 May 1927. It was one of the last, for sales of the Tin Lizzie were already falling.

The Fifteen Millionth
Ford

In the spring of 1927 a prize of $25,000 was offered to the first aviator to fly non-stop from New York to Paris. One who took up the challenge was Captain Charles Lindbergh of St Louis, Missouri (*above*). On 20 May, Lindbergh's *Spirit of St Louis* took off from Roosevelt Field, Long Island. The plane carried so much fuel it could barely leave the ground. Thirty-one and a half hours later, Lindbergh landed in Paris, and a few days later he was greeted by cheering crowds at Croydon Airport, London (*opposite, above and below*).

SHOES

Despite the rapid advance of aviation, the way to travel across the United States in the 1920s was by train. For the poor and the unemployed, this meant hopping a ride in the boxcar of a freight train, but for the rich it meant comfort that the hobos could barely imagine. One of the most famous, and most elegant of the inter-city expresses was the Twentieth Century Limited (*opposite and right*), that ran daily from Penn Station, New York City, to Union Station, Chicago.

David Wark Griffith (*left*) was the father of the modern cinema. He brought elegance, drama and a host of new techniques to the silent film. His two masterpieces were *Intolerance* (*opposite, above*) and *The Birth of a Nation* (*opposite, below left*). Politically, Griffith was both a bigot and a racist. As an American film director he was without rivals. (*Opposite, below right*) A poster for *The Birth of a Nation,* featuring its star, Lillian Gish.

W. GRIFFITH'S
MORTAL MASTERPIECE
THE
BIRTH
OF A
NATION
WITH SOUND

Hollywood heroines came in two flavours in the days of the silent movie – the sweet and the savoury. Blanche Sweet (*above, left*) was well named, though her roles tended to be strong and determined. Theda Bara (*above, right*) was more savoury, a heavy-eyed 'vamp' who played Cleopatra, Poppaea, Sappho and Cigarette ('mascot' of the French Foreign Legion). In *The Tiger Woman* she was labelled 'The Vampire of the Season'.

Whatever the role, whatever the flavour, they all had mouths like Cupid's bow. Alla Nazimova (*above, left*) was a Russian actress who specialised in distressed and wronged women. Lillian Gish (*above, right*) was the darling of them all, the Bernhardt of the cinema. She made her stage debut at the age of five in a play called *In Convict's Stripes,* and her film debut in an early D.W.Griffith film, *An Unseen Enemy.* Her most famous films were *The Birth of a Nation, Broken Blossoms* and *Orphans of the Storm.* She won an Academy Award in 1971, and was still starring in films in the 1980s.

Male movie stars were muscular, fearless men who occasionally stopped fighting to smoulder with passion. Among the strongest were Francis X. Bushman (*above, left*) and Ramon Novarro (*above, right*). Both starred in the silent version of *Ben Hur,* made by MGM in 1926, with Bushman playing the villainous Messala and Novarro playing the hero. The film was a box office and critical success. *The New York Times* described it as a 'masterpiece of study and patience, a photodrama filled with artistry'.

Other heroes were more limited in their roles. William S. Hart (*above, right*) played cowboys – good cowboys, who rode straight and shot straight and dealt straight. It was the spirit of the thing rather than Hart's acting that made his films successful. Douglas Fairbanks (*below, right*, seated) was the movie hero *par excellence*. When he died in 1939, the film critic C.A. Lejeune wrote of him: 'Behind those acrobatic stunts and that schoolboy exuberance, there was real genius. His leaps, and fights, and swift, violent trajectories were thrilling to watch...but they had about them the quality of beauty and surprise...'

If popularity is the only criterion, Mary Pickford (*above, left*) is without doubt the greatest movie star there has ever been. At the height of her career she was known as first 'America's Sweetheart', and then, as the market developed, 'The World's Sweetheart'. The public adored her, but at a price. They wanted to see her play but one role – the downtrodden waif who found love and riches at the end of Reel Six, or Eight, or Ten. (*Above, right*) Pickford in just such a role – with Howard Ralston in the 1920 film *Pollyanna*.

Clara Bow (*above, left*) was in a different league. She was the 'It' girl, with her bob, her saucer eyes, her bathing suit, her dimples and her jiggle. She represented a mixture of the new emancipated woman and the old flirtatious girl. The public allowed her greater freedom of movement than they gave Mary Pickford. She could be concerned and caring, as in *True to the Navy* (*above, right*), and provocative and pouting, as in *Mantrap* (*right*) with Percy Marmont (left) and Ernest Terrence (right).

There were many Hollywood stars. Some were caught on celluloid for a few hours, but the films they made and the memories of them have gone forever. Few now remember Pauline Frederick (*above, left and right, and left*). The films she made were what *Variety* brushed aside as 'factory-made releases', but the fans held her in their hearts for a brief while.

Louise Brooks (*above and right*), however, became a screen goddess years after she had given up acting. The Hollywood studios did not know what a talent they possessed in her, and it was left to the German director G .W. Pabst to realise her magic. *Die Büchse von Pandora* (*Pandora's Box*) was made in 1929. 'Imagine Pabst choosing Louise Brooks when he could have had me,' said Marlene Dietrich, thrusting modesty aside. The film became a classic. Brooks became immortal.

Cecil Blount DeMille was an unsuccessful playwright and actor before he discovered Hollywood, with his colleague Sam Goldwyn. Together they founded Paramount Studios and made the first American feature film – *The Squaw Man* – in 1914. DeMille's trademark was to mix religion and sex, violence and high moral themes. He was a master of the crowd scene, and a lover of lavish spectacle. In 1923 he made *The Ten Commandments* (*above, left*) with Theodore Roberts as Moses (*below, left*).

DeMille was the mogul's mogul – a man who believed intensely in the power of the cinema to shape people's opinions and to open their eyes to what he regarded as the truth. There is little that is subtle about DeMille or his films, but he left the United States in no doubt as to the power of Hollywood, and the need to respect that power. (*Right*) DeMille on the set of one of his early films *The Call of the North*, with Wallace Reid.

The cinematic world is divided into two halves – those that believe Charlie Chaplin was the greatest silent comedian, and those that know Buster Keaton (*opposite, above left and right*) was infinitely greater. Keaton never laughed at life. He struggled thoughtfully with fate in all his films, seldom avoiding catastrophe, but trying to learn from each and every crisis. (*Opposite, below*) A scene from *The Cameraman,* made in 1928. (*Above, right*) Keaton as an amateur sleuth in *Sherlock Junior* (1924). (*Below, right*) Perhaps Keaton's greatest film – *The General* (1927).

Harold Lloyd was the most successful silent film comedian of the 1920s. Like Chaplin and Keaton, he played one character in all his films – a keen, ambitious, extrovert young man, who held a distorting mirror up to the all-American boy of the time. His film career began as a $3-a-day extra: at the height of his fame he was taking 75 per cent of box office takings. (*Left*) Lloyd in *The Freshman*, a 1925 silent classic in which he played a shy college boy who scores the winning touch-down in an all-important football game.

One of the trademarks of Lloyd's character was his irresistible enthusiasm, his refusal to accept defeat, his belief that he could do anything – even turn his hand to car mechanics (*below, right*). Lloyd's most famous film was *Safety Last* (*above, right*) made in 1923 for his own company. The plot was simple – a small-town boy goes to the big city, hoping to win the girl he loves by entering a contest to climb a skyscraper.

In 1923 a seventeen-year-old dancer named Josephine Baker joined the chorus of a Broadway musical called *Shuffle Along*. The dancer was more successful than the show, and two years later she went to the Théâtre des Champs-Elysées, Paris, to star in *The Negro Review*. Paris was delighted. Few had seen dancing so exotic, so exciting, so powerful. And few had seen stars so scantily clad. Josephine not only danced, she sang in a voice that alternated between the decadent, the lustful and the crazy, but was always mesmerising.

Josephine stayed in Europe. The French adored her. The Germans, or, at least, the German authorities, were more reticent: she was banned from the Munich stage for 'indecent public behaviour'. Berlin responded more enthusiastically. Her banana skirt created a storm of enthusiasm, and, when Harry Kessler saw her at a party wearing only a diaphanous loincloth, he immediately wanted to write a pantomime for her based on the *Song of Solomon*.

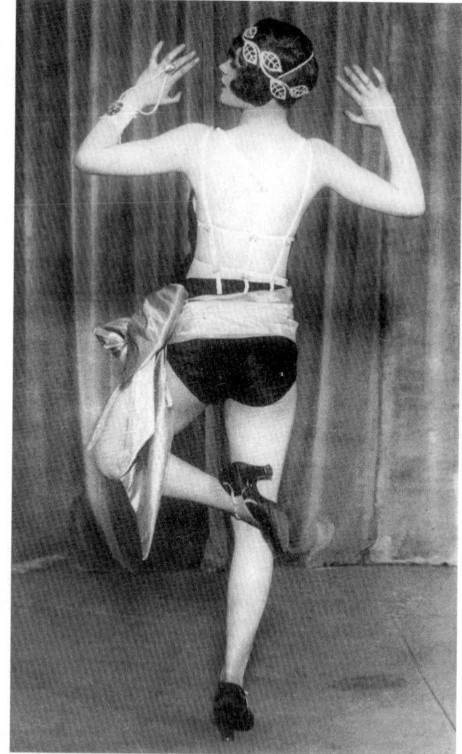

It was the age of the long string of pearls, the low-backed dress, and the fur-lined hem (*above, left*); of cocktails and laughter; of the ukelele and the flivver; of jazz and the movies... It was also the age of the dance – the shimmy, the drag, the yam and, above all, the Charleston. People danced wherever there was space to turn round – in clubs, in dance halls, on top of cars, in their front rooms. The US was dance crazy.

One of the sensations of 1925 was the Black Bottom, a manic variation on the Charleston, though not always as provocatively performed as by Jean Rai (*opposite, right*). The Bunny Hug demanded the flexibility of a contortionist. (*Right*) Miss Bee Thompson wears a two-pronged bumper to ensure that her partner's body keeps its distance, June 1923. Which of the two suffered more if he didn't isn't clear.

Asa Yoelson was reckoned by millions of Americans to be the finest entertainer of the 1920s, an opinion he also shared. For, as Al Jolson, he starred in Broadway shows, on the radio, and in the first talking picture *The Jazz Singer* (*opposite*). Jolson's speciality was to 'black up' (*above*), appearing as he had done in hundreds of minstrel shows before the First World War. He had a powerful voice (and a piercing whistle), but it was the energy with which he delivered a song that made him unforgettable – down on one knee, hands clasped together, belting out *Sonny Boy*. Few could resist Al Jolson.

Paul Robeson was to many the greatest male singer of the age. He had a voice that combined power with subtlety, and a repertoire that included black spirituals, operatic arias and Broadway musicals. He was also a fine actor. In 1925 he appeared in Eugene O'Neill's *Emperor Jones* (*left*). He won international acclaim for his portrayal of Othello, both in London in 1930 and, ten years later, in New York.

Marian Anderson (*right*), who was born in Philadelphia in 1902, came from a poor family. She possessed a magnificent contralto voice before which prejudice and racism crumbled. In 1929 she gave a recital at Carnegie Hall. It took another twenty-five years, however, before she became the first black singer to perform at the Metropolitan Opera House, New York. Later President Eisenhower appointed her as delegate to the United Nations.

In the 1920s and 1930s the Algonquin Hotel, on 59 West 44th Street, became the regular meeting place of New York's literary set. Prominent among them was the columnist and writer Dorothy Parker (*above*). The group called themselves the Algonquin Round Table. Among its members were Ernest Hemingway, William Faulkner, Ring Lardner, Scott Fitzgerald, Walter Crane, Eugene O'Neill, Robert Benchley, Robert E. Sherwood, Alexander Woollcott, George S. Kaufman and Edna Ferber.

Peter Arno (*above*) was an exceptional member of the Round Table for he was a cartoonist rather than a writer. Like Parker and many of the others, Arno was a regular contributor to *The New Yorker* magazine. There was an almost incestuous side to the group's professional relationships, for Parker, Woollcott and Benchley frequently (and favourably) reviewed the work of their fellow members.

The writers who best captured the feelings of a generation of disillusioned middle-class young Americans after the First World War were Scott and Zelda Fitzgerald (*above, right*). Scott (*above, left*) was the more famous of the two. His two masterpieces – *Tender Is The Night* and *The Great Gatsby* – brought critical acclaim and financial success, but Zelda's increasing mental instability and his own drinking plunged him into bouts of deep depression. (*Opposite*) In happier times, Scott, Zelda and their young daughter perform a kick step by the Christmas tree, Paris 1925.

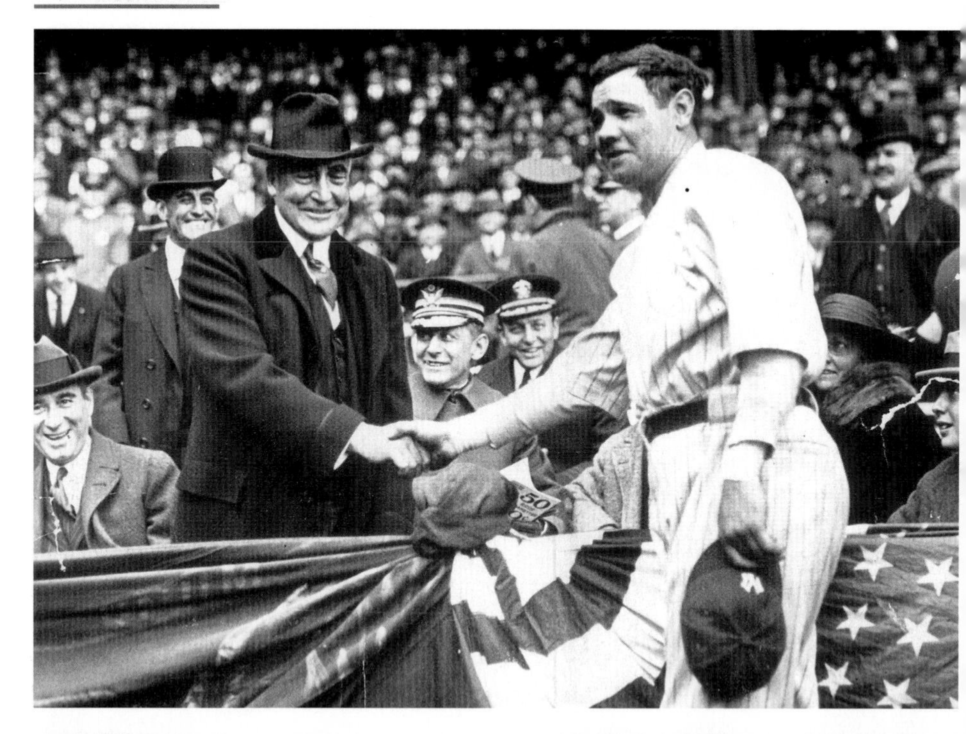

The American baseball star Babe Ruth (*opposite, below left*) was seldom out of the sporting headlines. In January 1921 the Boston Red Sox sold him to the New York Yankees for $125,000, transferring at a salary of $20,000. By 1930 Ruth was earning more than the President. (*Opposite, above*) Ruth shakes hands with President Warren Harding, 24 April 1923. (*Opposite, below right*) The Babe's wife and daughter (Ruth) with Nick Affrock,1925. On the golf course, the all-American hero was Bobby Jones (*right and above* – in white cap). Jones won the US Open in 1923, 1926, 1929 and 1930, and the British Open in 1926, 1927 and 1930.

16

CRASH AND RECOVERY 1929–1941

In the wake of the Wall Street Crash came the worst economic depression in American history. Factories halved their work force, delivery trucks lay idle, gleaming new skyscrapers were empty of tenants. Among the worst hit were the farmers. Land in the South and the Mid West had long been over-ploughed. Now the topsoil was crumbling and disappearing in the winds that whipped across the continent. In the words of Alistair Cooke: 'the western sky billowed with the terrifying "black rollers", and the farmers saw the punishment of the Old Testament God in "the whirlwind by day and the darkness at noon" ' (*right*).

Budweiser
LANDS

Introduction

Reality was dreadful, make-believe had never been so good. In the years after Wall Street shuddered and crashed, farm workers, engineers, shopkeepers, bankers, salesmen and college graduates joined the same bread queues, warmed themselves as best they could round the same wood fires under the same bridges, and rode the same boxcars crisscrossing the States in search of a week's work, a day's work, a couple of hours of labour in exchange for a meal and a cup of coffee.

At times it seemed the whole country was unemployed. Armies of men moved like choking ants across the dustbowl of the Mid West, blindly heading wherever it was rumoured there was work to be found. The Okies and the Arkies piled their scant belongings onto ancient trucks, and nosed their way west to California to pick oranges and peaches for a few cents a barrel. The Bonus Army of unemployed war veterans camped in the heart of Washington, DC, almost shaming the Government into action before they were moved on in their hundreds by the forces of law and order.

President Herbert Clark Hoover was unjustly blamed for the Depression that he had done little to cause, and which he could do nothing to relieve. The nation turned to F.D.R., who told them they had nothing to fear but fear itself. The Roosevelt New Deal created work – building roads, schools, bridges, houses. Banks reopened. Factories took on hands. Land that had been neglected was cultivated once more.

Through bad times and good, the radio and the gramophone and the movies offered escapism of the highest quality. You paid your money and you made your choice – Fred and Ginger, Duke Ellington at the Cotton Club, Mickey and Minnie, Laurel and Hardy, Burns and Allen, Amos 'n' Andy, the Rockettes at Radio City Music Hall. If life was regularly grey, pretence was always Technicolor.

And, all the while, the monuments kept rising – the Empire State building, Mount Rushmore, the Hoover Dam, the Hollywood Bowl, Mount Palomar Observatory, the Rockefeller Center, the Golden Gate Bridge. Few mourned the death of Prohibition in 1933. Even fewer wept for Al Capone when he was finally convicted (of tax evasion). A couple of top crime-busters made their first appearances on the world stage – J. Edgar Hoover and the FBI in the 1920s, Clark Kent and *Superman* on the eve of the Second World War.

And in 1939 a young MGM star made her first Technicolor feature film. The star was Judy Garland, the film *The Wizard of Oz.* For Judy, for Dorothy and for all Americans there was still hope that *Somewhere Over the Rainbow* dreams really could come true.

(*Opposite*) Herbert Hoover makes his inaugural address at the Capitol in Washington, DC, 4 March 1929. Five months later the Stock Exchange crashed. In happier times Hoover had presided over a highly successful scheme to relieve European food shortages (*above*). As US President, however, he faced almost insoluble problems. (*Right*) A cartoon of 1930 satirising Hoover's Farm Relief Programme which is depicted as a scarecrow with a shotgun attempting to scare off hard times. 'It may not be perfect,' says Hoover, 'but I'm sure it'll help quite a bit.'

In the summer of 1932, in the depths of the Depression, veterans of the First World War gathered in Washington, DC, to demand that the US Government keep its promise in paying a war bonus. The Bonus Army camped on the lawn below the Capitol (*left*), while the Senate debated their case. When the Senate ruled that the bonus would not be paid, 2,000 veterans stayed on in protest (*opposite, below*). During the next two weeks, the veterans erected a shanty town in the very centre of the city and along the Anacostia River.

On 28 July, the Government acted. President Hoover authorised Federal troops and police to move in, clear the site and disperse the protesters. Members of the Bonus Army who resisted were arrested, as in the case of John Cage (*above, right*). Hoover declared that the Bonus Army had been infiltrated by Communists and criminals. Fighting broke out and one veteran was killed. The shanty town and the tents were set on fire. Federal troops were commanded by General Douglas MacArthur and Major Dwight Eisenhower.

When life was at its worst for millions of Americans, a team of photographers set out to record the suffering and privation. Among them was Dorothea Lange, who had started her professional career as a society photographer. Her images of rural America told a bitter story.

(*Opposite, above left*) A sharecropper near Chesnee, South Carolina, July 1937. (*Opposite, above right*) Refugees from the droughts of Texas on their way to California, August 1936. (*Opposite, below*) Jobless men queueing for work, San Francisco, January 1938. (*Above, right*) Cutting lettuce in the fields of Salinas, California, June 1935. Farms where work was available were like oases in the desert. (*Below, right*) A farmer and his wife from Missouri look for work in California, February 1936.

Russell Lee was another photographer who travelled across the United States recording the everyday lives of those plunged into poverty. (*Above*) Jim Norris and his wife, October 1940. They were among hundreds of migrants who had moved from Texas and Oklahoma to set up a community at Pie Town, New Mexico. (*Left*) A union official holds the rations of butter and beans that are supposed to feed a family of three for two weeks, March 1939.

(*Above*) The kitchen, dining room and bathroom of an agricultural worker's home in one of the shacks of Oklahoma City, July 1939. (*Right*) The 'band' takes a break during a square dance held in McIntosh County, Oklahoma, June 1939. The suffering created by unemployment and poverty remained until America entered the Second World War.

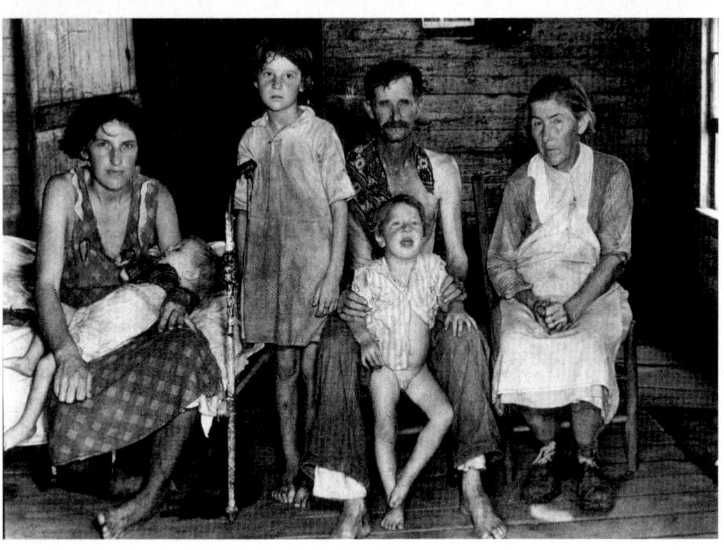

Walker Evans began his career as an architectural photographer, but, like Lange and Lee, turned to recording the struggles of American rural life in the 1930s. He was employed by the US Government Farm Security Administration to work in the South, taking pictures of the sharecroppers. (*Above, left*) Morgantown, in the coal mining region of Scott's Run, West Virginia, June 1935. (*Below, left*) Bud Fields, a cotton sharecropper, and his family, Hale County, Alabama, 1935.

(*Right*) A sharecropper's cabin in Hale County, Alabama, 1936. In 1938 Evans left the FSA and worked with James Agee on *Fortune* magazine. In 1941 he published many of the pictures he had taken in the Deep South during the 1930s in a book called *Let Us Now Praise Famous Men*. After the Second World War Evans returned to architectural photography, though he also compiled a stunning collection of studies of people in the New York subway.

In 1933 Hoover was succeeded by President Franklin D. Roosevelt. Roosevelt promised Americans a New Deal, a return to work, assuring them that 'happy days are here again'. (*Opposite, above*) Roosevelt visits a farm in Mandan, North Dakota, August 1936. (*Opposite, below*) Roosevelt with a member of his New Deal 'brains trust', Rex Tugwell, in Greenbelt, Maryland, February 1937. (*Above, left*) Young men leave for one of the work camps set up by the New Deal, 1933. (*Above, right*) A Rural Electrification Administration (REA) Co-operative in Rush County, Colorado, 1940.

A major part of Roosevelt's New Deal was a programme of large-scale public works, but at least one project began during the Hoover administration. In 1931 the Reclamation Bureau started constructing the Hoover Dam on the Nevada–Arizona line. The aim was to harness the power of the Colorado River (*above*), producing electricity and providing water for much-needed irrigation schemes.

The dam (*above*) was finally completed in 1935, and was renamed the Boulder Dam – it being a time when few Americans wished to celebrate the ill-fated and incompetent name of poor Herbert Hoover. It was a massive achievement. Men drove tunnels through the canyon bedrock, holding the river in them while the spillway above was formed – 700 feet (220 metres) high and made of 4,440,000 cubic feet (165,000 cubic metres) of concrete. History has its own rough justice. In 1947 the dam reverted to its original name, the Hoover Dam.

San Francisco's Golden Gate Bridge was opened in 1937. It had taken just over four years to design and build, and, at 4,200 feet (1,375 metres), was the longest bridge in the world. On 27 May, the day the Golden Gate Bridge was officially opened, 200,000 pedestrians made the half-hour long crossing. Fifty years later 250,000 gathered for a sunrise party to celebrate the anniversary of the Bridge. It buckled under the weight, but fortunately did not break.

The Empire State building (*left*) on Fifth Avenue, New York, was designed by Shreve, Lamb and Harmon back in the heady days of the late 1920s. It took two years to build and was opened on 1 May 1931 by Alfred E. Smith, head of the firm that built the 1,245 feet (410 metre) high skyscraper. It was hoped that the top of the building could be used as a mooring mast for airships, so that international flights could start from the very centre of the city.

Many of the men who built it (*right*) were below average height since it was reckoned that it was an advantage to have a low centre of gravity when working at such a height. (*Above*) The view from the top of the Empire State building, looking downtown towards Wall Street. Though no longer the tallest building in New York, the Empire State still offers the best views of the city, towards all points of the compass.

A generation before the fantasy world of Disneyland and the mad world of Las Vegas, a huge amphitheatre was built in the scrub-covered hills behind Los Angeles. It was the Hollywood Bowl (*above*) and it was a monument to the age of mass entertainment in which it was built, an age when millions swarmed to movie palaces, dance halls, to Coney Island – anywhere that promised a good time.

The Bowl had its own symphony orchestra, troupe of dancers and choir. It had parking space for hundreds of cars, and, usually, good weather. It offered concerts, operas, film shows and a mixed bag of 'spectaculars'. It also offered religious services to suit almost all denominations and faiths. (*Above*) The annual Easter Sunrise service at the Hollywood Bowl, 1938.

Gutzon Borglum was a sculptor who believed 'American art ought to be monumental in keeping with American life'. In 1927 he began work on the Mount Rushmore National Monument (*right*). Half a million tons of rock were removed from the granite face of the Needles, near Rapid City in South Dakota before the softer under-rock was reached. Here Borglum fashioned his staggering 60 foot (20 metre) high heads of four American presidents – (from left to right) George Washington, Thomas Jefferson, Theodore Roosevelt (who happened to be a friend of Borglum) and Abraham Lincoln.

Amelia Earhart (*right and opposite, above*) was born in Atchison, Kansas, in 1898. Thirty years later she became the first woman to make a solo flight across the Atlantic, from Newfoundland to Burry Point, Wales. She was the most famous woman aviator of the age, following her Atlantic crossing with a flight over the Pacific. (*Opposite, below left and right*) Earhart in the cockpit of her plane at Culmore, near Derry, Ireland, May 1932. Five years later Earhart's plane was lost over the Pacific during her attempt to fly round the world.

In 1925 the Tennessee Legislature passed a law prohibiting the teaching of the Theory of Evolution in schools. A few months later John Scopes, a high school teacher, was charged with breaking the law. His trial (*below, left*) in Dayton, Tennessee, received widespread publicity. Anti-Evolutionists massed inside and outside the courtroom, and set up their own bookstall in the main street (*opposite*). Clarence Darrow (*above, left*, seated on the right) was appointed attorney for the defence. The year before he had saved Leopold and Loeb from the electric chair in a sensational trial for kidnap and murder.

Darrow described the Scopes case as 'the first of its kind since we stopped trying people for witchcraft'. His opponent was William Jennings Bryan, a man who believed in the literal truth of the Bible. Darrow and Bryan almost came to blows, lunging at one another and shaking their fists. Scopes was found guilty and was fined $100. Bryan died of a cerebral haemorrhage a few days later.

The Depression dragged in its wake appalling industrial confrontation between labour and management. Wages were cut, the working week was lengthened. Workers expressed their anger in strikes, sit-ins and occasional running battles with their employers. (*Above, left*) A striker fights Ford Company security men at Dearborn, Michigan, 1932. (*Above, right*) Chicago police fire at strikers in the Chicago Hardware Company premises, 20 July 1938. (*Centre, left*) A sit-in at the General Motors Fisher Body Plant, Flint, Michigan, 1937. (*Below, left*) Troops protect workers during a strike at the American Republic Steel Works, 1937.

(*Above, right*) Police use tear gas against women who have joined picket lines at the Newton Steel Company, Monroe, Michigan, 10 June 1937. (*Below, right*) Police attempt to break up a gathering along the San Francisco waterfront on the eve of a General Strike which involved 200,000 workers, 1934. But the masses had little industrial muscle. There were 15 million unemployed in the United States.

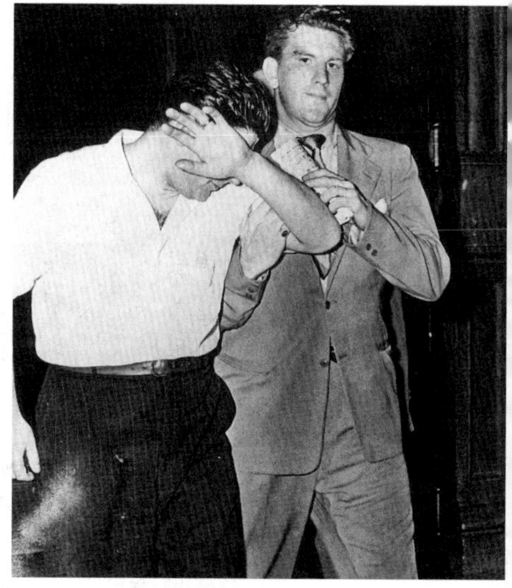

John Edgar Hoover (*above, left*) was appointed Director of the Federal Bureau of Investigation in 1924. He was a man who loathed all those who imperilled the American way of life, which he believed included a great many people. (*Above, right*) Richard Eichenlaub, a suspected Nazi, is led away by a member of the FBI, July 1941. (*Left*) The identification division of the FBI, 1935.

(*Above*) A narcotics detective makes his report on a collection of drugs and drug-taking equipment at the New York Police Department's Bureau of Narcotics, March 1939. (*Right*) Members of a suspected Nazi spying ring sit behind FBI officials in Brooklyn Federal Court, July 1941.

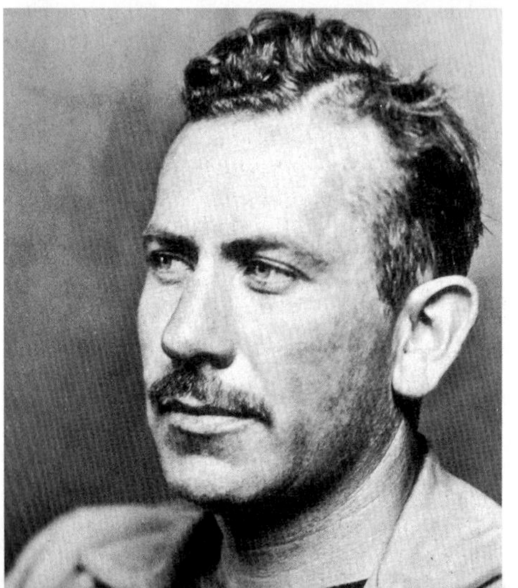

In 1939 John Steinbeck (*left*) wrote *The Grapes of Wrath*, a novel that movingly portrayed the sufferings of a family of farmers from the Dust Bowl of Oklahoma who set out to make a new life in California. The following year it was made into a film, described by the New York critic Howard Barnes as 'a genuinely great motion picture which makes one proud to have even a small share in the affairs of the cinema'.

The film was directed by John Ford. Its star was Henry Fonda (*opposite, above* – in centre with John Carradine and John Qualen). (*Above*) The Joad family prepare to set out on another leg of their long journey. (*Right*) Jane Darwell and Russell Simpson as Ma and Pa Joad: 'We're the people that live. Can't lick us. We'll go on forever, Pa, because we're the people.'

It was a rich time for American literature with a wide range of great works. (*Opposite, clockwise from left*) Sinclair Lewis, author of *Dodsworth* and *Elmer Gantry*; William Faulkner, author of *As I Lay Dying, The Sound and the Fury* and *Absalom, Absalom!*; Damon Runyon, who created a world of lovable gamblers and small-time hoods; and Pearl Grey, better known as Zane Grey, whose *Riders of the Purple Sage* sold over 2 million copies. (*Above*) Upton Sinclair, whose novels such as *The Jungle* exposed the desperate conditions of America's working classes.

It was a golden time for the Hollywood studios. Costs were cheap, technology was rapidly improving, and the studio bosses had the power to keep most of their stars in order. One of the most successful studios was Warner Brothers, run by Harry M. Warner (*left*) and Jack L. Warner. They produced a range of costume dramas and films that dealt with social issues. (*Above*) Yet another premiere night at the Warner Brothers Theatre on Wilshire Boulevard, Los Angeles, in the 1930s.

(*Above*) Jack L. Warner with Ann Sheridan (*right*) and Bette Davis. Davis was one of the few stars with an independent voice, successfully battling with the studio chiefs to escape the artistic straitjacket that came with most Hollywood contracts. (*Left*) Louis B. Mayer, co-founder, with Sam Goldwyn, of Metro-Goldwyn-Mayer Pictures. Mayer was a cinematic and commercial genius, but he ruled MGM with an iron hand.

In 1933 RKO Studio fortunes were considerably improved when Merian C. Cooper and Ernest Shoedsack made *King Kong*. The story was a simple update of the old fairy tale *Beauty and the Beast*. The acting bordered on the melodramatic. The special effects were primitive by modern standards, but the film became a classic. (*Right*) Kong battles with the US air force. (*Far right, above*) A happy ending for Bruce Cabot and Fay Wray. (*Far right, centre and below*) Desperate moments for Fay Wray.

Busby Berkeley was a choreographer and film director who specialised in kaleidoscopic routines involving dozens of chorus girls (*left, below and opposite*). They varied from the kitsch to the dazzling, from the delightful to the sinister.

'What do you go for, to see a show for, take a bet – you go to see those beautiful dames...' – lyrics from *Dames*, one of the songs in the film *42nd Street*. And there were plenty of them in the films of the 1930s. Dorothy Lamour (*left*) was dark and exotic; Veronica Lake (*below, left*) was blonde and sultry; Joan Crawford (*below, right*) was simply dramatic.

Bette Davis (*right*) gave the studio bosses plenty of trouble, the movie fans hours of joy. Jean Harlow (*below*) was the 'blonde bombshell' who gave the men in her films plenty of trouble. And there were many, many more...

For the female moviegoer there was much to fantasise over, though they might have been surprised to discover how many of the objects of their dreams were gay. (*Above, left*) Cary Grant and Randolph Scott in sportive mood by the pool of the Santa Monica home they shared, 1935. (*Below, left*) Tyrone Power pauses for breath on a publicity shoot. The studios like to parade their stars as happy, healthy people.

James Cagney (*right*) was one of the most successful Hollywood actors of the 1930s, both artistically and financially (he demanded $4,000 a week). Between 1929 and 1941 Cagney made many major films, including *Public Enemy, Blonde Crazy, A Midsummer Night's Dream* and *Angels With Dirty Faces.* Of his performance in *The Roaring Twenties,* which Cagney made in 1939, Graham Greene wrote: 'Mr Cagney of the bull-calf brow, is as always a superb and witty actor.'

Stan Laurel's partnership with Oliver Hardy began in 1927 when they appeared together in a Hal Roach short called *Slipping Wives*. For the next three years they made a film a month. In 1931 came their first full-length film, *The Rogue Song*. The magazine *Picturegoer* thought that 'three-quarters of an hour of this comedy team is too much'. The movie-going public disagreed. The two characters, with their mutual antagonism (*above*) and alternating friendship, pulled in big audiences throughout the 1930s.

Their screen personae reflected their real-life relationship. There were years when they disliked working together and tried to go their separate ways. (*Above*) A scene from the 1930 comedy short *Brats*, directed by James Parrott, though one of the writers on the film was Hal Roach, later to direct many of their most successful films. In 1951 Roach sold the films he had made with them to TV for $750,000. Stan and Oliver received nothing.

Unlike some of its two-legged stars, Hollywood had little trouble with its four-legged friends. They seldom demanded more money, or flounced off the set, or had immoral private lives. The most famous were Lassie (*opposite*) and Rin-Tin-Tin (*above*). Rin-Tin-Tin was the first of the wonder dogs – rescuing children, catching thieves, tracking down desperadoes. Lassie came later. She (or rather 'they') made seven feature films, and later starred in a TV series.

In 1936, when Louis B. Mayer suggested to Irving Thalberg (Head of Production at MGM) that it might be a good idea to consider filming Margaret Mitchell's novel *Gone With the Wind,* Thalberg replied: 'Forget it, Louis, no Civil War picture ever made a nickel.' Three years later the film was made. When it was released it made a fortune. Vivien Leigh as Scarlett O'Hara, and Hattie McDaniel as her Mama (*above, left*) both won Oscars. Clark Gable (*below, left* – with Vivien Leigh) received an Academy Award nomination for his performance as the gallant Rhett Butler.

The production was impeccable. Costumes, sets, lighting and photography were among the finest Hollywood has ever created. The set pieces – the fund-raising ball at which the newly-widowed Scarlett outrages society (*above, right*), and the Confederate wounded covering the centre of Atlanta (*below, right*) – were magnificent. The film's writer (Sidney Howard), director (Victor Fleming), photographer (Ernest Haller) and production director (Lyle Wheeler) also won Oscars.

In the same year as *Gone With the Wind* MGM produced *The Wizard of Oz.* It failed to make a fortune, and won only a single Oscar (for best song – *Somewhere Over the Rainbow*). Generations have loved it, though the critics were harsh – 'the light touch of fantasy weighs like a pound of fruitcake soaking wet'.

(*Opposite, below*) Mervyn Leroy (in hat), producer of the film, and Victor Fleming (in chair) discuss sketches for set designs of *The Wizard of Oz*. (*Opposite, above*) Judy Garland as Dorothy and Ray Bolger as the Scarecrow come under the evil eye of Margaret Hamilton as the Wicked Witch of the West. (*Right*) Garland and Jack Haley (the Tin Man). Haley's role posed problems. Bolger was originally cast as the Tin Man but swapped roles with Buddy Ebsen (the original Scarecrow). Ebsen was allergic to the metal paint and had to be replaced by Haley.

RADIO CITY
RADIO CITY
"STELLA DALLAS"

Radio City Music Hall, New York (*opposite, above and below right*), was the last word in 1930s luxury. It was a temple to showbiz, luxuriously appointed, glittering like a million diamonds, bright and brash with music and dance. Stars came and went, but the Music Hall's most famous act remained – the Rockettes (*right and opposite, below left*). The Rockettes were reckoned to be the world's greatest precision dancers, kicking their way in perfect unison across the footlights of the gleaming stage.

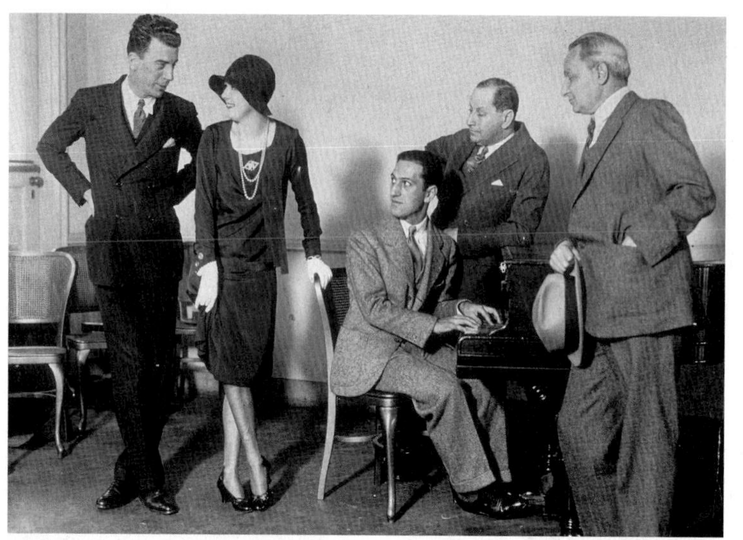

In the face of intense competition (Rodgers and Hart, Jerome Kern, Irving Berlin, Cole Porter and a dozen others), George Gershwin (*below, left*) emerged as the finest songwriter of the 1930s. With his brother Ira he wrote a litany of songs that have never been equalled (*'S Wonderful, Our Love is Here to Stay, Fascinating Rhythm, Someone to Watch Over Me...*). (*Above, left*) Gershwin at the piano with (left to right) Jack Donahue, Marilyn Miller, Sigmund Romberg and Flo Ziegfeld, 1927. (*Opposite*) Gershwin composing *Porgy and Bess* in 1935.

After dark, the place to go in New York City was the Cotton Club (*below*). And the reason for going there was to hear Duke Ellington (*left*) and his Orchestra. Ellington's music in the 1930s and early 1940s was the best that big band jazz has ever offered. The numbers were the finest Ellington wrote, the band was the best he had, the setting was the most exciting.

And if you couldn't get to Harlem, you might be lucky enough to find a club where Louis Armstrong (*above*) was playing. The early New Orleans years were behind him, and he had yet to develop into a top entertainer, but his trumpet had never sounded better. And, wherever you went, you'd find the fans (*right*).

In 1930 Martha Graham (*opposite, left*) founded the Dance Repertory Theatre. This enabled her to establish a company of dancers who would use every aspect of the body and the mind to dramatic purpose. For the next sixty years she remained at the forefront of American modern dance. Like Graham, Fred Astaire had a long dancing life. He began as a vaudeville dancer, partnered by his sister Adele, back in the 1910s. Later in life he became an accomplished film actor. But the best of Astaire lives on in the RKO films he made in the 1930s, with choreography by Hermes Pan (*above* – on left), partnered by the exquisite Ginger Rogers (*opposite, right*).

Orson Welles was the *enfant terrible* of many media in the 1930s. He had yet to revolutionise the motion picture with *Citizen Kane*, but had already shocked America with his radio adaptation of H.G. Wells's *The War of the Worlds*. Welles brought the story up to date, and set it in New Jersey. The play was unannounced, and opened with a news flash that sounded to thousands of listeners as though aliens had indeed landed in New England. Many fled from their homes, and there were later reports of suicides.

(*Opposite*) Welles, with arms raised, rehearses members of the Mercury Theatre of the Air, the radio repertory company that he directed and that was responsible for *The War of the Worlds*. (*Above*) Orson Welles (in shirtsleeves and braces) with Agnes Moorehead (left) and other members of the Mercury Theatre, 1938. Agnes Moorehead was later to play the part of Kane's mother in Welles's masterpiece *Citizen Kane*.

Joseph Paul DiMaggio was born in Martinez, California, in 1914. He was one of the greatest baseball players of all time, known to the fans as 'Joltin' Joe' and 'the Yankee Clipper'. He was a powerful hitter and an elegant centre fielder who played fifteen seasons with the New York Yankees. In the 1941 season he recorded a hit in fifty-six consecutive games (a world record), and was successful in having the most runs batted in in 1939 and 1940. His later claim to fame was becoming the husband of Marilyn Monroe. Of him she wrote: 'he winces easily'.

CYCLONE
COOKS

'We'll go to Coney, and eat polony on a roll...' – lyric from the song *Manhattan* by Lorenz Hart. Coney Island was the place where working-class New Yorkers went in their hundreds of thousands during the summers of the 1930s and early 1940s. The golden sand, the boardwalk, the amusement arcades acted like magnets for all those who wanted sun and fun. (*Left*) Arthur Fellig's (better known as the photographer Weegee) crowded Coney Island scene in the summer of 1940 – 'they came early and stayed late...'

17
ARSENAL OF THE WEST 1941–1960

(*Right*) Paris, August 1944. American infantry march down the Champs Elysées in a victory parade. Diplomacy and the intransigence of General de Gaulle allowed Free French troops a day to liberate the city officially, and then the GIs swept in. It had been an heroic struggle from the beaches of Normandy to the world's most glamorous city. Thousands of American troops had died in the ten weeks since D-Day. Here at last was a rest from fighting and an unforgettable moment of glory.

Introduction

The United States rose to the demands of the Second World War as the uncrowned heavyweight champion of the world. Since the end of the 1914–18 War, American politicians and patriots had sworn never again to allow their country to be dragged into the squabbles of Europe. There was plenty of support for the American Nazis who wished to keep the US neutral even after the War had started. But the Japanese attack on Pearl Harbor in December 1941 forced the heavyweight to put on the gloves.

Three and a half years later came the knockout blows, delivered on Hiroshima and Nagasaki. The Manhattan Project had brought some of the finest minds to the Nevada Desert to develop the weapon that was to terrorise the world for the next sixty years.

The mass production techniques that had been perfected during the Second World War were maintained in the peace that followed. No sooner was an idea conceived than it was commercially available. The juke box, colour TV, the microwave, the long-playing record, even the humble hula-hoop (which began life at $5 and sold so well that the price fell to 50 cents) rolled off the assembly line, and into and then out of the stores.

The same efficiency saved the citizens of West Berlin from what many Americans regarded as a fate worse than death – Communism. When the Soviet Union closed rail and road links to the city in June 1948, the Berlin Air Lift brought 7,000 tons of food and fuel every day to the beleaguered outpost of capitalism. Ironically, Dwight D. Eisenhower – previously popular as the Commander-in-Chief of the Allied Forces against Germany – became the likeable 'Ike'.

America was happy with itself, constantly inventing new ways of displaying its genius. The first McDonalds and the first Kentucky Fried Chicken outlets opened. Detroit built a staggering variety of beautiful, gas-guzzling automobiles. The American standard of living was the envy of the rest of the world. It was the land of good teeth and apple pie, of the world's finest athletes, of the fender guitar and rock 'n' roll, of streamlined life.

But in the South there were stirrings of a movement that was to threaten to blow the nation apart in the years ahead. On 1 December 1955, a seamstress named Rosa Parks got on a bus and sat in the wrong seat. For Rosa was black and the seat was reserved for white folks.

In the words of President Franklin D. Roosevelt, it was 'a moment of infamy' that would live forever in history. On Sunday 7 December 1941 Japanese dive bombers attacked the American naval base of Pearl Harbor on Oahu Island, Hawaii (*left, above and below*). Eight battleships, three destroyers and one hundred and seventy-seven US planes were destroyed. A fortnight later, Roosevelt signed the US declaration of war against Germany and Italy (*opposite*). He had repeatedly promised his people: 'your boys are not going to be sent into any foreign wars'. Events now forced his hand.

The American recovery after the horrors of Pearl Harbor was staggering. The navy fought its way through the Pacific in a series of major battles. (*Opposite, above*) The aircraft carrier USS *Yorktown* receives a direct hit from a Japanese plane during the Battle of Midway Island, June 1942. (*Opposite, below*) The crew of the USS *Lexington* abandon ship while a destroyer waits alongside to pick up survivors, June 1942. (*Above*) The USS *Franklin* begins to sink, 19 March 1945. The ship had been hit by a *kamikaze* dive bomber, setting off the ammunition store. More than seven hundred members of the crew died.

The workhorse of the daylight US bombing raids on Germany was the Boeing B17 'Flying Fortress' (*left, and opposite, above*). The plane was a formidable invader, carrying its load of 500 lb bombs (*below, right*). (*Below, left*) A US mechanic attends to the lower gun turret, 'somewhere in England', 1944.

(*Right*) The nine-man crew of one of the first Flying Fortresses to arrive in England, 4 September 1942. Roosevelt had promised his allies 60,000 planes a year. In 1943 the United States produced 86,000.

It was one of the best kept secrets of the war. German High Command had their suspicions, but never knew where the Allies would begin their invasion of northern Europe. (*Left, above and below*) American assault troops approach the Normandy coast and wade ashore at Omaha Beach. (*Opposite, above*) Members of the Allied Expeditionary Force dig in on a Normandy beach, 14 June 1944. (*Opposite, below left*) General Dwight D. Eisenhower, Supreme Commander of the AEF, on board a warship heading for Normandy. (*Opposite, below right*) At home, New Yorkers anxiously await news of the progress of the invasion.

(*Above*) American tanks enter the Sicilian city of Palermo, July 1943. It was the first breach in the perimeter of Hitler's European fortress. (*Left*) Residents of the Italian village of San Vittore greet the liberating American troops, 23 February 1944. By this time most Italians considered the Nazis more an occupying force than an ally.

(Above) An American convoy rattles through Normandy, 9 September 1944. It was a moment that many French had hoped and prayed for over the previous four years. *(Right)* An impromptu celebration for US troops and the citizens of Cherbourg, June 1944. Much of the city had been destroyed in the previous weeks' fighting, but that detracted little from the joy of liberation.

Glenn Miller (*left*) was a trombonist and bandleader who ran a tight outfit. In the United States his biggest hits were *Moonlight Serenade* and *In the Mood*, exploiting the sweet and swinging sounds of his band. In 1942 Miller formed the Glenn Miller Army Air Force Band and was posted to Europe to entertain American and Allied service personnel.

The band was a huge success, broadcasting regularly and playing many concerts at air bases and army camps. It grew in size, adding a large string section (*above*) to the brass and saxophones (*right*). Miller himself became a casualty of war, when his plane was lost over the English Channel in 1944.

Like the navy, the US army fought its way from island to island in the Pacific. (*Above*) Assault troops establish a beachhead on the island of Okinawa, April 1943. (*Left*) US troops administer medical care to local islanders, 21 April 1945. (*Opposite*) One of the most famous images of the Second World War – Joe Rosenthal's photograph of US marines raising the flag at Iwo Jima, March 1945.

Perhaps the best kept secret of the war was the Manhattan Project – the development of the atomic bomb at Los Alamos, New Mexico (*opposite, below*). The head of the team of scientists was Robert Oppenheimer (*above and left*). (*Opposite, above*) An A bomb test at Bikini Atoll in the Pacific, 25 July 1945 – two weeks before Hiroshima.

After the destruction of the cities of Nagasaki and Hiroshima, the Japanese surrender was swift. The formal process was conducted on board the USS *Missouri* in Tokyo harbour on 2 September 1945. (*Above*) Soldiers and sailors on board the USS *Missouri* watch the arrival of the Japanese delegation. They were received by General Douglas MacArthur, who said: 'It is my earnest hope and indeed the hope of all mankind, that from this solemn occasion a better world shall emerge out of the blood and carnage of the past.'

(*Above, right*) The Japanese delegation – led by the Japanese Foreign Minister Mamoru Shigemitsu (in top hat and carrying walking stick) and General Yoshijiro Umezo. (*Below, right*) General MacArthur signs the Japanese surrender document.

To ease the appalling suffering of the people of Europe after the Second World War, a scheme of aid was proposed by Senator George Calett Marshall (*below, right*). Initially, the scheme centred round the delivery of emergency food supplies (*below, left*). Later, Marshall Aid money was used to help redevelop European agriculture.

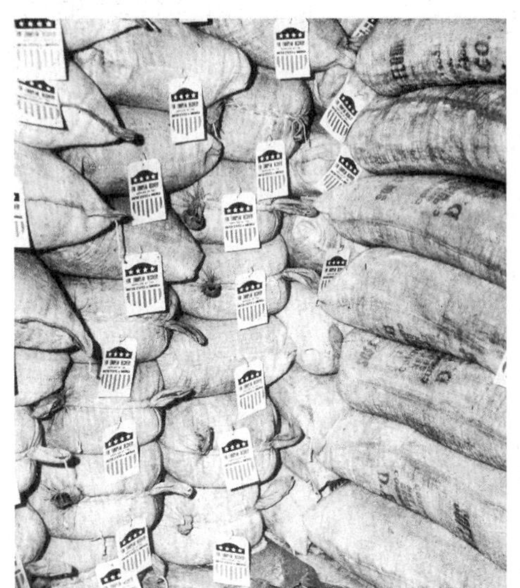

In January 1947 Marshall was appointed US Secretary of State by President Truman. (*Opposite, above*) Watering young trees in a Marshall Aid nursery, Greece, 1947. (*Right*) The first cargo of wheat arrives at Genoa, Italy, 1948. There was a secondary aim to the Marshall Aid programme – to halt the rise of Communism in Mediterranean states. Marshall was awarded the Nobel Peace Prize in 1953, and died in 1959.

On 25 June 1950, North Korean troops crossed the 38th Parallel that divided North and South Korea. It was the beginning of the first major clash between Communist and capitalist forces since the period immediately following the Bolshevik Revolution in Russia thirty years earlier. It was a bitter struggle that began with a series of North Korean victories, but later settled into a war of attrition with both sides digging in where they could (*below, left*).

(*Opposite, above*) An American 155mm howitzer goes into action, 22 October 1952. The Americans (*above*), with the South Koreans, bore the brunt of the war, though other allies from all over the world were sent to fight the North Korean 'Reds'. (*Right*) A weary survivor of the fighting, 5 July 1950. The war dragged on for three more years.

The division of Europe into zones of American and Soviet spheres of influence, and the Korean War, created an atmosphere of fear in much of the world. In 1953, when Julius and Ethel Rosenberg (*opposite, below right*) were found guilty of leaking nuclear secrets to the Soviet Union, they were executed. Among those to take advantage of the fear was Senator Joseph McCarthy (*above* – on right, with his assistant Ray Cohn). McCarthy presided over a witch-hunt of suspected Communists in the United States, trampling on the rights of those he accused. McCarthy enjoyed the fame his persecutions brought him (*opposite, above*). One of the few to oppose – and eventually expose – McCarthy was the broadcaster Ed Morrow (*opposite, below left*).

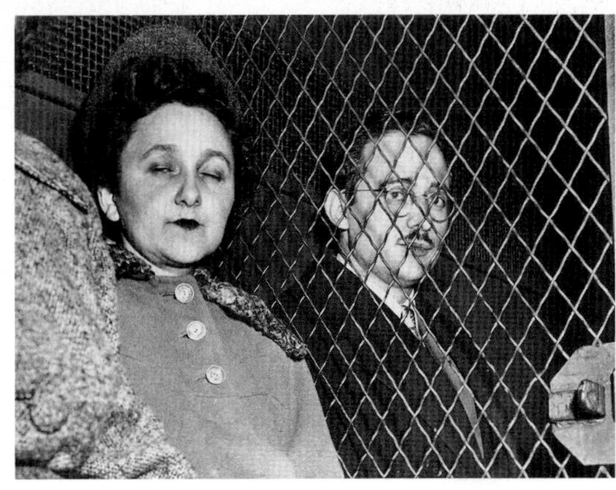

In November 1952, the former US General Dwight Eisenhower won a landslide victory for the Republicans in the presidential election. Four years later he was back (*opposite*), and the crowds still loved him. (*Above and right*) Sections of the crowd at Madison Square Garden for a Republican election rally, 5 November 1956. America still liked 'Ike' and he was re-elected.

They started as a vaudeville act called Six Musical Minstrels, led by their mother Minnie. Later they were known the world over as the Marx Brothers, stars of radio, musical comedy and, above all, film. (*Left*) Adolph 'Harpo' Marx steaming with lust in a scene from their last film *Love Happy*. (*Opposite, above*) Leonard 'Chico' Marx in the same film. (*Opposite, below*) Henry 'Groucho' Marx in the 1951 film *A Girl in Every Port*.

WINDSOR
THEATRE
STAGE ENTRANCE

HORSE
OWNER

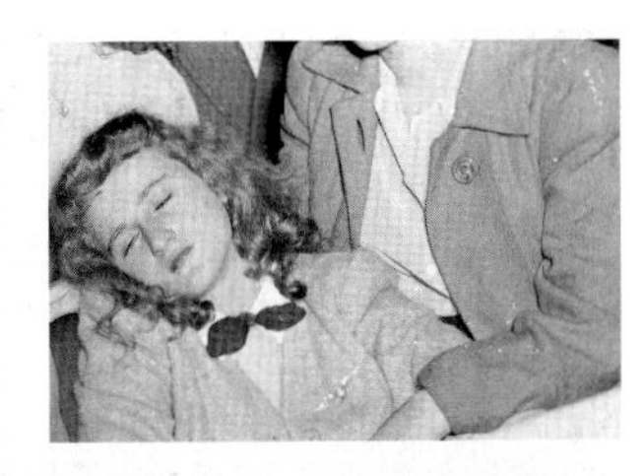

Francis (Frank) Albert Sinatra (*opposite*) served his apprenticeship as vocalist with the great swing bands of Tommy Dorsey and Harry James in the early 1940s. By the mid-Forties he was ready to launch his new career, as a solo crooner. Whatever dreams he had must all have come true at the Paramount Theatre in New York. The fans and bobby-soxers queued round the block to get in, and, once in, found it impossible to contain their adulation for their idol (*above*). For some the occasion was too much. What started as a joy (*top, left*), turned into an overwhelmingly tearful experience (*top, centre*) from which the only escape was unconsciousness (*top, right*).

OPERAT

In the late Thirties a new dance craze hit the United States. It was flamboyantly athletic and overwhelmingly exhausting. It was called the Jitterbug, a mixture of fast jazz dance steps and acrobatics (*opposite and right*). It travelled with American servicemen and women, wherever they went, convincing some Europeans that their liberators from Fascism were little removed from the old barbarian hordes.

The most famous American sporting hero of the 1940s was Joseph Louis Barrow, who fought under the name Joe Louis. Louis (*above*) won the World Heavyweight title in 1937, beating James J. Braddock. He served as a GI in the war (*opposite, below*) but kept punching and held the title for twelve years, defending his title twenty-five times and beating, among others, Jersey Joe Walcott at Madison Square Garden, New York, on 7 December 1947 (*opposite, above*). Louis eventually lost his title to Ezzard Charles.

Radio and film audiences reached their peak during and just after the Second World War. Millions went to the movies or listened in every week to their favourite entertainers. Among the top US artists were the comedian Bob Hope (*above, left*) and the singer Bing Crosby (*above, right*), whose series of 'Road' films were an easily digested mixture of comedy, music and light romance.

The younger generation of performers included a red-haired singer, impressionist and manic comedian named Danny Kaye (*above, left*), master of vocal dexterity and *mittel*-European characterisation. Like Hope and Crosby, Dean Martin and Jerry Lewis (*above, right* – left and right respectively) were a double act who mixed song and comedy, though Lewis was far more of the true clown than wise-cracking Hope. Jerry Lewis and Deano shared an uneasy partnership, however, and went their separate ways in the late Fifties.

NBC

(*Opposite, above*) Fanny Brice (left) and Judy Garland appear on the Maxwell House Radio Show for NBC, 1942, a unique combination of two unique voices. (*Opposite, below left*) Betty Grable was voted the American No. 1 Pin-Up during the Second World War. As a publicity stunt her legs were insured for $1 million. (*Opposite, below right*) The singer Dinah Shore had her own radio (and later television) series that ran for many years. (*Above*) The closest of harmony was provided by the Andrews Sisters (from left Patty, Maxine and Laverne), here conducted by Al Ritz of the Ritz Brothers in 1940. (*Right*) Dorothy Lamour (*left*) and Betty Hutton in costume for the 1943 Paramount film *And the Angels Sing*.

The world of popular music has yet to recover from the explosive arrival of rock 'n' roll in the early 1950s. It had its origins in the country and western music of such singers as Hank Williams and the jazz of Louis Jordan, but it took off as no music had ever done before. The most successful performer was Bill Haley (*above*), a former hillbilly singer who recorded a number called *Rock the Joint* in 1952. Then followed two enormous hits – *Rock Around the Clock* and *Shake, Rattle and Roll.* Authority condemned the music as evil, thereby guaranteeing its success.

Johnnie Ray (*right*) was a balladeer whose emotional style earned him the nicknames 'Cry Guy' and 'The Nabob of Sob'. Modestly he would often admit that he felt his contribution to the world's happiness was perhaps not as great as that of the evangelist Billy Graham. Ray's greatest hits were the aptly named *Cry, Hey, There!* and *Just Walkin' in the Rain.*

But the King of them all was Elvis Aaron Presley (*left*). Presley was discovered by Sam Phillips of Sun Records, who heard a record Presley had made for his mother in 1953. The rest, as they say, is history – history that includes Presley's highly publicised two years in the army (*opposite, above*), and his range of outstanding hits: *Heartbreak Hotel, Hound Dog, Love Me Tender, All Shook Up, It's Now or Never, King Creole* and dozens more.

Elvis was adored for his ability to mix white country and western music with black rhythm and blues, and for his innate sexuality. Fans queued anywhere and everywhere for a chance to see him, touch him, get his autograph (*right*). His films – some of them good, most of them execrable – included *Jailhouse Rock, Loving You, GI Blues* and *Flaming Star* (*far right*).

The era of the big bands was almost over. With the birth of the cool, in came small combos and the whole new musical world of bop, pioneered by the alto saxophonist Charlie Parker. Dizzy Gillespie (*left*) was a hard-blowing trumpeter who worked with Parker in the late Forties but went on to front his own group. Like many other exponents of modern jazz, Gillespie's music was aimed as much at the intellect as the feet. The king of the cool was the trumpeter Miles Davis (*opposite, below right*) whose albums with Gil Evans were classics of the 1950s.

Stan 'the Man' Kenton (*right*) was among those who kept the big band sound alive, playing what Kenton himself called 'progressive jazz'. And for those who wanted to hear what it was really all about, there was the Count Basie Band (*above*), still doing what it had always done best – swinging all night.

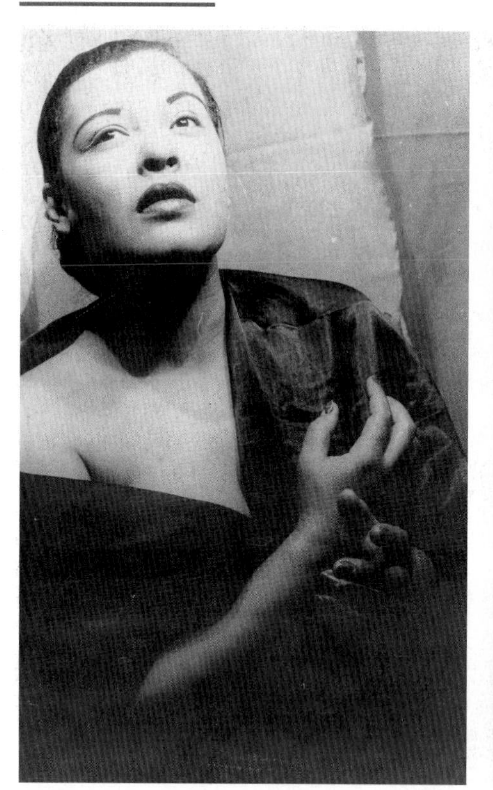

There is no way of measuring who has been the greatest female jazz singer of all time. There are many contenders, few with such passionate supporters as Billie Holiday (*above, left*), c. 1950. Her life was one of pain and suffering, of a desperate search for love that met only bitter betrayal – all of which found its way into her voice. More accomplished as a cabaret singer was Eartha Kitt (*above, right*), who made her film debut in 1954 in *New Faces*. Her abnormal vibrato and sexy delivery fitted the 'vamp-style' numbers that she sang, but she was clearly a performer, which Holiday never was.

For the full range of emotion, from joy to despair, there have been few to match Ella Fitzgerald (*above*). Ella was the musician's singer, her meticulous diction coupled with a fluency of improvisation and feeling for jazz that left listeners breathless. Her career spanned many decades. She sang with all the top bands. But her greatest legacy is perhaps the albums she made with Nelson Riddle in the 1950s – the *Songbooks* of Rodgers and Hart, Gershwin, Cole Porter and Duke Ellington.

(*Opposite, above*) In 1940 MGM pictures celebrated their 25th anniversary – Louis B. Mayer and a nebula of stars face the camera and the cake. (*Opposite, below*) It was a productive time for Paramount Studios on Marathon Street, Hollywood, with Adolph Zukor in charge. (*Above*) Six Goldwyn Girls flash their smiles before leaving for England to publicise Danny Kaye's comedy *The Kid from Brooklyn*. (Front, left to right) Karen X. Gaylord and Martha Montgomery. (Rear, left to right) Diana Mumby, Mary Brewer, Mary Eilen Gleeson and Irene Vernon.

PARAMOUNT · PUBLIX · CORPORATION
· WEST COAST STUDIOS ·
NO PARKING

Though the studio system began to crumble in the face of the TV competition to the cinema, there was still plenty of talent behind the camera in the Forties and Fifties. John Ford directed some of the finest westerns of all time – notably his trilogy starring John Wayne (*Rio Grande, She Wore a Yellow Ribbon* and *Fort Apache*). (*Above, left*) Ford wraps up warm on the deck of the USS *Reluctant* during the filming of *Mister Roberts* in 1955. (*Above, right*) Howard Hawks, with his poodles Trix and Susie, 19 February 1949, the year he made *Red River*.

The American film director John Huston watches technicians at work on the set of *Moulin Rouge* (*above, right*), the film biography of Toulouse-Lautrec, 1952. (*Below, right*) Orson Welles – star, writer, producer and director of *Citizen Kane* and producer and director of *The Magnificent Ambersons*, a powerful portrait of a vanished way of American life.

In the 1940s and 1950s the finest westerns starred John Wayne (*left*). The self-styled King of the Cowboys was Roy Rogers (*right* – with his wife Dale Evans). A singing cowboy from the silver screen with a passion for boots was Gene Autry (*far right*). William Boyd (*above*) played Hopalong Cassidy from 1935 until TV tired of him.

Hollywood could still boast that it had more stars than there are in the heavens. (*Left, clockwise from top left*) Ava Gardner, Lauren Bacall, Marilyn Monroe and Grace Kelly. A tough bunch of hombres – (*right, clockwise from top left*) Marlon Brando, Humphrey Bogart, Gregory Peck and Charlton Heston.

James Dean made his screen debut in the 1955 production *East of Eden*. He was an immediate sensation, the quintessence of disaffected American youth. He made only two more films – *Giant* (*opposite*) and *Rebel Without a Cause* (*right*), both in 1955. He died a few weeks later in a car crash, but lived on as a cult figure and a symbol of youthful rebellion and insecurity.

In the 1950s Walt Disney, the cartoonist, film-maker and creator of Mickey Mouse, decided it was time to bring some of his screen fantasies to life. He chose a plot of land in California and there built Disneyland. It was a mixture of fairyland, the Wild West, King Arthur's court and Never-Never Land. An autopia freeway (*above, left*) took visitors round the site, past fairgrounds (*below, left*), a sixteen-storey model of the Matterhorn and Sleeping Beauty's castle (*opposite*).

The sands of the desert were ever more brilliantly illuminated. Las Vegas (*above and opposite, above*) became the glittering Mecca for all who worshipped showbiz or gambling. The big hotels (The Sands and Caesar's Palace) were the venues for America's top entertainers.

Those who believed in Lady Luck tried their hands at anything from roulette (*right, and opposite, below*) to blackjack to the humble one-armed bandit. It made little difference. The pocket and the wallet emptied in any case.

Revolution followed revolution in the 1950s. Some of the most popular were those involving convenience foods, a boon and a blessing to the all-American housewife and her hungry all-American family. The first McDonald's hamburger store was opened by the firm's founder Ray A. Kroc in Chicago in 1955. It was an immediate success, and Kroc opened many more branches, all selling the 15 cent hamburger (*above*).

When he died in 1956, Clarence Birdseye (*right*) had long played his part in the development of convenience foods. Back in 1924 he had founded the firm which still bears his name. Working as a fur trapper, he noticed that food remained fresh if kept at low temperatures. Four years later he sold out to the General Food Corporation for $22 million.

Howard Hughes (*opposite, above left*) was an aviator and film maker, a multi-millionaire who created two American phenomena in the late 1940s. The first was the *Spruce Goose* (*above*), the world's largest seaplane.

The second was Jane Russell (*above, right*), the film star who starred in Hughes's production of *The Outlaw*. The posters for the film caused a scandal, as did Russell's underwear (designed by Hughes himself). (*Opposite, below*) Hughes at the flight controls of the *Star of California* with Joseph Bartles and Fred Summerwell, 1952. From then on the world saw less and less of Hughes, who ended his days as a recluse.

The days of the luxury liner lived on into the 1950s, largely thanks to the SS *United States*. It had been sixty-eight years since the States had last held the Blue Riband trophy for the fastest transatlantic crossing – back in 1884, when the *Amerika* held it for a few months, after making the crossing at an average speed of 17.82 knots. In July 1952, the *United States* sailed from the US to Le Havre in France at a speed of 35.59 knots.

(*Opposite*) The *United States* arrives at Le Havre. (*Right*) The superliner is towed into port. The ship's designer was William Francis Gibbs who claimed that his vessel was the fastest and safest ever built. The voyage had taken three days, ten hours and forty minutes.

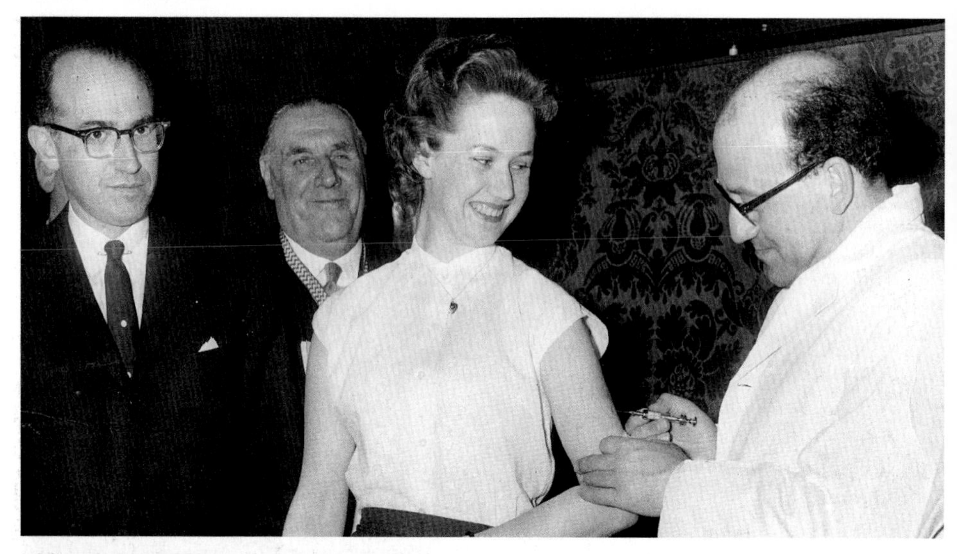

In the mid-1950s the American scientist Dr Jonas Edward Salk (*left*) developed the first vaccine against poliomyelitis, a disease that had crippled thousands of adults and children every year. Prior to this preventative measure, there was little that could be done for sufferers. Some were given ultra-violet treatment (*opposite*). Others spent years in iron lungs. (*Above*) The Salk vaccine is administered to a woman at London's County Hall, 6 May 1959.

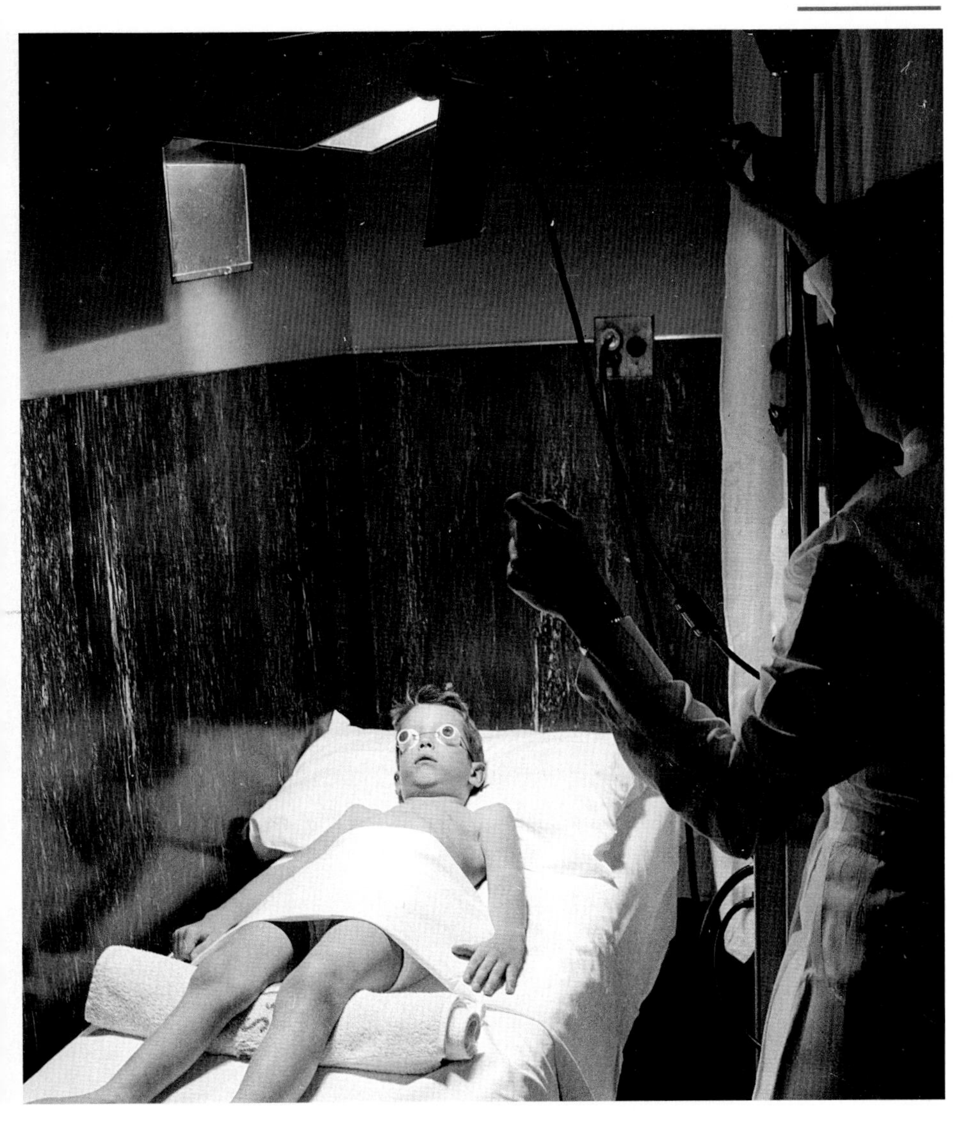

Frank Lloyd Wright (*top*) was the dean of American architecture. He was a daring innovator to the end, whose last work was the Guggenheim Museum of Modern and Contemporary Art in New York (*above and right*), completed just four months before his death in April 1959.

Modern literature was in good American hands. Among the top novelists were Truman Capote (*above*), here relaxing in his cluttered Brooklyn apartment in 1958. James Baldwin published *Go Tell it On the Mountain* in 1954 and *Giovanni's Room* in 1957. He lived for a while in Paris before returning to the US in 1957 and working as a black activist.

A mixed posy of writers – (*right, clockwise from top left*) Erskine Caldwell, still going strong with *A Lamp for Nightfall* and *Love and Money*; Arthur Miller, who wrote two of his finest plays – *The Crucible* and *A View from the Bridge* in the 1950s; the poet Ezra Pound, who escaped a trial for treason, but left the States for Italy; and Norman Mailer, who showed rare modesty by declaring 'some of my pieces are mediocre'.

Ernest Hemingway reaped rich rewards in the 1950s, winning the Pulitzer Prize in 1953 and the Nobel Prize for Literature in 1954. In 1952 he published *The Old Man and the Sea*, reckoned by many to be his finest novel. (*Above*) Hemingway in expansive mood at a bar in Pamplona, Spain, the setting for his book *Fiesta*. (*Opposite*) Hemingway at a bull fight in Madrid, 12 August 1960. The end was almost in sight.

Ever since the 1920s Edna Ferber (*left*) had been one of the major American novelists, with works that included *Showboat, Gigolo, So Big* (for which she won the Pulitzer Prize) and *Cimarron*. In 1943 she published *Saratoga Trunk*. Patricia Highsmith (*above*), who spent most of her adult life in Europe, specialised in beautifully crafted tales of murder, beginning with *Strangers on a Train* and moving on to the first of the Ripley books, *The Talented Mr Ripley*.

Clare Boothe Luce (*above*) was a satirist who was fascinated by politics. She was one of America's wittiest playwrights and a forthright journalist. Her anti-Nazi play *Margin for Error* was filmed during the Second World War. Most of the stories of Eudora Welty (*right*) were set in the American South, in a small Mississippi town that resembled her own birthplace. She wrote several novels, but her most powerful writing was in short stories such as *Petrified Man* and *Why I Live at the PO.*

American composers produced music that spanned the entire musical spectrum – from the tuneful to the bizarre, from the brash and noisy to John Cage's total silence. Roy Harris (*left*) wrote music that was ruggedly American, including fifteen symphonies, concertos, and much chamber music.

John Cage (*above, left*) studied with Schoenberg. He was interested in the sounds of the 'distorted piano', the normal instrument with objects placed inside, and bizarre uses of percussion instruments. Aaron Copland (*above, right*) was one of Nadia Boulanger's pupils. There was nothing minimalist about his work. He wrote ballets, oratorios, film scores, operas and symphonies – all of them in a richly American idiom.

Richard Rodgers and Oscar Hammerstein Jnr (*above*) together wrote a string of Broadway hits, including *The King and I* (1951) and *The Sound of Music* (1959). (*Far left*) Oscar Hammerstein chats with Mitzi Gaynor, star of the film version of *South Pacific*. (*Left*) Rodgers conducts.

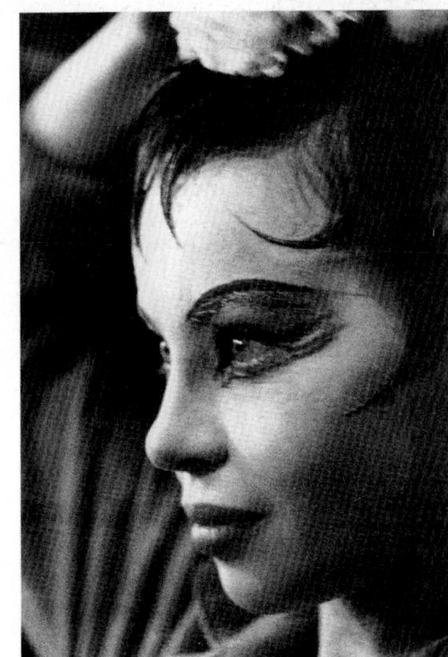

The lyricist Alan Jay Lerner and the composer Frederick Loewe (*above and right*) were another superbly accomplished Broadway team, responsible for a host of hit shows, including *My Fair Lady* and *Brigadoon*. (*Far right*) Leslie Caron, star of the MGM 1958 film version of Lerner and Loewe's *Gigi*.

For all round musical brilliance (as composer, pianist and conductor), few had the panache and excitement of Leonard Bernstein (*left*). As resident conductor with the New York Philharmonic Orchestra (*opposite, above left*) he made a series of recordings of a wide range of the classical repertoire. In 1958 he wrote the score for *West Side Story*. Natalie Wood starred in the film version (*opposite, above right*). The brilliant choreography (*opposite, below*) was the work of Jerome Robbins.

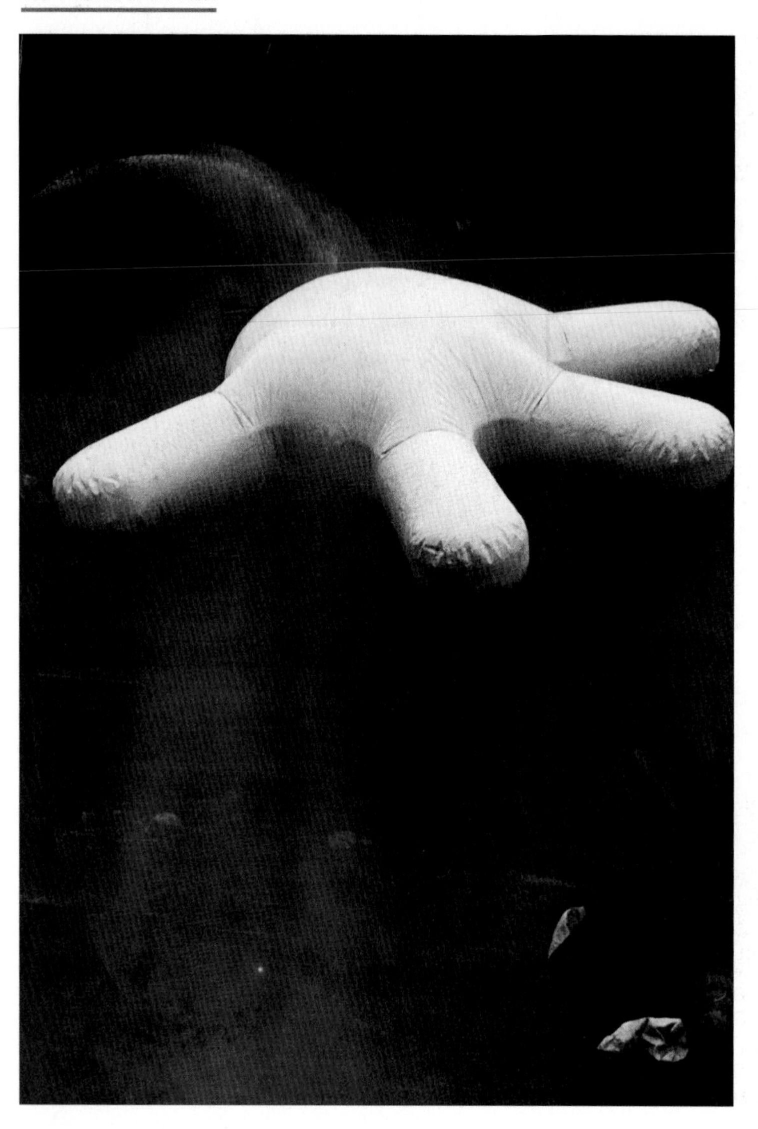

In the 1940s and 1950s Weegee had already catalogued much that was unusual in American city life, particularly in New York City. His images are often distorted, giving people a new perspective on much that they might otherwise take for granted. (*Left and opposite, below left and right*) Weegee's record of Macy's giant clown figure being inflated before decorating the store. (*Opposite, above*) Plaster busts of famous American personalities include one of Weegee himself, bottom row with cigar.

18
FREE AT LAST
1960–1970

On 20 July 1969, the Italian film star Gina Lollobrigida reported: 'Nothing in show business will ever top what I saw today.' What she saw was the Stars and Stripes flying on the surface of the moon (*right*). The *Apollo 11* team had set out from pad 39-a at Cape Kennedy four days earlier. The flight to the moon had taken three days. On their tenth lunar orbit, Neil Armstrong and Edwin 'Buzz' Aldrin entered the lunar module which took them to the moon's surface. They stayed two hours and twenty-one minutes

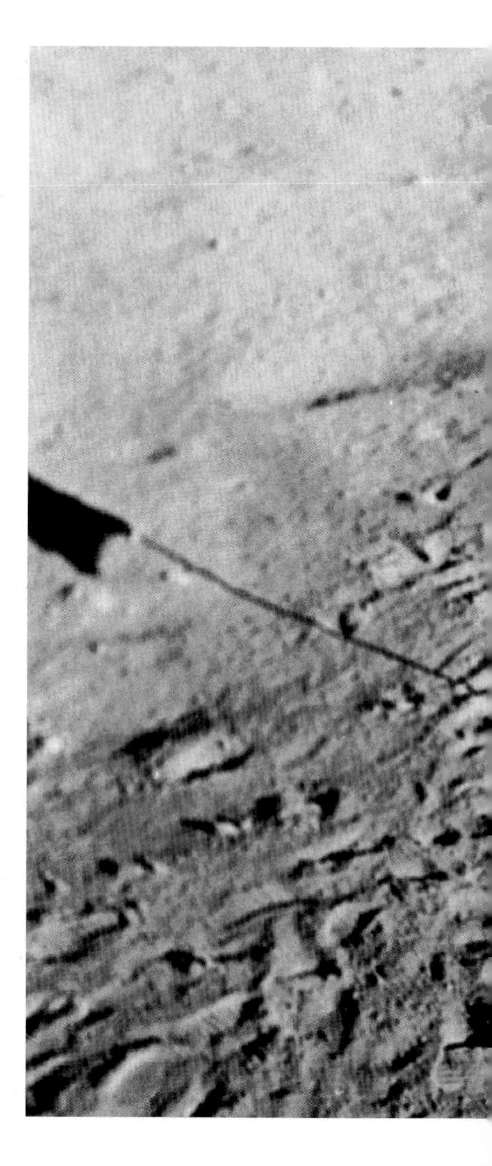

Introduction

The pendulum of history swung to and fro for the United States – from triumph to tragedy, from shame to glory, from elation to despair. The song that typified the decade was Bob Dylan's *The Times They Are a'Changin'*, and the changes were often horrifically dramatic.

Glory came to Neil Armstrong and his fellow astronauts and to the whole NASA team who put a man on the moon late in August 1969. It was one small step for man, one giant leap for mankind, though where that leap landed is still uncertain. There was glory too for Muhammed Ali, the most extraordinary and the most exciting boxing champion the world has ever known. And it seemed, for a couple of years, that there would be glory for John Fitzgerald Kennedy, the thirty-fifth and youngest President of the United States.

He took credit for aborting the Soviet Union's attempt to establish missile basis on Cuba, for championing the cause of the West in Berlin, and for supporting the Civil Rights movement. Almost alone among the Kennedys, he appeared to lead a charmed life until a bullet (magic or otherwise) killed him on that awful November day in Dallas. Where were *you* on the day Kennedy died?

The war in Vietnam bore all the hallmarks of the ancient Crusades – a proud cause tainted with commercial motives, a vast invading army, an infidel enemy and an incomprehensible defeat. What was new was the degree of anarchy and agnosticism at home. There were draft-dodgers and flag-burners, hippies and druggies, massive pop festivals (of which Woodstock was the biggest), sit-ins, love-ins and drop-outs. An older generation shook its head in disbelief, for something had gone very wrong.

In sport, however, things went very right. America conquered the world at tennis, golf, swimming, and almost every game where the outcome depended on an individual performance. And new ideas continued to flow from the brains of its inventive people – the Pill, lasers, the Jumbo Jet – which revolutionised holidays – the pogo stick, the Twist, and a million ways of using plastic.

But for many American citizens, the Sixties were memorable for a man and a movement. The man was Martin Luther King Jnr, and the movement was the powerful and peaceful struggle to obtain equal rights for America's black people. On 25 March 1965, King addressed 25,000 people at the end of their famous Selma to Montgomery march: 'They told us we wouldn't get here,' he said. 'There were those who said that we would get here only over their dead bodies, but all the world today knows that we are here and that we are standing before the forces of power in the state of Alabama saying "We ain't goin' let nobody turn us around."'

It was a moment for history to relish.

By the summer of 1960, the forty-three-year-old senator from Massachusetts was ready to make his move. John F. Kennedy had been groomed for high office since he was a young man. On 12 July he left New York, with his wife Jacqueline (*above, left*) for the Democratic Party Convention in Los Angeles. It had already been a long campaign. On 5 January, Kennedy had addressed delegates and a film crew during nominations for the Democratic presidential candidate (*opposite, above*). (*Below, left*) Kennedy shakes hands with a supporter in Boston.

(*Right*) With the nomination safely in his pocket, Kennedy processes in triumph. Ahead lay the election.

A million West Berliners gathered to hear President Kennedy's speech on 26 June 1963. 'There are some who say in Europe and elsewhere "we can work with the Communists",' he said. 'Let them come to Berlin. And there are even a few who say that it's true that Communism is an evil system but it permits us to make economic progress. Let them come to Berlin.' (*Above*) Kennedy (left) with Willy Brandt and Chancellor Adenauer tours West Berlin, and (*opposite, below*) visits the Brandenburg Gate.

Two years earlier tension had mounted between the two superpowers over the question of Berlin. Kennedy and the Soviet Premier Nikita Khrushchev met in Vienna but failed to resolve the situation. Two months later the Berlin Wall was built. In October 1961 Soviet and American tanks faced each other in what threatened to escalate into a major crisis. (*Above, right*) President Kennedy pays a visit to the newly constructed Berlin Wall. (*Below, right*) Kennedy addresses a press conference during the Berlin crisis.

In October 1962 American reconnaissance planes flying over the Caribbean identified what appeared to be missiles on the decks of the Soviet cargo ship *Fizik Kurchatov* (*opposite*). Since the Revolution of 1959, Cuba had been seen as a hostile neighbour by the United States. Kennedy demanded that the ship and the missiles return to the Soviet Union. On 24 October, Kennedy faced the television cameras (*above, left*) to announce a blockade of Cuba.

For a week the Cuban Missile Crisis shook the world. At times war between the United States and the Soviet Union seemed terrifyingly possible. Eventually, however, Khrushchev ordered the ship to return. The following month, another US plane flew over Cuba and photographed the area which it was believed had been prepared for the missiles (*opposite, below*). The photograph identifies the 'abandoned launch positions' (centre), and the missile storage area (right).

On 22 November 1963 President John F. Kennedy was assassinated in Dallas. A few hours later, the former Vice President Lyndon B. Johnson was sworn in as Kennedy's successor on board *Air Force One* (*above*). Kennedy's funeral took place three days later. (*Opposite, above*) Jacqueline Kennedy, with her children Caroline and John, on the steps of the Capitol, Washington, DC. Robert Kennedy is on the left. (*Opposite, below*) The Kennedy family watch as the President's coffin passes by. (*Opposite, below right*) Chancellor Erhard of West Germany, General de Gaulle and Emperor Haile Selassie salute JFK.

Robert Allen Zimmerman became famous throughout the world in the 1960s as Bob Dylan (*left*). His early songs – *Blowin' in the Wind* and *The Times They Are a-Changin'* – were seized upon by the young as anthems of the age. Dylan (he was never called 'Bob') became tired of his enforced role as spokesman for an entire generation and turned to rock 'n' roll. Success pursued him, and the critics hailed him as a poet rather than a songwriter.

After a motorcycle accident in 1966 Dylan briefly retired from the music business, but returned with two more albums in the late 1960s – *John Wesley Harding* and *Nashville Skyline*. By the Seventies, Dylan was mixing country and western with rock 'n' roll, Judaism with Evangelical Christianity, and one drug with another. (*Above*) Dylan with Joan Baez at a concert in the State Prison in Clinton, New Jersey, December 1975. (*Right*) Dylan at a press conference in London, 28 April 1965.

In the 1960s the Civil Rights movement swept across the southern United States, challenging bigotry and repression with dignity and determination. The guiding hand and inspiration in much of this was Martin Luther King Jnr (*opposite, above* – facing the microphones in Birmingham, Alabama). In August 1963, 200,000 people gathered in Washington, DC (*above*), to hear one of King's most powerful speeches – 'I have a dream...' (*Opposite, below*) Civil Rights activists turn their backs on the jet from a water cannon.

The strength of feeling among black Americans forced President Lyndon Johnson to consult with leaders of the Civil Rights movement. (*Above*) Johnson and King discuss the Voting Rights Act, 1965.

Tension remained, however. On 15 August 1965 violence erupted on the streets of Watts, Los Angeles (*opposite, below*). For five days the district was at the mercy of rioters, looters and arsonists. It took 20,000 National Guardsmen to restore order. Thirty people died, hundreds were injured, more than 2,000 were arrested. President Johnson's response was strong: 'It is not enough simply to decry disorder. We must strike at the unjust conditions from which disorder flows.' (*Right*) A bulldozer clears some of the debris from the streets of Watts, 25 August 1965.

'Last Sunday, more than 8,000 of us started on a mighty walk from Selma, Alabama...They told us we wouldn't get here. And there were those who said that we would get here only over their dead bodies, but all the world knows today that we are here and that we are standing before the forces of power in the state of Alabama saying, "We ain't goin' let nobody turn us around".' From a speech by Martin Luther King on the steps of the Alabama State Capitol, Montgomery, 25 March 1965.

(*Above*) The head of the Civil Rights march from Selma to Montgomery, Alabama, 24 March 1965. (*Right*) Some of the marchers prepare for a night's rest – 'My feets is tired, but my soul is rested...'

There were others who advocated the use of different methods to achieve black freedom and black power. Malcolm X (*left*) was angered by the patience and orderliness of the crowds addressed by Martin Luther King. He called for direct action, for a show of force against white racism, for the overthrow of the established order, and he found support among members of the Black Muslims. Later, Malcolm X founded his own Black Panthers, 'the Children of Malcolm'.

The Black Power movement spread. At the Mexico City Olympics in 1968, Tommie Smith (centre) and John Carlos (right) gave the Black Power salute (*right*) when they were awarded gold and bronze medals respectively in the men's 200 metres. Like Smith and Carlos, the Australian silver medal winner Peter Norman (just in the picture, left) wore a Civil Rights badge. Both Smith and Carlos were suspended from the US team.

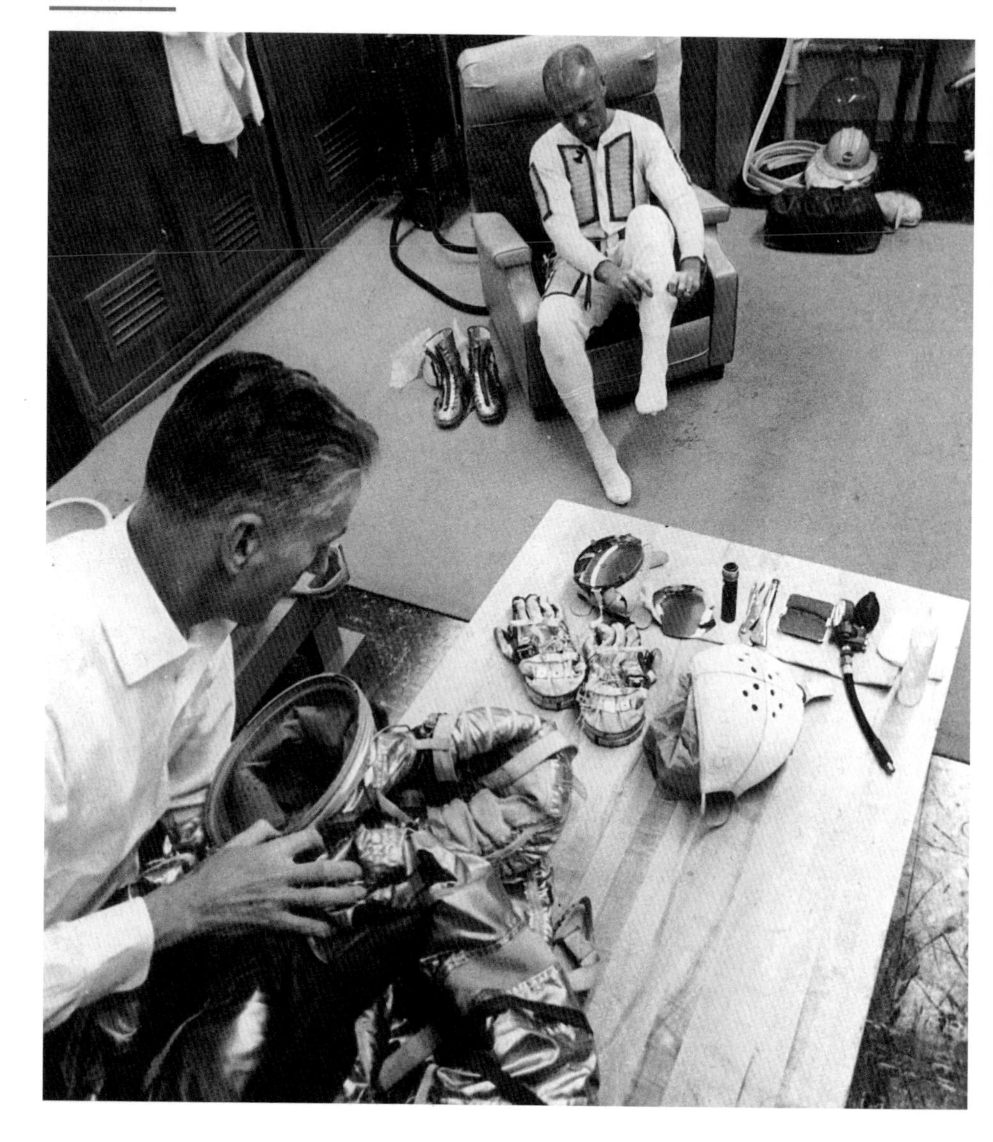

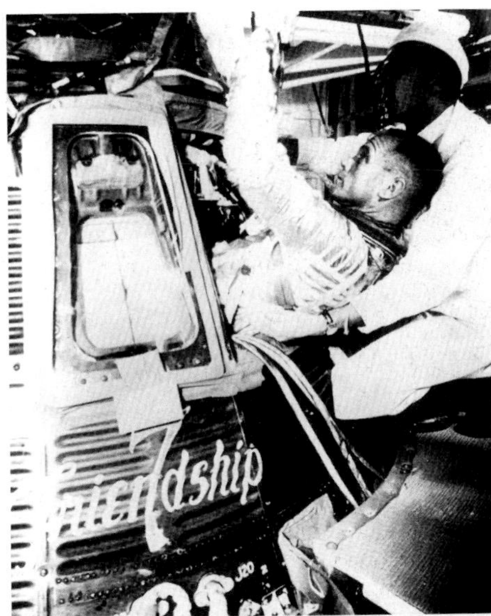

In February 1962 John Glenn became the first American to orbit the earth. (*Opposite*) Glenn prepares for his flight in *Friendship 7*, while Joe Schmitt checks his equipment. (*Above, left*) Glenn leaves Mission Control on his way to the Mercury spaceship, Cape Canaveral. (*Above, right*) Glenn is loaded into the spaceship for his 130,000 kilometre flight. (*Below, right*) The launch site at Cape Canaveral in August 1962. Glenn's flight was said to be 'smooth and easy', and lasted five hours. He orbited the earth just three times.

(*Left*) Neil Armstrong leads 'Buzz' Aldrin and Michael Collins out of the Cape Kennedy Space Centre at the start of their *Apollo 11* mission to the moon, 16 July 1969. (*Below, left*) 'Buzz' Aldrin sets foot on the moon. (*Below, right*) Armstrong reported that the surface of the moon was 'fine and powdery'.

Aldrin and Armstrong landed on the moon at 10.56 p.m. Eastern Daylight Time. Armstrong's comment as he stepped down ('That's one small step for man, one giant leap for mankind') became one of the most quoted remarks of the 20th century. (*Above*) From left to right: Armstrong, Collins and Aldrin smile for the cameras after their return to earth. It was an heroic achievement, for they then had to speak to Richard Nixon, President of the United States.

The US space programme was in full swing and a year later it was the turn of *Apollo 13* (*left*). (*Opposite, below left*) The launch control centre at Kennedy Space Centre during the earlier *Apollo 12* launch, 1969. (*Opposite, above*) The crew of the *Apollo 13* – Fred W. Haise, John Swigart and James Lovell – wait to be hoisted on board the USS *Iwo Jima* after splashdown, 17 April 1970.(*Opposite, below right*) The object of all their endeavours – the moon.

By the mid-1960s, American commitment to the war in Vietnam was total. The fear that Communism might infect the whole of South-East Asia had dragged the United States ever deeper into a conflict that they were doomed not to win. (*Above*) US infantry take cover in a trench on Hill Timothy, 11 April 1968. (*Left*) Taking out the wounded. In an increasingly hostile country, American losses were heavy.

For many young American troops the strain, the terror, the suffering and the isolation from home were unbearable. (*Above*) An American marine silently weeps in a US helicopter. (*Right*) Marine Chaplain Eli Tavesian gives Communion to marine Louis A. Loya at a forward command post in Hue, Vietnam, 1968.

The entire country was torn apart. Neither troops nor civilians could distinguish friend from foe. Civilians were rescued, evacuated, evicted, massacred in the confusion and panic that so often prevailed. The whole of Vietnam became a combat zone. (*Left*) A US marine carries an elderly Vietnamese woman to a waiting helicopter as her village is evacuated, 23 March 1970.

(*Above*) A wounded Vietnamese refugee is lifted aboard an American helicopter, 20 March 1965. (*Right*) Young refugees seeking a new home, somewhere in Vietnam. In parts of Vietnam where a matriarchal society existed, it was considered the duty of daughters to look after their younger brothers. In the south, it seemed that all roads led to Saigon, the one place in Vietnam usually free from the actions of the Vietcong.

END THE DRAFT-
LET YOUNG MEN LIVE
I AM NOT A COMMUNIST AND I STILL OPPOSE THE WAR IN VIETNAM

WAR IS HELL. DON'T GO.

Like Vietnam, the United States was torn apart. (*Opposite*) Three views of protest – John Wilson attends a meeting to organise an anti-war rally; 100,000 demonstrators march against the Vietnam war; and a San Francisco student's placard reads 'WAR IS HELL. DON'T GO'. (*Right*) William Rogers, Secretary of State, appears before the Senate Foreign Relations Committee. (*Below, left and right*) More protest.

Among the top American television shows of the 1960s were *I Love Lucy, The Ed Sullivan Show, The Waltons, The Monkees* and *Happy Days* (featuring 'the Fonz'). To many *Star Trek* was in a class of its own, splitting infinitives and boldly going where no TV series had gone before. Audiences were delighted by the lugubrious view of life in the universe articulated by Mr Spock, played by Leonard Nimoy (*left*).

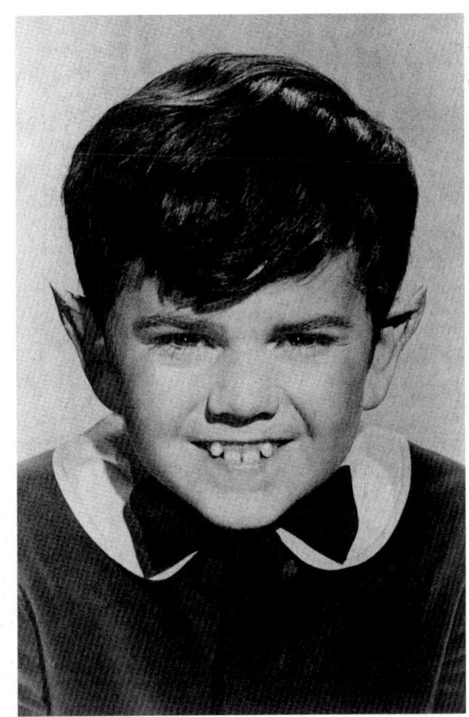

Lovers of fantasy were also offered the tongue-in-cheek antics of Adam West as *Batman* (*above, left*), biffing, bamming and ker-powing his way through the evil plans of The Joker, The Riddler, Penguin and Catwoman. A third star to be fitted with extra large ears was eleven-year-old Butch Patrick (*above, right*), who played the part of Eddy, youngest member of the TV Munster family.

America, as ever, was a land of the haves and the have-nots. For those that succeeded (*above, left*) life was exceedingly good – a fine house, a gleaming car, an attractive partner and somewhere between two and three children. On the streets of Harlem, life was different (*below, left*), with the majority of the population underfed, overcrowded, unemployed or overworked. Wherever children were raised, however, Dr Benjamin Spock (*opposite*) offered help and advice, though there were those who blamed him for the draft-dodging, flag-burning generation.

Dr Benjamin
SPOCK
Decent
&
Indecent
OUR
SPOCK

The first Boeing 747 jumbo jet airliner (*above*) rolled off the production line in 1969, and went into service in 1970. It ushered in a new age for travellers, business executives and holiday makers, and led to huge reductions in air fares. (*Opposite, above*) Flight crew attend to the wishes of first-class passengers on board a 747, 23 January 1970. (*Opposite, below left*) Technicians check one of the engines on the first Pan Am 747 to arrive in London. It took them two hours to get the engine started. (*Opposite, below right*) An engineer prepares a 747 engine for welding, California, 25 March 1969.

For decades there had been talk of a new bridge over the mouth of the East River, to link Brooklyn and Staten Island. Work began in the late 1950s on the Verrazano-Narrows Bridge, named after the Italian explorer Giovanni da Verrazano who sailed along this stretch of the coast in 1524. The bridge (*above*) took five years to build and was the last link in a super-highway designed to take traffic from New England clear of Manhattan to join the expressways heading south.

The first traffic across the bridge was an official motorcade (*above*) on Saturday 23 November 1964. The bridge has the world's longest suspension span – 4,260 feet (1,430 metres), though the whole structure is some three miles in length. It can also carry an enormous volume of traffic on its twelve lanes – six on an upper deck, and six on a lower deck.

And still they came...the endless supply of Hollywood heroes. The sex symbols of the Swinging Sixties included (*opposite, clockwise from top left*) James Coburn, James Earl Jones, Kirk Douglas and Steve McQueen. Sidney Poitier (*right*) was both actor and director, and a star who did a great deal to raise the status of black actors in Hollywood. He was criticised, however, for mostly playing middle-class, professional and inherently 'good' characters.

Warhol's influence was strong in the 1960s American art world. (*Above*) Roy Lichtenstein stands in front of *Whaam!* at the Tate Gallery in London, 5 January 1968. (*Left*) Claes Oldenburg rests beside his outsize tube of toothpaste in the Düsseldorf Kunsthalle, 20 April 1970.

(*Above*) A commissionaire at the Royal College of Art, London, contemplates Tom Wesselmann's *Mouth*, November 1971. (*Right*) Robert Rauschenberg, the avant-garde sculptor, 2 February 1964.

In the face of the Beatles, Motown, Dylan and rock, jazz somehow survived. In New Orleans jazz relied on old-timers like Ernest 'Punch' Miller (*opposite*). In New York and around the world it relied on Thelonius Monk (*above*), and the indefatigable Duke Ellington (*right*).

There were plenty of voices to be heard in the world of pop. The arrival of the LP back in the 1950s had given the record industry a mighty lungful of fresh air. Top of the soul charts for much of the Sixties was Stevie Wonder (*left*). The Supremes (*opposite, above left*) with Diana Ross (centre) made it big with *Baby Love*. The Temptations (*opposite, above right*) had a big hit with *My Girl*. (*Opposite, below left*) Martha and the Vandellas and (*opposite, below right*) Smokey Robinson on the *Sound of Motown* TV show, 13 March 1965.

ROBINSON

He was still the greatest. On 25 February 1964 Cassius Clay (yet to become Muhammed Ali) fought Sonny Liston for the Heavyweight Championship of the World. (*Above*) Clay predicts that he will beat Liston in the eighth round. He didn't – Liston retired in the seventh round. (*Opposite, above*) Clay (left) and Liston slug it out. (*Opposite, below*) At the end of the fight, Clay's joy is unconfined.

Male American tennis stars found the top tournaments hard going in the 1960s and early 1970s. Arthur Ashe (*left*) won the Australian Open in 1970, but the men's competitions were almost all won by Australians.

In women's tennis it was a different story. Between 1966 and 1975, Billie-Jean King (*left and opposite, above*) won the Wimbledon Championship five times, the US Open four times, the French Open and the Australian Open once. Billie-Jean combined speed and stamina, accuracy and immense power. She also did much to raise the status of and remuneration for the women's game.

If pickings were poor for the United States in the world of tennis, they were extremely rich on the golf courses of the world. Jack 'the Golden Bear' Nicklaus (*above*) won eight major titles in the 1960s, including the US Masters three times. Arnold Palmer (*opposite*) won both the US Masters and US Open in 1960, and the UK and US Opens in 1962. In 1966 US golfers swept the board – Nicklaus won the UK Open and US Masters, Billy Casper won the US Open, and Al Geiberger won the PGA.

The challenging mood of the Sixties gave impetus to the crusade for women's rights, though there were still plenty of men (and women) who preferred to see women in their traditional role as mother, housewife and sex object. (*Opposite*) Hugh Hefner, publisher of *Playboy* magazine and owner of many Playboy clubs, with a bevy of bunny girls, 18 July 1962. (*Above, right*) Bella Abzug, the lawyer and politician, in passionate feminist mode, New York City, 1970. (*Below, right*) Betty Friedan, whose book *The Feminine Mystique* did much to raise the consciousness of women. (*Below, left*) American feminist writer Gloria Steinem.

At the age of fourteen, Allen Ginsberg (*left*) had declared: 'I'll be a genius of some kind or another, probably in literature. Either I'm a genius, I'm eccentric, or I'm slightly schizophrenic. Probably the first two.' Twenty-five years later many reckoned he was all three. Subsequently, Ginsberg joined The Beats, a group of writers, poets, painters and musicians, all rebelling against the perceived horrors of middle-class life.

Another prophet and advocate of an alternative lifestyle was Dr Timothy Leary (*above*), the Harvard professor who urged young people to 'turn on to the scene, tune in to what's happening, and drop out'. Both Ginsberg and Leary (*right*) believed drugs helped.

The high water-and-mud-mark of the hippie scene was the Pop Festival at Woodstock (*opposite, above and below, left and right*) on 600 acres of land near Bethel in New York State, from 15 to 17 August 1969. It was advertised as three days of 'peace and music'. As well as that, there were three deaths, two births and four miscarriages – about average for a town of 200,000 people.

19
NIGHTMARE YEARS 1970–1985

Of the fifty United States, only Massachusetts and the District of Columbia (scene of his downfall less than two years later) failed to fall for Richard Nixon's political charm in the presidential election of November 1972. Senator George McGovern was swept aside as Nixon promised that he would 'get on with the great tasks that lie before us', and pledged to secure a 'peace with honour in Vietnam'. (*Right*) Nixon gives his famous victory salute at the Inaugural Ball to celebrate his election to a second term in office, 26 January 1973.

Introduction

My Lai, Watergate, Kent State and Wounded Knee were best forgotten. The world of dreams was far more satisfactory. Hollywood was reborn with a clutch of films that made fortunes – *The Godfather I* and *II*, the *Star Wars* trilogy and the almost inexhaustible *Rocky* series.

Little Jimmy, youngest of the Osmonds, had his tremolo chart-topping moments of fame, but little Michael of the Jackson Five made a far bigger and longer-lasting name. Sinatra retired again and again. Elvis was seen to be alive, if no longer kicking, in supermarkets, parking lots, and flitting through the glitz of Las Vegas. A new generation of superstars carried the flag for America – John Travolta, Bruce Springsteen, Madonna, and Diana Ross.

Tricky Dicky Nixon fell from grace and came within a sweaty whisker of impeachment, while his minions went to gaol in a political scandal unparalleled in the history of the United States. Ronald Reagan rebuilt the Republican cause, riding through the frozen waste of the Cold War like a gun-slinger through a B-movie Western. There were signs that the breadth and depth of the American economy were about to face down the Soviet system, and that American culture was beginning to overrun those parts of the world that had hitherto managed to resist the Burger and the Mouse.

The nation was still torn asunder by events in Vietnam, 7,000 miles away. America struggled and suffered both as villain and victim. Returning veterans found themselves condemned by 'love children', punks and Flower People, and given the briefest of heroes' welcomes by mainstream Americans. When the unthinkable happened, and President Johnson brought the troops home to leave Saigon to the Communists, the nation went into shock.

Then came the 200th anniversary of the founding of the United States, and the combination of American resilience and worldwide mastering of public relations once again swept gloom and internal divisions aside. No country has ever rivalled the US when it comes to mounting a glamorous and spectacular display of Might and Right. The celebrations were followed by the Los Angeles Olympics in 1984, where American athletes went for gold and won it with astounding success.

Fifty years after the Crash of 1929, Wall Street powered into a golden decade, where fortunes were made in a market that went inexorably upward. Valets parked the stretch limousines. Marinas bulged with the yachts of the new rich. Private helicopters buzzed like swarming bees over the major cities of every state.

The nightmare began to give way, and Americans returned to the sound sleep and sweet dreams of unavoidable prosperity that they had enjoyed for a couple of hundred years.

The twin towers of the World Trade Center in Lower Manhattan, New York City (*left and opposite*), were, briefly, the tallest buildings in the world when they opened in January 1973. Each tower is one hundred and ten storeys high, and the pair cost $750 million to build. Swift elevators whisk those who can brave it to the 107th floor Observation Deck, 1,350 feet (450 metres) above street level.

A stroll across the plaza beneath the Towers is to be avoided during the depths of winter. Icicles falling from the tops of the Towers could prove lethal. The architect, Minoru Yamasaki, claimed that the building was the first of the 21st century – in which case it was completed twenty-nine years ahead of schedule, possibly a world record for architecture. Yamasaki also built the airport in St Louis.

In September 1972, Mark Spitz (*above*) won seven gold medals at the Olympic Games in Munich, West Germany. The twenty-two-year-old swimmer won four golds on his own, and the remaining three as a member of winning relay teams. The rest of the American Olympic contingent managed to collect only twenty-six more gold medals between them.

Eight years later, in the Winter Olympics at Lake Placid, New York State, Eric Heiden (*above*) won five gold medals in the speed skating events. His victories (and that of the US ice hockey team over the Soviet Union) touched off an explosion of national pride. At Radio City Music Hall the audience spontaneously began singing *The Star Spangled Banner*, interrupting a stage performance of *Snow White*.

Relations between the United States and the Chinese Republic had been cold and intermittent since the Revolution of 1949. In February 1972, however, Richard Nixon became the first US President to visit Beijing. He met Chairman Mao Zedong (*above and opposite, below*), and visited the Great Wall of China with his wife Pat and the US Secretary of State, William Pierce Rogers (*opposite, above*). The visit was one of Nixon's greatest political successes. At one point a Chinese band was moved to play *America the Beautiful.*

It took just six months from February 1974 to bring down Nixon's administration. In March Nixon was named as co-conspirator in the Watergate scandal. By June there were calls for his impeachment (*left*). (*Above and opposite*) A desperate Nixon appears on national television.

(*Above*) The US Senate panel begins the Watergate hearings, 18 May 1973 – front row (from left to right): Senators Howard Baker, Sam Irvin, Chief Counsel Watergate Committee Sam Dash, and Senators Herman E. Talmadge and Daniel Inouye. Among the fallen: (*opposite, above left*) John D. Ehrlichman leaves the US District Court, Washington, DC, after sentence; (*opposite, above right*) John Mitchell, the disgraced Attorney-General; (*opposite, below left*) convicted Watergate burglar James McCord. (*Opposite, below right*) The financial costs of Watergate.

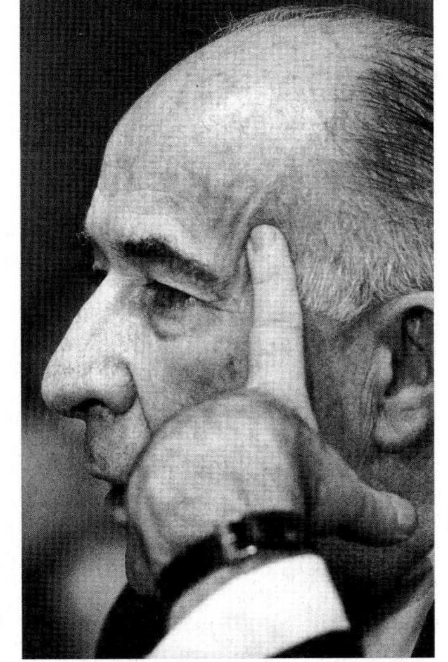

DISBURSEMENTS
KALMBACH 250,000
STRACHAN 350,000
PORTER 100,000
LIDDY 199,000
MAGRUDER 20,000
LANKLER 50,000
25,000
NOFZIGER 10,000
15,000
STONE 3,000
DOLE 5,000
OTHER
TOTAL

By early August 1974 it was all over. Nixon (*above*) became the first President in United States history to resign from office. He was replaced by Gerald Ford the following day. (*Left*) Chief Justice Warren Burger administers the oath of office while Betty Ford looks on.

The first tasks for Ford (*right*) were to regain public trust in the Presidency and rebuild America's self-esteem. 'I am acutely aware that you have not elected me as a President,' he said in a television speech, 'so I ask you to confirm me as your President with your prayers.' The nation never did elect him President, choosing Jimmy Carter instead two years later.

Some of the nightmare lifted in January 1973 with the signing of the Vietnam cease-fire agreement in Paris. The negotiations had been headed by Dr Henry Kissinger for the United States, Phan Dan Lam for South Vietnam (*above*), and by Hguyen Duy Trinh, the North Vietnam Minister of Foreign Affairs (*opposite, below right*). Two separate signing sessions had to be arranged as the South Vietnamese delegation refused to recognise the existence of the Vietcong.

(*Right*) The vast table in the Hotel Majestic around which the negotiations were conducted, 27 January 1973. (*Below, left*) US Secretary of State William Rogers signs the Paris peace treaty. More than 56,000 Americans had died in the war, and more than a million Vietnamese.

The road to the Paris peace talks had been long and hard. In the early Seventies protest against the Vietnam war reached its peak, with mass demonstrations by those who opposed America's involvement. (*Above*) Anti-war demonstrators in Washington, DC, are led away by police in riot gear, 5 May 1971. (*Opposite, above*) Vietnam war veterans make their protest in The Mall, Washington. (*Opposite, below left and right*) Two of the 200,000 demonstrators who marched in Washington on 26 April 1971.

HONOR FOR RESISTERS
AMNESTY FOR
WAR CRIMINALS

And then they came home...in glory and relief, on stretchers and on their own two feet. They were greeted by their loved ones (*right and opposite*), but often quickly forgotten by their country. A dreadful sourness curdled the aftertaste of Vietnam. Some came from the prison camps of North Vietnam. (*Above*) American prisoners of war report to US representatives at Gia Lam Airport, Hanoi, after the Paris cease-fire.

In September 1978, the leaders of Egypt and Israel met at Camp David, Maryland. Their meeting was hosted by President Carter, and resulted in a framework for peace in the Middle East.

(*Opposite, above and below*) The meeting at Camp David: (left to right in both pictures) President Mohamed Anwar al-Sadat of Egypt, Jimmy Carter, Prime Minister Menachem Begin of Israel. Camp David had been established as a presidential mountain retreat by Franklin D. Roosevelt back in the 1930s. (*Right*) Hugh Carey, Governor of New York, reports to the press on a meeting with President Carter at Camp David, July 1979.

A celebration of some of the best writing talent in the United States during the 1970s. (*Left, clockwise from top left*) Joseph Heller, author of *Catch-22*; Edward Albee, who wrote the Broadway play *Who's Afraid of Virginia Woolf?*; Ray Bradbury and Isaac Asimov, hugely successful science fiction writers. (*Opposite, clockwise from top left*) Tennessee Williams, whose many plays included *A Streetcar Named Desire* and *Cat on a Hot Tin Roof*; Harold Robbins, author of the raunchy *The Carpetbaggers*; the critic and journalist Tom Wolfe, who later wrote *The Bonfire of the Vanities*; and John Updike, whose Rabbit trilogy covered thirty years in the life of a car salesman.

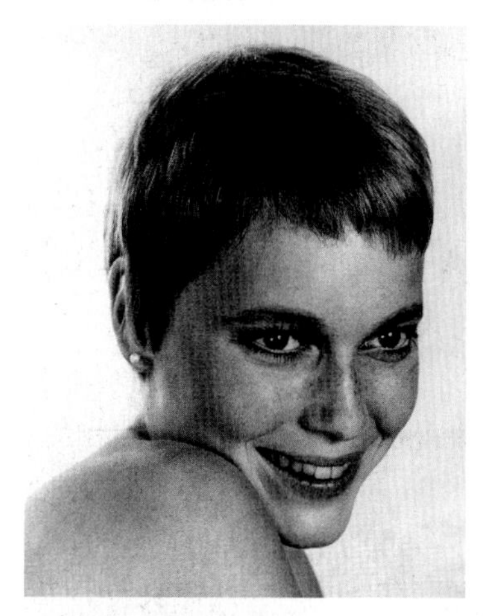

The fans still loved them, though their screen personae were designed to produce rather more lust than love. (*Opposite, clockwise from top left*) Mia Farrow, Raquel Welch and Faye Dunaway. (*Right, clockwise from top left*) Jodie Foster as the twelve-year-old-prostitute in *Taxi Driver*; Meryl Streep; Sigourney Weaver, playing the part of Ripley in the 1979 film *Alien*; and Brooke Shields.

It was the age of the singer-guitarist. A million or more young Americans spent their weekend afternoons and their evenings in shed or garage or bedroom, recreating the works of their musical heroes, or plucking out songs of their own. There were plenty of giants to emulate. Neil Diamond (*above, left*) had a big hit with *Red Red Wine.* Simon and Garfunkel (*below, left* – Art Garfunkel is on the left) topped the charts with *Bridge Over Troubled Water,* but then split up, much to the disappointment of their fans.

Joni Mitchell (*above, left*) came down from Canada with a clutch of songs that included *Both Sides Now*. James Taylor (*above, right* – on the left) had a string of hits that included *Fire and Rain, Sweet Baby James, Carolina on My Mind* and *Steamroller*. Carole King (*above, right* – on the right) wrote and recorded *Tapestry*, one of the most beautiful (and successful) albums of the Seventies, with songs that included *I Feel the Earth Move, You've Got a Friend* and *(You Make Me Feel) Like a Natural Woman*.

The cameras loved them, the fans loved them, the backers loved them once the box office receipts rolled in. (*Opposite, clockwise from top left*) Robert de Niro as Michael in *The Deer Hunter*; Robert Redford; Warren Beatty; and Al Pacino, taking a walk in casual clothes down Madison Avenue, New York City. (*Above, right*) Martin Sheen. (*Below, right*) Dustin Hoffman, playing the *Washington Post* journalist Carl Bernstein in the 1975 movie *All The President's Men* – in which the co-star was Robert Redford.

By the Seventies cinema technology had reached a degree of sophistication that led Warners to think they could make a convincing screen version of *Superman*. The actor chosen for the role was Christopher Reeve (*left*). Alas, ambition o'er vaulted achievement. It was hard to believe a man could fly. *The New Yorker* was especially harsh: 'It's cheesy-looking...the story never seems to get started; the special effects are far from wizardly...'

But Reeve (*above and below, left and right*) played the lead with immense charm and verve, whether in the persona of Clark Kent or as the superhero himself. And nobody complained about the money the film took at the box office.

They were known as the Jackson Five, though there were really six of them – and they truly were brothers. Outshining the rest of the fraternity was Michael. He came to the fore back in 1969 when he and his brothers recorded *ABC* and *I Want You Back*. In the early 1970s came *Ben*, his first solo hit. Ten years of growth and fame followed, with one press release after another insisting that stardom wasn't having any noticeable effect on him.

The rest of the Jacksons were gradually pushed into the background. From the late 1970s onwards, the spotlight narrowed steadily until Michael was left alone in its terrifying beam. (*Above*) The Jacksons in happier days: (from left to right) Jackie, Tito, Jermaine, Marlon, Randy and Michael. For Michael, the terrors and horrors of the 1980s were still a decade away.

Andy Warhol (*left*) was famous for more than fifteen minutes. From the mid-Sixties to his death in 1987 he was at the forefront of avant-garde film making, art, photography and publishing. After highly personal film versions of *Frankenstein* (1973) and *Dracula* (1974), he turned to portrait painting (notably of Mao Zedong and Marilyn Monroe), reviving the technique of repetitive images that he had used in earlier screen prints.

In 1977 came Warhol's portraits of the *Princess of Iran* (*above*), which he produced at the age of forty-six. An earlier Warhol war-horse was his monster piece of soap box art which he somewhat unnecessarily called *The Brillo Boxes* (*right*).
His reputation and influence were enormous. Few of his contemporaries could match the breadth of Warhol's creative field or his devotion to art.

In July 1975 Soviet and American astronauts met somewhere in space. Whatever the fears and tensions between them on earth, the two powers were able to arrange a joint mission involving *Soyuz* and *Apollo* spacecraft. (*Above*) Russian astronaut Valeri Kubasov (right) shakes hands with his American counterpart Thomas Stafford, 12 July 1975. (*Opposite*) The Soviet *Soyuz* spacecraft seen from *Apollo*. The two craft made two joint orbits of the earth before going their separate ways.

50

It was a tough time down on the ground for the United States, but out in space triumph followed triumph. In 1973, Dr Owen Garriott (*opposite*) made a record seven-hour space walk during his fifty-nine-day stay in the Skylab space station. Three years later, in July 1976, a US Viking spacecraft landed on the surface of Mars. The pictures it sent back (*above*) were remarkable for their clarity and beauty.

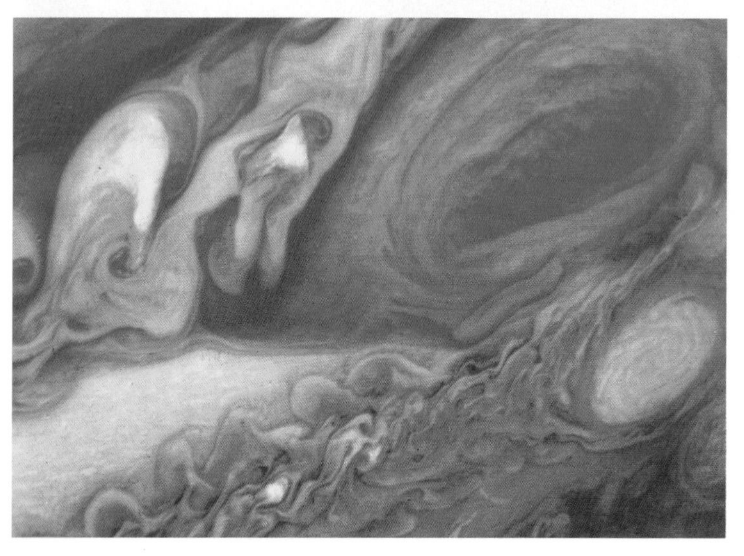

In the late Seventies, NASA scientists turned their attention to the planets Saturn, Uranus and Jupiter. *Voyager 1* (*above, left*) was launched in 1977. The pictures it sent back enabled scientists to discern 'rings' around Uranus similar to those round Saturn. Two years later, *Voyager 2* (*opposite, above* – in a simulation) set out. This time cameras revealed rings round Jupiter – a whirling mass of rocky debris, eighteen miles thick and 5,000 miles wide.

The quality of the pictures sent back by *Voyager 2* was breathtaking. (*Opposite, below*) The Great Red Spot on the planet Jupiter and the turbulent region to the west, as seen by cameras on board *Voyager 2*. (*Below, right*) Another picture of the Great Red Spot, in the region of Jupiter that extends from the planet's equator to its southern polar latitudes.

There were those who labelled him a spoilt brat and a 'bad sport', but John McEnroe (*above, left and right*) was the man who inaugurated a new golden age for American tennis – when he wasn't arguing with the umpire (*left*).

Jimmy Connors (*above, left*) reached his peak in 1974, when he won the Wimbledon Championship, the US Open and the Australian Open. Chris Evert (*right, and above, right*) was as cool on court as McEnroe was fiery. She won the US Open four years running from 1975.

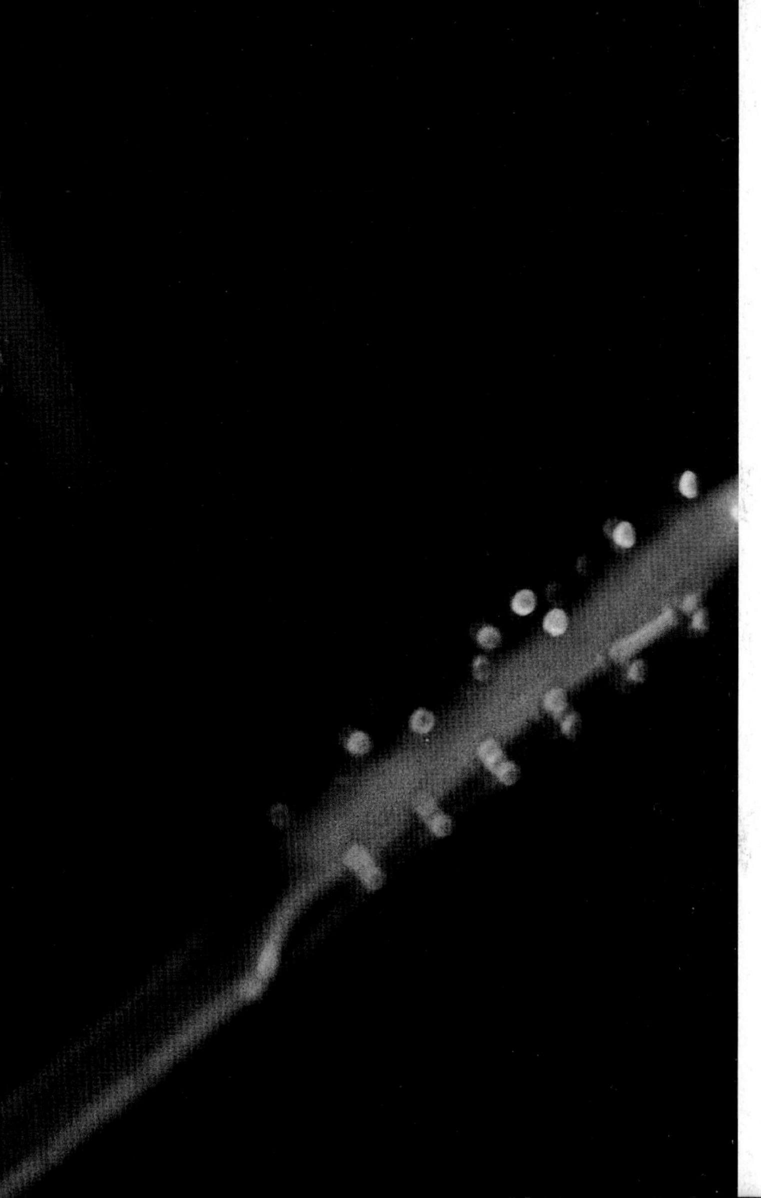

Jimi Hendrix (*left*) just made it into the Seventies. He was twenty-seven years old when he choked to death after mixing drugs and alcohol at a flat in Shepherd's Bush, London, on 18 September 1970. The previous month, Hendrix had performed at a pop festival where the stars had included Chicago, Emerson, Lake and Palmer, the Doors, Joni Mitchell, Leonard Cohen, Miles Davis and Joan Baez. Even in such brilliant company Hendrix was supreme. More than thirty years later, he remains the outstanding black rock guitarist and singer for millions of fans.

ERA ERA ERA
NYU
IN MEMORY OF THE VOICES WE HAVE LOST
LESBIAN HERSTORY ARCHIVES

FREEDOM FROM RELIGION
SEXUAL FREEDOM
FOR ALL
NORTH AMERICAN MAN
LOVE ASSOCIATIO

LESBIANS & GAY MEN
DEMAND:
NO U.S. INTERVENTION
IN
EL SALVADOR

Few political issues escaped the bright and witty attention of gays. Whatever the cause, gays and lesbians were there in their finery (*right*). (*Opposite, above*) Over 10,000 gays and lesbians march along Fifth Avenue, New York, in boisterous mood – their march marked the anniversary of a police raid on the Stonewall Inn, a gay bar. (*Opposite, below left*) Gays lobby for sexual freedom and (*opposite, below right*) no US intervention in El Salvador. (*Above*) Gay priests join the pilgrimage that will hopefully end in 'Gay Rights Now', New York 1980.

20
REBUILDING THE DREAM 1985–2000

The United States took its self-imposed international duties very seriously as the 20th century neared its end. It seemed there was no one else capable of maintaining the world's peace. Peace-keeping was an expensive business. Sophisticated weapons had proliferated and you did not have to be a superpower to pose a threat to millions of people. There were plenty of terrorists scattered round the world. (*Right*) A Stealth B-2 bomber makes its menacing appearance at Northrup Air Base, California.

Introduction

As in the great days of 1849, fortune hunters trekked to California in the 1980s and 1990 to Silicon Valley where computer empires sprouted overnight like magic mushrooms. Bill Gates made enough money from Microsoft to buy entire countries, and in his wake came the Internet bounty hunters who, it seemed, could pluck millions of dollars out of thin air. America invented the CD, and then, incredibly, left it to the Japanese to exploit the invention. The development of synthetic genes and genetically modified food split national opinion.

There were lasers to write in the sky and mend people's bodies, and Stealth bombers to glide unseen through the sky and break people's bodies. NASA revived its space missions with the launch of *Voyagers I* and *II*, boldly going where no hardware had ever gone before, and bringing back pictures of infinite space and infinite beauty.

The States had its victories overseas. The Soviet empire came metaphorically tumbling down and the Berlin Wall – which had long seemed America's last frontier – was literally dismantled. Iran became the new bogeyman, but the Gulf War of 1991 proved the destructiveness of US firepower. Successive administrations blew hot and cold over the problem of Cuba, the pea under Old Glory's mattress. The Wonderful World of Disney was exported to France where it eventually struck its customary gold.

In sport there were victories at home and abroad. Hard on the heels of Grand Slam champions Connors, McEnroe, Billie Jean King and Evert, of an earlier age, came Sampras and Navratilova, the latter one of the new wave of immigrants – sports stars who found America the perfect training ground. 'Tiger' Woods became the first black golfer to don the Green Jacket. 'Flo Jo' Griffith and Carl Lewis hit the tape harder and faster than anyone in the world.

For many Americans, the dream could best be rebuilt by a return to the old ways and the Old Religion. The last few years of the millennium saw a rebirth of aggressive Christianity – pro-life in its anti-abortion stance, pro-death in its belief in capital punishment. Some sects withdrew from mainstream life altogether, seeking to set up their own communities. Where these attempts ended in tragedy (as at Jamestown and Waco), or clashed with that other keystone of the American way of life, the family (as in the case of the Moonies), they achieved a considerable notoriety.

Ronald Wilson Reagan was the oldest candidate ever to be elected to the US Presidency. He was sixty-nine when he hit the election trail in the spring and summer of 1980 (*above*). He owed his victory to three things – his promise to 'put America back to work', his ruggedly patriotic foreign policy and the expectation that he would cut taxes. Added to this, Reagan possessed considerable personal charm, a useful relic of his Hollywood days. (*Opposite, above*) Union support at a 1980 campaign rally. (*Opposite, below*) The placards read: 'HOW DO YOU SPELL TAX RELIEF? R-E-A-G-A-N', and 'WIN WORLD RESPECT WITH REAGAN.'

REAGAN-BUSH
TEAMSTERS
FOR
REAGAN

HOW DO YOU SPELL
TAX RELIEF?
R-E-A-G-A-N
WIN WORLD
RESPECT!!
WITH
REAGAN
YOUTH
FOR
Ronald
REAGAN
WIN
WITH

It was a good time to back America. Across the world the Soviet dream was crumbling. By the late 1980s Mikhail Gorbachev was presiding over the collapse of what Reagan had dubbed 'the evil Empire'. In December 1987 the two leaders met in Washington, DC (*above and opposite*), to sign a treaty that was aimed at reducing the size of both their nuclear arsenals.

The summit lasted three days, and, after signing the treaty, Reagan and Gorbachev exchanged pens. 'We can only hope,' said Reagan, 'that this history-making agreement will not be an end in itself, but the beginning of a working relationship that will enable us to tackle other issues.' But time was running out for Mikhail Gorbachev. In December 1991 the Soviet Head of State was forced to resign. Reagan had already gone.

The United States had long abandoned its former policy of avoiding entanglement in the world's conflicts. When the bitter civil war broke out in Lebanon, United States marines were hurried to Beirut (*above, left and right*). They formed part of an international peace-keeping force, facing this role with a mixture of toughness and humour – the sign (*above, left*) reads 'WELCOME TO RADAR SPRINGS, LEBANON. MAYOR CWO2 [Z] LOZADA. POPULATION 12.'

(*Above and right*) US troops in Haiti show the flag and hand out candy. They were part of a group of 144th Special Force squad sent out to keep the peace.

Frank Oz (on the left) and Jim Henson (*left*) created the Muppets, a motley collection of animals and freaks whose music and humour delighted children and adults alike in the 1980s and 1990s. Everyone had a Muppet favourite – Fozzie Bear, Animal, Zoot, Waldorf and Statler. But the stars of the show were Kermit the Frog (*opposite, below left* – in the crushing embrace of his muscular lover), and Miss Piggy herself (*opposite, below right*). (*Opposite, above*) Kermit and the Great Gonzo as a pair of investigative reporters in *The Great Muppet Caper*, 1981.

(*Opposite, above*) General H. 'Stormin' ' Norman Schwarzkopf, commanding officer of the US Joint Forces in the Persian Gulf, addresses members of the 354th Tactical Air Force Wing. (*Opposite, below*) American Air Force F-15 C fighters fly over a Kuwaiti oilfield set on fire by Iraqi troops. (*Above*) US troops, back from the Gulf War, march past (left to right) General Schwarzkopf, President George Bush, Barbara Bush, Vice-President Dan Quayle and Marilyn Quayle.

Twelve years of Republican rule ended on Wednesday 4 November 1992 when Bill Clinton (*above*) was elected President of the United States. His victory over George Bush was crushing – Clinton gained three hundred and seventy electoral votes, Bush one hundred and eighty-six. (*Left*) Clinton with his running mate, Al Gore, on the campaign trail, 1992.

Later, the world was to discover that Clinton relied as heavily on his wife Hilary as Reagan had done on Nancy. But, for the moment, the spotlight cast only a cursory beam on Hilary and Chelsea Clinton at Clinton's inauguration (*above*). (*Right*) A famous handshake – Israeli Prime Minister Iitzhak Rabin and Palestinian leader Yasser Arafat meet on the White House lawn, 29 September 1993.

In 1993, a group of Branch Davidians, led by David Koresh, were besieged by FBI and ATF agents in their compound at Waco, Texas (*above*). Tension built up, for the Davidians had threatened to kill themselves. As the days passed, and negotiations broke down repeatedly, the press arrived in their dozens. (*Left*) Heavily armed ATF agents on the morning of the eighth day of the siege.

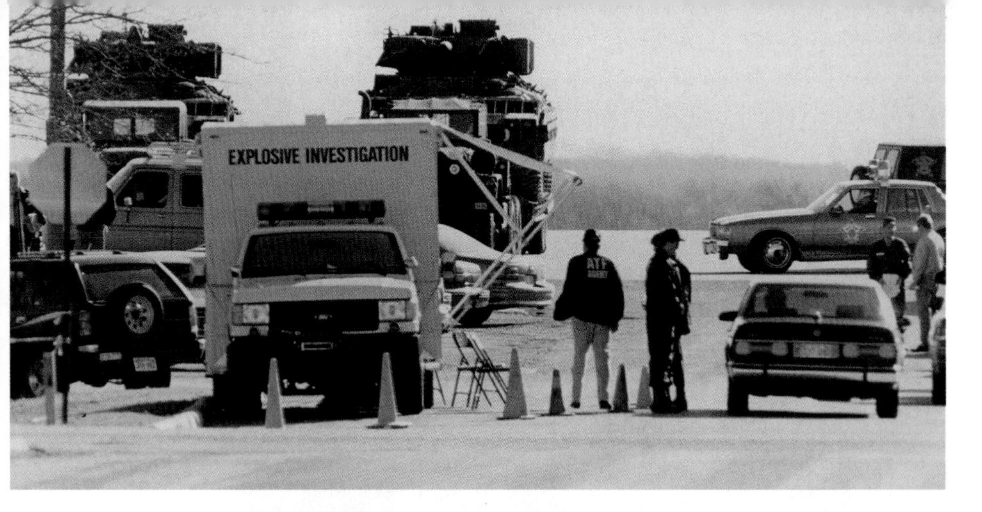

(*Above*) The scene on the tenth day. In the background are two Bradley infantry combat vehicles awaiting action. The lorry in the foreground belongs to the team that hope to remove the explosives the Davidians held in the compound. It ended in disaster. Shots were exchanged. The compound exploded. The Davidians were annihilated. (*Right*) A Chinook helicopter flies over the blazing wreckage of the compound.

Three golden moments from the 1996 Olympic Games in Atlanta, Georgia. (*Above, left*) US swimmers celebrate after winning the gold medal in the 4x100 metres relay: (left to right) Amy van Dyken, Angel Martino, Amanda Beard and Beth Batsford. (*Below, left*) Repeat performance for the US women's gymnastics team: (left to right) Jaycie Phelps, Amanda Border and Shannon Miller. (*Opposite*) Carl Lewis, an eight-times Olympic gold medallist, sails through the air on his second 'jump of the night' during the men's long jump finals.

USA
Atlanta 1996
2374

The American hero of the Seoul Olympics was Florence Griffiths 'Flo Jo' Joyner, who won a clutch of medals, and whose ebullient spirit and flamboyant performances brought crowds to their feet. Three of her medals were gold. In the 4x400 metres relay (*left*), she won silver.

(*Right*) Flo Jo's haul of medals: 100 metres, 200 metres, 4x100 metres relay and 4x400 metres relay. (*Below, left and right*) Joyner's joy is unconfined as she celebrates her victory in the women's 100 metres at the Los Angles Olympics in 1984. Her world record performances of 10.49 seconds in the 100 metres and 21.34 metres in the 200 metres stood until her tragic death in 1998 at the age of thirty-eight.

Some achieve greatness with awesome rapidity. Eldrick 'Tiger' Woods was only nineteen when he blasted off from the first tee in his first US Masters competition at the Augusta National Golf Club, 1995 (*left*). He was then already US Amateur champion.

(*Right*) Two years later he had won the Masters and was waiting to be presented with the coveted Green Jacket. (*Below*) A moment of doubt. Woods was nine strokes ahead of his nearest rival when he played the fifth hole in the final round of the 1997 US Masters. He drove into a bunker, struggled to reach the green and bogeyed the hole. It didn't matter – he still won.

Michael Jackson in dangerous thriller-killer mode, 15 October 1993 (*left*). He was performing in a concert in São Paulo, Brazil, on the Latin American leg of his 'Dangerous' World Tour. Whatever the problems in his private life, Jackson's popularity never waned during the 1990s. (*Opposite*) Singer and actress Madonna waves to her fans as she arrives at the Shrine Auditorium, Los Angeles, for the world premiere of her film *Evita*, 14 December 1996. Whatever her popularity, Madonna's problems in her private life never waned during the 1990s.

KEEP THE LOVE ALIVE
LANCASTER PA.
THERE IS A LIGHT THAT NEVER GOES OUT
NEIL
GARTH
WALL
TONY
PENNSYLVANIA

Keeping AIDS in the public consciousness. (*Opposite*) The AIDS quilt was the largest in the world when it was displayed for the first time in Washington, DC, 11 October 1992. Each of its 20,000 panels commemorated a different AIDS victim. (*Above, right*) American visitors to Brussels join a candlelit rally to mark World Aids Day, 1 December 1998. (*Below, right*) WAKE UP! THE AIDS CRISIS IS NOT OVER. Some of the participants in a march on Washington, DC, for Lesbian and Gay Rights lie down in protest on Pennsylvania Avenue, at the gates of the White House.

NASA

The Hubble Space telescope (*right*) was named after the American astronomer Edwin P. Hubble. It was launched into space in April 1990, but began to malfunction. In a mission that combined technology and improvisation with equal brilliance, the space shuttle *Endeavour* docked alongside to make repairs, 9 December 1993 (*opposite*).

Among the many trouble spots that engaged American attention and demanded American presence was Bosnia. When fighting broke out between the Bosnians and the Serbians, US troops flew in. (*Left*) President Clinton visits his troops, 13 January 1996.

(*Right*) A Bosnian soldier with horse and cart threads his way through American tanks, 9 January 1996. (*Below, left*) Women holding paper doves stand alongside a security official during a peace demonstration in Sarajevo. (*Below, right*) Richard Holbrooke, chief US peace negotiator, announcing a key deal regarding the future of Bosnia at a press conference in New York City, 1995.

On 23 December 1997, Madeleine Albright (*left*) became the first female US Secretary of State. She was faced with what seemed to many an overwhelming task, in a world where many areas had become increasingly unstable. (*Opposite, above*) Madeleine Albright and Yasser Arafat shake hands on the steps of the Palestinian Authority's Ministry of Education, prior to the talks aimed at restarting the Middle East peace process.

(*Below, right*) Madeleine Albright with the Israeli Prime Minister Benjamin Netanyahu (extreme left) after a three-hour discussion on the urgency of the peace process. Israeli Foreign Minister David Levy is second from left, Defence Minister Yitzhak Moredechai is on the extreme right.

Four years after the Bosnian crisis it was the turn of Kosovo. (*Left*) A US soldier stands guard at an American camp near Tiraia, 22 April 1999. America was seeking to bolster NATO's peace-keeping mission. (*Opposite, above*) One of the twenty-four Apache helicopters at Tiraia. (*Opposite, below left*) Ethnic Albanians in carts and tractors struggle to escape the fighting in Patina. (*Opposite, below right*) American soldiers in Tirana, Albania, during the Kosovo crisis.

A batch of Hollywood's finest and latest: (*above, left*) Kevin Spacey – *Seven* and *American Beauty*; (*below, left*) Tim Robbins – *The Player* and *The Shawshank Redemption*; (*below, right*) Morgan Freeman – *Robin Hood, Prince of Thieves* and *The Shawshank Redemption.*

(*Right, clockwise from top left*): Bruce Willis – *Die Hard* and *Hudson Hawk*; Richard Gere – *Pretty Woman* and *An Officer and a Gentleman*; Harrison Ford – *Witness, Patriot Games* and *The Fugitive*; and Kevin Costner – *JFK* and *Dances with Wolves.*

Last heroines of the 20th century. (*Left, clockwise from top left*) Kim Basinger – *9$^{1}/_{2}$ Weeks* and *LA Confidential*; Uma Thurman – *Dangerous Liaisons* and *Even Cowgirls Get the Blues*; Gwyneth Paltrow – *Seven* and *Blood and Bones*; and Sharon Stone – *Basic Instinct* and *Bad Girls*.

(*Right, clockwise from top left*) Michelle Pfeiffer – *The Fabulous Baker Boys* and *Frankie and Johnny*; Demi Moore – *GI Jane* and *A Few Good Men*; Julia Roberts – *Pretty Woman* and *Erin Brockovich*; and Meg Ryan – *Sleepless in Seattle* and *When Harry Met Sally*.

Throughout the Eighties and Nineties, movie audiences steadily increased. The worst was over for Hollywood. Film makers rediscovered some of the old magic. One of the most commercially successful was Steven Spielberg *(left)*. In the Seventies, he had directed *Jaws* and *Close Encounters of the Third Kind*, two films that played strongly on the audience's emotions. In 1982 came a piece of old-style screen magic – *E.T.* It took a fortune at the box office and reminded millions that movie-going could be a sweet experience.

Martin Scorsese (*above, left*) preferred harder, leaner drama, anything from *Raging Bull* to *The Last Temptation of Christ.* Spike Lee (*above, right*) was a highly individual director, one of the few genuinely black voices in Hollywood. Oliver Stone (*below, left*) was considered by many to have rewritten history with his film about the assassination of Kennedy – *JFK.* Mel Brooks (*below, right*) specialised in pastiche and parody, from *Young Frankenstein* to *Blazing Saddles.*

President Bill Clinton had much on his mind in 1998. There were the problems in the Balkans, in the Gulf, in Grozny – in fact, all over the world. And some of the troubles were very near to hand. They were of a personal nature. There were moves to impeach the President following allegations of sexual harassment from Paula Jones. (*Left*) The President ponders his future prior to addressing a forum on the role of NATO. At that time, Kenneth Starr, the lawyer later to confront Clinton, was very much in the ascendant.

But the biggest headlines were reserved for Clinton's flirtation with the former member of the White House staff, an intern named Monica Lewinsky (*above*). What actually passed between the two nobody seems to know for certain (least of all the President himself), but the allegations of sexual impropriety and of subsequent perjury did much to weaken the country's belief in Clinton as an honest or credible Head of State.

Index

The Hulton Getty Picture Collection:
Alan Band: pp 642(t), 643; Gary Franklin: pp 712(tr), 787, 792, 823(tr), (bl); Peter Gould: p. 777(tr); Ernst Haas: pp 22-7, 30-31, 65, 625, 630(r), 639(bl), 655, 667(tr), (b), 685(t), 743, 758(b); Peter Keegan: p. 736; Kobal: pp 558(t), 762(br); *Observer*: pp 681(br), 719(bl); Doug McKenzie: pp. 778-9; Kevin Weaver: pp. 813(bl), 817(br); Weegee: pp 580-81, 688-9.

Allsport: Tony Duffy, pp 802, 803(t); Mike Powell, p. 803(bl), (br).

Archive Photos: Pp 98, 120, 121(r), 138, 139(b), 142, 160, 176(l), 210, 212-15, 324-6, 346-7, 382-5, 460-61, 462(b), 469, 483(tl), (b), 493, 530-31, 546(bl), 550-51, 554-5, 564-5, 568-9, 570, 576-7, 604(b), 624, 633, 636, 637(bl), 642(b), 644-7, 648(t), 653, 660, 662, 663®, 665(t), (bl), 727 (bl), 730-31, 741(b), 742(t), 744, 745 (bl), (br), 746-7, 810.

Fotos International/Archive Photos: Munawar Hosain, pp 818(t), 821(br); Bob Grant, pp 819(tl), (bl), (tr), 820(br); Frank Edwards, p. 820(tl); Kostas Alexander, pp 820(tr), 821(tl); Fotos International, pp 821(bl), 822, 823(tl).

Reuters/Archive Photos: Bob Rhia Jnr, pp 782-3; Rick Wilking, pp 789, 814; Carole Devillers, p. 791(t); Jeff Christensen, p. 791(b); Pat Benic, p. 794(t); Terry Bochatey, p. 795; Jim Bourg, p. 796(t); Jeff Mitchell, pp 798(t), 799(t); John Kuntz, p. 798(b); G.Reed Schumann, p. 799(b); Gary Hershorn, pp 800(t), 805(t), (b); Jerry Lampen, p. 800(b); Wolfgang Rattay, p. 801; Mike Blake, p. 804; Str. Marchos Pacheco, p. 806; Fred Prouser, p. 807; Mike Theiler, p. 808; Yves Herman, p. 809(t); Vidal Medina, p. 809(b); Win McNamee, p. 812; Corrine Dufka, p. 813(t); Reuters, p. 813(br); Jim Hollander, p. 815(t); Avi Ohayon, p. 815(b); Arben Celi, p. 816; Petr Josek, p. 817(t); Yannis Behrakis, p. 817(bl); Larry Downing, p. 824; Tim Aubry, p. 825.

Victor Malafronte/Archive Photos: Pp 818(br), (bl), 819(br), 820(bl), 821(tr).

About the pictures in this book

This book was created by The Hulton Getty Picture Collection which comprises over 300 separate collections and 18 million images. It is a part of Getty Images, Inc. with over 70 million images and 30,000 hours of film. Picture sources for this book include:

Hulton Getty, Archive Photos and **FPG** (archival photographs and film)
Allsport (sports photography)
Liaison Agency (news and reportage)
Online USA (celebrity photography)

All are part of Getty's press and editorial sales channel, **www.gettysource.com**
In addition to gettysource suppliers, images were supplied by Gettyone Stone, The Image Bank and Telegraph Colour Library, who are all part of Getty's online solution for creative access, gettyone, **www.gettyone.com**

How to buy or license a picture from this book

All non-Hulton images are credited on the Acknowledgements page.

Picture licensing information

For information about licensing any image in this book, please phone **+ 44 (0)20 7579 5731**, fax: **44 (0)20 7266 3154** or e-mail **chris.barwick@getty-images.com**

Online access

For information about Getty Images and for access to individual collections go to **www.hultongetty.com.**
Go to **www.gettyone.com** for creative and conceptually oriented imagery and (in third quarter 2000) **www.gettysource.com** for editorial images.

Buying a print

For details on how to purchase exhibition quality prints call The Hulton Getty Picture Gallery, phone **+ 44 (0)20 7276 4525** or e-mail **hulton.gallery@getty-images.com**